A BRIEF HISTORY
OF THE
ISLE OF MAN

SECOND EDITION (REVISED)

Loaghtan Books
Caardee, Dreemskerry Hill
Maughold
Isle of Man
IM7 1BE

Published by Loaghtan Books

2nd edition (revised) published: March 2017

Typesetting and origination by:
Loaghtan Books

Printed and bound by:
Lavenham Press

Website: www.loaghtanbooks.com

ISBN: 978-1-908060-16-7

In loving memory of my father,
who took great interest in this book while it was
being prepared, but sadly did not live to see its
publication

Front cover: Near Corrin's Tower, Peel, looking south west

Rear cover: Ramsey and the north; Scotland is visible across the sea

Title page: Eary Cushlin, looking towards the Calf

CONTENTS

THE ISLE OF MAN

The sketch map below is intended only to give a rough idea of the location of some of the places mentioned in the text. Those travelling by car would be advised to use the 1:50,000 Ordnance Survey (OS) Landranger Map, sheet 95 (the pink one). Walkers should use either the OS map or the 1:25,000 Public Rights of Way and Outdoor Leisure Map published by the Isle of Man Government.

In recent years various conventions have been adopted to refer to the Isle of Man in a shorter form. Man, Mann and Mannin have all gone in and out of fashion, and are still in common usage and largely interchangeable, at least in English. 'Man' is the result of dropping the 'Isle of', while 'Mannin' is what the Manx call their island in their own language; 'Ellan Vannin' means 'Isle of Man' in Manx. 'Mann' appears to be a shortened and anglicised form of 'Mannin'.

The term 'Man' is ambiguous as it is also an acceptable way of referring to 'Mankind' and might easily cause confusion if the reader can't tell whether the author is referring to the land or the people living on it. Mannin would be more appropriate if the book were written in Manx. As it is not, and in an effort to be unambiguous, 'Mann' is used as the standard short form for 'Isle of Man' in this Brief History.

THE DAWN OF TIME

If you stand on the summit of Snaefell on a clear day you can see seven kingdoms, or so the story goes: Mann (of course), England, Wales, Scotland, Ireland, the ocean, which is Neptune's Kingdom and heaven, the Kingdom of God. From Snaefell you can see the great panorama of neighbouring islands circling around Mann in the centre, like the rim of a tea cup circling the bubbles in the middle. If the light is right – and it doesn't happen often – the islands of Britain seem close enough for you to reach out your hand and pluck Scafell Pike from the Lake District or cradle the Mountains of Mourne in the palm of your hand.

The birth of an island

What people don't think about when admiring the fabulous view is that Mann and its neighbouring islands are all joined together under the sea. The Isle of Man, the rest of Britain, Ireland, most of continental Europe, half of Iceland, and even Russia and China are part of what is called the Eurasian plate. It is a huge landmass, and one piece of the jigsaw of tectonic plates which make up the Earth's outer layer or crust. The tectonic plates float on the semi-molten rock which makes up the earth's mantle. Because they float they bump against each other and when they do they cause earthquakes and volcanoes, and create or change mountains and valleys.

That's the situation now, but 500 million years ago things, as you would expect, were very different. The Isle of Man is now on latitude 55 degrees north but was then on the other side of the world on latitude 60 degrees south, between where Cape Horn and Antarctica is today. It was part of a small landmass called Avalonia which also included what was to become England, Wales, and the south and east of Ireland. Scotland and the north and west of Ireland were part of a continent called Laurentia which also included

The Chasms. Some of the oldest rocks on Mann

North America and Greenland. Avalonia and Laurentia were separated by the Iapetus Ocean which was roughly as wide as the Atlantic between Newfoundland and Ireland today.

Over the next 90 million years the bed of the Iapetus Ocean was covered with layer upon layer of sediment which gradually hardened to form what is known as the Manx Group of rocks. These are some of the oldest rocks on the island, and include the rocks in the Maughold Brooghs, Ramsey and Sulby Glen, Injebreck, Snaefell and The Chasms. On Mann the oldest rocks of all are two narrow bands running from Glen Rushen north east to around Barregarrow, and from near The Stacks, north east through South Barrule to Ramsey. These are about 480 million years old. To put that in context, at that time almost all life on earth lived in the sea, although plants which lived on land were just beginning to develop.

All the time the rocks in the Manx Group were being formed, the two continents, Avalonia and Laurentia, were drifting towards each other. They eventually collided about 410 million years ago, crumpled at the edges and formed the Caledonian Mountain range which probably equalled the size of the Himalayas today. The collision of the two continental plates also brought together the northern and southern parts of the British Isles. Most of Mann comes from Avalonia, but one small part comes from Laurentia. The rocks along the coast between Niarbyl and Peel have their fellows in North America. If you stand on the rocks to the north of Niarbyl beach you are standing on the same rocks as those in the Adirondack Mountains in New York.

Niarbyl beach showing the rocks from Avalonia (grey rocks bottom right) and Laurentia (yellow rocks top left)

The huge Caledonian Mountain range, which contained the Isle of Man together with the rest of the British Isles, still lay south of the equator. The sun, wind and rain eroded the mountains while rivers moved large quantities of dark red sand and pebbles and dumped them in low-lying areas. Over time the water evaporated and the sand compressed into rocks to become what is now known as Peel Sandstone. The rock is only found in the area around Peel, which is obviously where it got its name, and does not, for example, extend even as far as Poortown, only a couple of miles away to the south east. Sandstone is a freestone, which means that it can be cut in any direction, unlike something like slate which only splits easily along the grain. Peel Sandstone is the only freestone on Mann and was often used in buildings. It is however very soft and erodes easily, so modern buildings in the area tend to be built of an imported stone, of similar colour but less friable.

The rock formations which were to become the Isle of Man continued to drift northwards until, around 330 million years ago, they reached the equator. Warm shallow tropical seas teeming with marine life and including huge numbers of shellfish covered most of what would become Mann. Shells are made out of calcium carbonate and it is layers of ancient shells which form the carboniferous limestone now found around Castletown. Limestone is particularly hard wearing and much of the old part of Castletown, including Castle Rushen and Langness lighthouse, was built using the local limestone. A dark variation of the limestone known locally as 'black marble' was quarried at Poyllvaaish, a mile or so west of Castletown. Poyllvaaish marble was used for various decorative purposes – and not only on Mann. In 1704, Poyllvaaish marble was exported to Liverpool to be used as flagstones for the floor of St Peter's church. The site is now the Liverpool One shopping centre, but the place where the entrance to St Peter's church used to be is marked by a gold cross on the floor.

Millions more years passed and the land which was to become Mann continued its progress northwards. Not much

Above: Langness lighthouse; fishing vessel Nancy Ellen *passes heading for Castletown with lobster pots on board.*
Left: Poyllvaaish quarry
Below: Port Erin's millennium monolith made from Poyllvaaish marble

happened to change its essential composition until it reached its current location. The world had gradually been getting colder and, about two million years ago, experienced the start of the Ice Age. Huge glaciers spread down from the arctic covering most of Britain with sheet ice. The ice advanced and retreated several times, sometimes covering the whole of what was to become Mann, sometimes covering only part of it. The ice scoured out valleys, rounded off hills and dumped rock debris as the ice melted. The northern end of the island, beyond what is now the A3 road between Ramsey and Kirk Michael, is formed entirely from glacial deposits. As the ice moved southwards from the pole, it pushed soft debris such as earth and pebbles in front of it, rather like sweeping dust with the edge of a ruler, or pushing wrinkles in soft cloth. Solid ice pushing earth in front of it creates what are

Tholt-y-Will, and the giant deer which might once have lived there

called moraine ridges. The hills around Bride are what remains of glacial moraine and show the southern limits of the last glacier to reach Mann.

The first Man on Mann

After the glaciers finally withdrew, they left Mann roughly the same shape that it is now, although still not yet an island. At first it would also have been bare of vegetation or animal life. Then algae and mosses would have colonised the bare ground, followed by plants such as those which live in the arctic today. Once such hardy plants had broken down the rock to create soil, less hardy vegetation would have started to grow, insects and small animals would have moved in and eventually a new ecosystem would come into being, complete with grazing animals and predators – including Man.

Palaeolithic or Early Stone Age people were nomads, following plentiful sources of food, whether that was ripening plants, or animal herds. Such people lived in portable skin shelters, but no record is left of their presence on the island. Glaciers obliterate entire landscapes, never mind the fugitive remnants of nomadic families with no settled home. As animals sought the best grazing, so they would have been followed by hunters. The first people to make Mann their base could well have walked here.

It was the Ice Age which turned Mann into an island. About 15,000 years ago the climate became warmer and the ice sheet melted. The sea level rose and gradually flooded the valleys between what was left of the peaks of the Caledonian Mountain range. The land link between the Isle of Man and Ireland ended about 12,000 years ago; that between Mann and the UK about 2,000 years later. The difference between what was then the land level is noticeable even today, as large ships travelling north to south or vice versa across the Irish Sea, almost invariably pass to the west of the Isle of Man. Not only is the route more direct, the sea is also much deeper there.

At the beginning of the Mesolithic period or Middle Stone Age, mammoths, giant deer and great bears inhabited large parts of what became the British Isles – the remains of hippos and cave lions have even been found under Trafalgar Square in London. However something, possibly climate change, possibly a meteor strike, happened to make the very large animals die out. As the climate gradually grew warmer the cold tundra, which had been the character of the land after the ice receded, began to give way to trees. Mixed deciduous woodland, not unlike that which now colonises the Manx national glens, would have spread over much of the island, with pine and birch trees on many of the uplands.

Some of the last of the giant deer seem to have survived for centuries longer on the Isle of Man, perhaps protected by the fact that Mann, now an island, was difficult for predators to get to. Giant deer were thought to have been extinct in continental Europe by 8,000 BC, but an almost complete skeleton of one was found at Ballaugh in 1815 which has been dated to about 7,000 BC. This means that the giant deer survived on Mann then for about twice as long as the dodo has been extinct today. Like the dodo, the giant deer possibly owed its final demise to the arrival of Man. People settled on the island around 7,000 BC and a single giant deer could have fed an extended family for at least a fortnight. The skeleton from Ballaugh was given to the Edinburgh museum, but another example, found at Close y Garey in 1887, is on display at the Manx Museum. Probably because of their huge antlers, giant deer are occasionally known as Irish Elk. The title is inaccurate. Neither Irish nor an elk, the animal's nearest modern relative is the fallow deer.

Seafaring settlers

The first people to live on Mann after it became an island would have been hunter-gatherers like their Palaeolithic predecessors. Why they came to the Isle of Man we don't know but the immigration could not have been undertaken lightly. The boats of the time were dug-out canoes and possibly portable hide boats similar to coracles, which were useful for a nomadic lifestyle along the coast. Whatever their reason for coming to Mann, the island obviously had suitable or even desirable living conditions as the visitors stayed.

The new island residents still lived a nomadic lifestyle with extended family groups following animal herds or moving to take advantage of plants in season. Everything the communities owned would have been light and portable. Clothes and shelters were made from animal hide, tools from horn, bone or flint, baskets were woven from reeds, grasses or supple twigs, rope was twisted from animal gut or creeping plants such as honeysuckle, needles were fashioned from antler or fish bone. Hunter-gatherers also did more gathering than hunting. Certainly they ate meat and fish whenever they could catch it, but most of their diet consisted of roots, leaves, berries, nuts, insects, eggs and shellfish. Anyone who has ever been camping will know that, once the tent has been removed, there is remarkably little left to show details about who has been living there and how, so traces of Mesolithic people are extremely fugitive. The most obvious permanent traces which hunter-gatherers leave behind them are evidence of flint working such as flakes of waste flint which experts call debatage, and broken flint knapping tools made out of antler or bone. Remains of this sort have been discovered at Billown and under Ronaldsway airport and are remarkably similar in style to Mesolithic tools found in Northern Ireland. It therefore seems likely that Mann's first settlers came from Ireland.

Mesolithic people were extremely skilled at fashioning flint into various tools and, as time went on, such tools became more sophisticated. Instead of shaping a single piece of flint into whatever the flint knappers wanted, they gradually came to use a combination of materials. Stone axes, for example, were developed during the Middle Stone Age, usually with a flint blade inserted through a wooden handle and bound in place with leather thongs, plant fibres, or animal sinews. The habit of combining materials to make more efficient tools is most obvious in the development of microliths. Microliths are small triangular pieces of flint, about the size of a penny, and were fixed into antler or bone handles to make a variety of different tools either with sharp points, such as spears, harpoons and arrows, or with barbed cutting edges such as knives or something which resembled a sickle.

The Mesolithic period lasted from around 9,000 BC to 4,000 BC during which time people slowly evolved from being foraging nomads to something part-way towards farmers. Over a period of time, hunter-gatherers began to favour one site over others, possibly because of some natural shelter, access to clean water, an abundant supply of plant food or good hunting grounds. They would still have left their favoured site from time to time, as the seasons changed, but would probably have returned to it as a semi-permanent home.

Living on an island the Manx would not have been able to cover the huge distances on land travelled by continental hunter-gatherers and would probably have relied much more on a diet of fish and seaweed. An island race would naturally take to fishing but frequent travel across the sea would have been risky and possibly viewed as unnecessary. There was probably regular contact with tribes in Ireland and Scotland however, in view of the similarity of tools. As many of the foodstuffs of Mann's indigenous people would have been concentrated into a relatively small area they may even have been one of the earlier people to adopt a more permanent way of life. Such a suggestion is backed by a recent find when extending the runway at Ronaldsway airport; archaeologists identified the remains of a wooden shelter about seven metres in diameter, dating to around 6,000 BC. The shelter also suggests that the Manx had more contact with their northern neighbours. The first permanent settlements in Britain appeared in Ireland and Scotland, but England and Wales had to wait until the Bronze Age for the creation of settled communities.

From foraging to farming

Of course hunter-gatherers didn't wake up one morning and decide that they would be farmers from now on. The Neolithic or New Stone Age lasted from about 4,000 BC to about 2,500 BC and it was during this time that people began to create the first permanent settlements and adapt to a different way of living. Communities began growing their own food and domesticating animals, rather than relying on what they could find and/or hunt. Again the question is why the change, and again we don't really know. One of the arguments put forward is that the population was increasing and the land could no longer support the lifestyle of a hunter-gatherer. If more people needed to be fed, then more food was required, and this meant either improving gathering techniques or deliberately encouraging and planting the right sort of plants to produce a bigger harvest. Growing their own would definitely make sense for an island race where a nomadic life had to be confined to a relatively small area and where the amount of dependable food gathered from the land was more obviously finite.

Above: Cashtal yn Ard long barrow.
Left and below: Belas Knap long barrow in Gloucestershire showing what Cashtal yn Ard would have looked like before its earth covering was removed. Glos. photographs © Melanie Stern

In a settled lifestyle the emphasis changed from portable to permanent. Things no longer needed to be light enough to carry, so could be made strong enough to withstand bad weather and accidental knocks without needing constant repair. Canoes dating from the Neolithic period have been found on the island; the most complete example was discovered at Ballakaighan in 1884, during remedial drainage work for the Manx Northern Railway. It closely resembled canoes of a similar age found near the Clyde. The canoe is heavy and although certainly portable not easy to carry for any distance. Houses too became more durable. Rather than dwellings being 'kits' of flexible poles and skins, they began to be built of heavier timber and stone with turf or thatched roofs.

The new ex-nomads already knew a lot about plants, but far less about how to make them grow. Simple ploughs called ards were first used during the Neolithic period. They were designed to make a shallow furrow in the ground and were hauled by people. Furrows speeded up planting so it became possible to cultivate larger areas of land. Hunting was unpredictable so communities learned to keep within a restricted area those animals they wanted for meat, milk, hide, wool, etc.

Dogs had long been tamed for their usefulness when hunting, but the first domesticated farm animals were likely to have been pigs, followed by goats and sheep. Some experts even think that goats would have been used as pack animals. Stone Age sheep would have been similar to the Manx Loaghtan, small and hardy, and would have been kept for their fleece and milk as much as for their meat. The Loaghtan, together with breeds such as the Gute, native to Gotland in Sweden, and the Soay, native to Shetland in Scotland, are the nearest modern equivalent of prehistoric sheep.

The new stationary lifestyle also made the use of pottery practical for the first time. Pots are time-consuming to make and, as they break, of little use to people constantly on the move, but have obvious advantages in a less nomadic lifestyle. Neolithic pots were made by coiling long strips of clay in a rising spiral and smoothing over the sides before hardening the result in a hot, controlled fire. People had been using fire for thousands of years but it was during the New Stone Age that they learned some of the sophistications needed to control its temperature. Neolithic pots were probably hardened in an early form of kiln called a clamp, where combustible material is stacked around the newly-made pots, and its burning is controlled under turf to retain the heat. Early Neolithic pots had no decoration, but later ones had designs marked on the clay such as scratched herringbone patterns, finger prints, or the impression of grains of wheat.

Loaghtan sheep at
The Grove Museum of Victorian Life

Only on Mann

One Neolithic settlement containing pottery fragments and some large pottery jars was found at Ronaldsway in 1943 when the airport was being built. The settlement was obviously fairly extensive as more was uncovered when the runway was extended in 2009 (see above). The Ronaldsway settlement showed distinctions thought to be unique to the Isle of Man, which indicates that the early Manx were developing independently from the people on the surrounding islands. The jars of the Ronaldsway culture are fairly crude, about 20 ins (50 cms) tall and about 11 ins (28 cms) in diameter with thick, straight-sided walls and round bases. Similar pots have been found at other sites throughout the island, including four at Billown in 1996.

The two halves of King Orry's Grave are separated by the B11 road

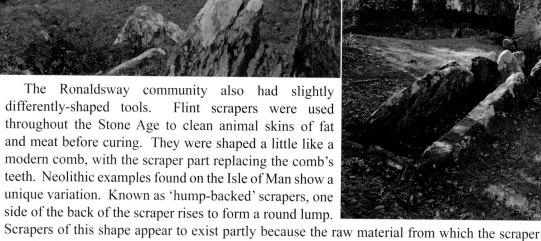

The Ronaldsway community also had slightly differently-shaped tools. Flint scrapers were used throughout the Stone Age to clean animal skins of fat and meat before curing. They were shaped a little like a modern comb, with the scraper part replacing the comb's teeth. Neolithic examples found on the Isle of Man show a unique variation. Known as 'hump-backed' scrapers, one side of the back of the scraper rises to form a round lump. Scrapers of this shape appear to exist partly because the raw material from which the scraper was fashioned was a rounded pebble, but also because Stone Age flint knappers discovered that the 'hump' fits neatly into the palm of the hand to make the scraper easier to hold and use.

The most unusual finds dating from Stone Age Ronaldsway are five oval slate plaques about 3 ins (7 cms) long and 1½ ins (3 cms) wide. Two of the plaques are decorated with chevrons incised into the surface and all are smoothed and polished. The trouble is that we don't know what they are! A similar plaque has been found at Ballavarry as well as plaque fragments in Onchan. Experts have suggested that the undecorated plaques are blanks awaiting decoration, and that the decorated ones, rather than being casually lost or thrown away, were carefully placed where they were found during some sort of ritual. Whatever is the truth, the Manx plaques are unique in Neolithic Britain.

The gradual development of permanent settlements meant that Neolithic people became builders, not only of permanent domestic accommodation, but also of structures with ceremonial significance. And the structures which survive best are those concerned with the supernatural, the afterlife, and the rituals which served both, just as cathedrals survive better than humble cottages today.

Dealing with the Dead

Most of the ceremonial structures found on Mann are similar to those found on Neolithic sites in other countries. Religion tends to be conservative, so although the way of life of people of the same religion may differ quite radically, their religious rites, observances and buildings tend to be much more similar. Even so, at least one of the Manx ceremonial sites is unusual and perhaps unique.

The Isle of Man has several well-preserved Neolithic sites, the most complete of which is Cashtal yn Ard. Dating from about 2,000 BC Cashtal yn Ard, when complete, was at least 130 ft (40 metres) long and 45 ft (14 metres) wide. Often referred to as a 'long barrow' Cashtal yn Ard is a long oval with a grave gallery of five compartments, and a forecourt at the western end marked by a semicircle of eight standing stones radiating out like horns. It was originally topped by a large flat stone and the whole covered with earth. Excavations have revealed flint, pottery and human bones, including part of a skull and upper jaw bone. The entrance to the burial chamber was from the west and facing the setting sun, but the original approach was from the east. The symbolism is therefore of life approaching death. The footpath to Cashtal yn Ard still approaches from the east and visitors must tread a path used for over four millennia.

Neolithic burial sites are usually on high ground and often visible from some distance away; Cashtal yn Ard commands a superb 360-degree view. Archaeologists surmise that the monuments act as a reminder of the tribe's ancestors, and, as they are at a point where earth and sky meet, mark a meeting place between this world and the next. Such sites also act as a beacon or notice board for neighbouring tribes; they announce that 'we are here, this is our place'. Whatever the reason Cashtal yn Ard has company. Another Neolithic burial, Ballafayle Cairn, of a slightly later

date, tops a neighbouring hill to the north east and is almost within line of sight of Cashtal-yn-Ard; certainly the trees which are near both sites can be seen from each. Whether the two were in use at similar times by different tribes, one took precedence over the other or they were used in series we can't be sure.

One Neolithic burial which seems to have been in use at the same time as Cashtal yn Ard is Gretch Veg, better known as King Orry's Grave. The ancient Manx peoples seem to have gone in for size, as both

Cloven Stones, Old Packhorse Lane, Baldrine

Cashtal yn Ard and King Orry's Grave are some of the largest barrows of their type in the British Isles. Despite its name, King Orry's Grave is nothing to do with King Orry. Most people imagine archaeological remains as being remote from civilisation, but King Orry's Grave is not like that at all. It has the B11 road running through the middle of it, cutting off the two ends in such a way that some people believe that there are actually two separate structures, built very close together. The eastern end is clearly visible by the road, but the western end, until recently, was in someone's back garden, or, more accurately, the cottage was built on the site in 1868 and subsumed the Neolithic remains into the garden. A rockery with one-upmanship! Another and similar tomb, and one which seems to have suffered a similar fate at the hand of developers, is the Cloven Stones at Baldrine.

The Isle of Man's most unusual Neolithic burial site is on Mull Hill near Cregneash and is a chambered tomb known as the Meayll Circle. Often marked on old maps as a stone circle the Meayll Circle is in fact a ring of six pairs of burial chambers arranged in two sets of three, making twelve chambers in all. There is a gap at each end of the circle with an alignment

The Meayll circle. Note the pairs of burial chambers

facing roughly north west/south east; the northern entrance faces Bradda Head and the sea.

Series of paired burial chambers with gaps between them are known elsewhere, but the tombs at the top of Mull Hill appear to be unique in that the burial chambers are arranged in a circle. Each of the six pairs takes the form of a T with the downstroke of the letter facing away from the centre of the circle. The downstroke acts as a passageway to the two burial chambers on either side and each T appears to be roughly paved. Apart from flint arrow heads, scrapers and knives plus the remains of at least twenty-six different burial urns, many of which contained evidence of cremated human bones, the Meayll Circle is particularly noted for yielding Neolithic pottery of the Ronaldsway type.

And the afterlife?

The permanence of burial sites and the way they were looked after suggests that Neolithic people respected their dead and had a growing reverence for the supernatural. It's during the late Neolithic that people first started building henge monuments. Henges are generally accepted to be sites of ritual activity possibly linked to increasing understanding of both the natural and supernatural worlds. A henge is like an inside-out fort. Like a fort it's usually a circle of ditches and banks sometimes with a stone or wooden structure in the middle. Unlike a fort the ditches are on the inside of the bank circle rather than the outside and so are of little use for defence in the traditional sense – although it has been suggested that rather than being built to protect those inside from what was happening outside, they were built to protect those outside from whatever was going on inside.

Most people think of henge monuments as being very large. Avebury in England, the Ring of Brodgar in Scotland or Rath Maeve in Ireland are all huge for example, but henges don't have to be big. It is use and appearance rather than size which denotes a henge. Archaeological work in Billown has discovered what is possibly a mini henge with an internal diameter of about 6 ft (1.8 metres). Building a henge was a considerable undertaking. Even a small one would have taken days, possibly weeks of work. They also required great social co-operation. Henge builders needed to be supported by their community, so the fact that they were built at all suggests that the society had an abundance of food and natural resources to be able to spare people for the work. The needs of the builders not only had to be met by the work of their peers, it also deprived the tribe of whatever contribution the henge builders might otherwise have been making. Henges started to appear in the late Neolithic but really developed during a period of history which had huge significance for the Isle of Man. The Bronze Age.

BRONZE AGE, IRON AGE,
AND WHY THE ROMANS NEVER CAME TO MANN

Although the Bronze Age can be dated as starting from around 2,500 BC when people first began to use bronze implements, the Neolithic lifestyle lasted relatively unchanged for several centuries. In fact the use of stone never completely died out during the Bronze Age, probably because stone, unlike bronze, was usually available locally. Nevertheless as stone tools were superseded by bronze equivalents, less care was taken in their manufacture and much lower status given to their use. There is some evidence that the Manx were quick to adopt a Bronze Age way of life, possibly influenced by communities in Ireland.

As an island people the Manx would of course have used boats and been familiar with their building, and it is during the Bronze Age that boats designed for sea travel – rather than coastal and river vessels merely being used for that purpose – began to be developed.

Jarlshof, Shetland. Late Bronze Age or Early Iron Age dwelling. The remains of several such communities have been found on Mann, but none so well preserved

Bronze Age boats were about 30 ft (9 metres) long and about 8 ft (over 2.5 metres) wide, flat bottomed but with a steep upward curve at the sides and at either end. Those few which survive are made of thick oak planks sewn together with yew withies and are both strong and very flexible. The joins are made leak-proof by stuffing them with moss and clay, and the seal is then covered with oak laths. Each vessel could carry probably about five tons of cargo, although historians are not sure whether such boats were sailed, or paddled using a single blade – oars were not known in Northern Europe at that time.

Sea-going boats meant easier and more frequent contact with people on the neighbouring islands, particularly as the Isle of Man would have been a convenient stopping point for ships travelling across the Irish Sea. Then, as now, the tidal streams entering the Irish Sea from the north and south, meet just south and west of Mann. Sailors would naturally head for the island to wait for a favourable current or slack water, or to ask the advice of local seafaring experts, such as fishermen. The Manx would therefore have come into contact with different nationalities who had differing lifestyles. One group originated in central Europe and is often called the bell-beaker folk from their style of pottery; their cups look a little like upside down bells. The customs and skills of the beaker people gradually began to influence communities around them and, before long, spread to the British Isles including the Isle of Man. An example of their very distinctive pottery was found in Barroose, just west of Baldrine, with scattered beaker remains also found at Ballachrink between Andreas and Jurby. The key fact about the beaker people is not however the fashion of their earthenware. They were also skilled metal workers, possibly introduced bronze to the Isle of Man, and almost certainly influenced its manufacture here.

Bronze provides an edge

Bronze is an alloy made of about nine parts copper to one part tin, although lead was added to the mix later in the Bronze Age to make the alloy runnier and therefore easier to pour into moulds. The Isle of Man was rich in lead, and certainly had copper deposits on Spanish Head, Bradda Head, around Laxey and on Langness, but tin is rare. Mann had none.

Bronze Age bronze makers had four main sources of tin in Europe. In order of importance these were: Cornwall and Devon, England; Erzgebirge (the name means ore mountains) on the German/Czech border; the Iberian Massif in north-west Spain and Portugal; Brittany in France.

Bronze pieces which experts think might have belonged to a bronzesmith have been found on the Isle of Man, at Ballagawne, not far from Port St Mary. In addition, a clay mould for casting a knife blade or spearhead has been found in the Crawyn Broochs in Ballaugh. Some metalworking was therefore undertaken in Mann in the first millennium BC and, as the island has no tin, trade must have supplied it.

Experts can tell that the tin used by Manx bronzesmiths came from Cornwall, but the Manx probably didn't get it direct from the Cornish. Ireland was a major producer of bronze items, having good supplies of copper and regular access to English tin. The Isle of Man had had trading and cultural links with Ireland since Neolithic times and many of the Bronze Age implements discovered on Mann show a marked resemblance to those found in Ireland from a similar period. It seems likely that the Manx traded with their Irish neighbours for the tin they needed.

Wheal Coates, tin mine near St Agnes, Cornwall, England

At first bronze was used only for small decorative items, as it was both costly and difficult to make. As their knowledge of how to work with bronze grew, however, smiths began to make bronze knives and axes and, later, cups, harness decoration,

Killeaba Mount, Ramsey

fittings for boats – in fact anything people wanted. Bronzesmiths even made bronze razors; one was found in a grave at Port y Shee, Braddan. It's very similar in style to those used in north-west Ireland and eastern Scotland at the time. Many bronze items were for display or ceremonial use only, and stone tools continued to be used for day-to-day tasks. In fact most of the Bronze Age implements which survive are grave goods, i.e. deposited with the dead like the Port y Shee razor, so their design and quality may not necessarily be typical of items intended for use every day.

Community life

During the Bronze Age the building of massive burial monuments which were a feature of the Neolithic gradually gave way to the construction and use of smaller barrows, although each still often contained more than one burial. In the early Bronze Age people were buried curled up lying on their side; the Bronze Age burial at Killeaba, Ramsey, for example, contained four crouch burials of three adults and a child. Over the next thousand years or so, customs changed and cremation became the norm, with the cremated bones interred in large urns; the Port y Shee grave mentioned above consisted of an urn containing cremated remains. If the outward signs of burial were more modest, the grave goods were not, and axes, bangles, pots and weaponry have all been founded buried with their owners or as offerings made to gods or ancestors.

It was during the Bronze Age that the landscape of the island began to take on a form which would be familiar today. The population increased, trees were cleared and fields and paddocks laid out. People needed to be able to visit each other and their fields, so primitive roads and trackways became much more a feature of the landscape. Fields were usually square so that they could be ploughed in either direction, and often were separated merely by boundary markers or occasionally a low bank. Livestock was usually herded rather than fenced, although Bronze Age communities would probably have used moveable hurdles to control small groups of animals when necessary. Communities mainly concentrated on farming, but also supplemented their diet with fishing and hunting, and continued to gather from uncultivated areas whatever they did not grow.

Bronze Age islanders lived in round houses with low stone or timber walls supporting a conical roof of turf or thatch; the exact materials varied according to what they could find. Such houses needed to accommodate extended families and their animals, so were often very large;

the floor area could be at least twice that of the average family home today. The hearth was in the middle of the floor and there was no chimney, so smoke found its way out through the roof as it could. This was not as daft as it sounds. Dry wood can burn with little smoke and a chimney creates a through draft, introducing more oxygen and so causing a fire to burn more fiercely. Such a fire does give off more heat, but uses more fuel and is also more dangerous under a large roof of highly combustible material. From their smelting work, Bronze Age people would have understood how to manage fire. For safety reasons they may well have chosen not to build a funnel chimney. In any case, the climate at the time is generally thought to have been warmer so fires in the round houses may have been more important for cooking than heating.

One of the most extensive collection of round houses on Mann is north and east of the Meayll Circle on Mull Hill. The circle itself was built during the Neolithic (see chapter 1) but people continued to live in the area well into the Bronze Age and possibly beyond. Some of the round houses even appear to be semi-detached, with walls adjoining neighbouring dwellings; the design makes sense – more warmth and the need for fewer building materials. The wind on the Isle of Man mostly blows from the west and the Mull Hill round houses were built in a hollow with their entrances facing north, and were therefore sheltered from wind and weather.

Bronze Age round houses were often used for centuries, presumably passed on through families. Several found at Ballanorris and Ballakaighan, near Castletown, were inhabited into the Iron Age. They would have taken a fairly large work force to build, and yet experts think that they were inhabited by probably a single extended family. This suggests a high level of co-operation between different families. The building of a round house during the Bronze and Iron Ages could perhaps have been organised rather like the barn raising which continues among the Amish communities in North America today.

An event like the building of a round house meant a lot of mouths to feed and mounds excavated at Clay Head, south of Garwick Bay, proved to be an open-air cooking site – a sort of Bronze Age barbeque used from around 2,200 to 1,050 BC. Bronze Age pottery wouldn't stand direct contact

Ewart Park sword forged by bronze sword smith Neil Burridge (www.bronze-age-swords.com). Neil's Ewart Park sword is similar in size and shape to the bronze-age sword found at Berrag, Jurby and shows how the Berrag sword may have looked when new.
Photographs © Neil Burridge

with fire so liquids had to be warmed indirectly. Stones were heated in a fire, removed using tongs made out of the forked branch of a tree, plunged quickly into washing water to remove ash and cinders and then dropped, still very hot, into liquid to heat it. The method is surprisingly quick and efficient. The Clay Head mounds were made largely of cooking stones which had eventually shattered after much use.

The Manx probably still had trading and marital ties with people from the neighbouring islands, and ideas as well as trade goods crossed the water. The thought that where you lived made a difference to who you were, or that different countries encapsulated and defined different races, was still in its infancy. One consequence of an increasing population and the growth of permanent settlements is that competition for the means to live also increased. Choosing a good site for a farm, and then investing time, effort and resources to build and maintain it, would have meant a distinct unwillingness to move unless absolutely essential.

Communities were based around family ties and almost certainly had their own laws and customs. Disputes must have occurred before the Bronze Age, but any fighting had been either with fists, or using tools which were designed for hunting and domestic use – spears, knives and axes. Only during the Bronze Age did implements begin to be made which had no purpose other than conflict. For the first time people began to make swords.

Us and them

British Bronze Age swords are usually described as leaf-shaped, although this would be ash rather than oak; Bronze Age swords in Europe are more often described as 'carp's tongue', where the blade is parallel for most of its length but narrows for the final third. Leaf-shaped blades are better for slashing, straight blades better for thrusting, particularly if they narrow at the end. A virtually complete leaf-shaped sword was found at Berrag, north east of Sandygate, and can be seen in the Manx Museum. The hilt would probably have been wood, or just possibly bone, and may have been wrapped with hide strips to provide a good grip. That's if the sword was intended for serious use, of course. Many were forged either as gifts for the gods or as a fashion statement to impress (and deter) visitors and potential assailants.

Cronk ny Merriu, Iron Age fort near Port Grenaugh

The Bronze Age Manx obviously felt the need to defend themselves and their island, and started to build hill forts; such forts were also built in the Iron Age. There are several hill forts on the Isle of Man, the largest and highest being the summit of South Barrule. There are also twenty or more promontory forts, built by erecting ramparts effectively fencing off part of the coast. Not only do such forts take less effort to build, as the cliffs protect one or more sides, they also double as look-out points – although they might be draughty. Cronk ny Merriu near Port Grenaugh is one such, and excavations there have shown that access to the fort was by a strongly-built gate.

The word 'fort' can however be misunderstood. Certainly such structures were intended for defence but they were also meant to deter by their impressive size and bulk. There were simply not enough people willing to co-operate in waging large pitched battles, and most fighting between tribes would have taken the form of raids on cattle and stores. Each fort constituted a huge expenditure of effort, but the statement of intent must have been worth it to protect the tribe's possessions. Within the fort on South Barrule are traces of over seventy round stone-walled huts. From about 200 BC people seemed to gather together in greater numbers and such a large collection of round houses possibly indicates an embryo town.

Going Grey

The beginning of the Iron Age marked much more than exchanging brown metal for grey. According to the pollen record, the climate appears to have grown colder, which probably meant that natural resources were scarcer and people had to work harder to survive. Competition between families and tribes may have intensified. Society also appears to have grown more hierarchical as such competition seems to have been spearheaded by powerful leaders. Rather than communal burial sites, which were more common in the Neolithic and Bronze Ages, burials from the Iron Age are more often of high-status individuals who were interred with a range of quality grave goods.

Iron is popularly considered to have replaced bronze as the metal of choice because it was much harder and therefore more useful for making edged tools. Modern bronzesmiths dispute this and state that properly forged bronze swords are a good match for iron blades. Interestingly, in *The Bible*, I Samuel 17, Goliath's armour is bronze, while his spear is iron. It seems obvious which he thinks will offer him the best protection against David. The real disadvantage with bronze, if it can be considered such, is that an item in bronze is heavier than the same item made of iron. To reduce the weight of bronze swords, the blades are often shorter than that of an iron sword – which could be a disadvantage in a fight. Even so, probably the main reason that iron took over from bronze is because bronze alloy includes tin which, being rare (see above), is expensive. Iron items were far cheaper to produce and, to start with, inferior to their bronze equivalent – rather like plastic taking over from bone or ivory. Iron ore is, however, relatively common and so there was no need to bargain with foreign powers for illusive tin.

Trade probably introduced iron to Mann, but the island is rich in iron ore, with surface deposits in Maughold. The Manx probably started exploiting their own mineral resources quite soon. Excavations at several Iron Age sites around the island have revealed moulds, finishing tools, ore and slag.

Life goes on

Despite the evidence of early industry, the Iron Age way of life was still largely agricultural with farmers raising sheep, cattle and pigs, and growing peas, beans and wheat. Grain for eating

Mal Lumkin cross, Kirk Michael. The runic/ ogham inscription is on the back

would probably have been stored in granaries raised off the ground while grain for planting was often stored in underground pits sealed with clay. The top layer of grain sprouted, used up the available oxygen and stopped growing. Without oxygen the storage pit was sterile as long as it remained sealed.

In Ireland at this time families had what might today be considered an odd arrangement when it came to child rearing. After the age of about seven, children were often placed with foster parents rather than raised within their own family. There were two sorts of fosterage; fostering for affection and fostering for payment. The idea was to strengthen family connexions and ensure that children learned skills which their own parents might not be able to teach them. Fosterage also tended to make society more peaceable; your neighbour would be less likely to attack you or steal your cattle if you were raising his heir. Girls stayed in fosterage until they reached fourteen, boys until seventeen – think of it as similar to a boarding school today. Some form of fostering was certainly known on Mann, as a combined Runic and Ogham inscription from Kirk Michael says: 'Mal Lumkun erected this cross in memory of Mal Mura his foster [mother]…Better it is to leave a good foster son than a bad son.'

Iron Age families lived in round houses similar to Bronze Age dwellings and, as well as the means for domestic metalworking, each house would almost certainly have contained one or more looms for weaving cloth; archaeologists regularly find loom weights when excavating Iron Age round houses. Historians estimate that it takes about a week's worth of spinning to make enough yarn for one day's weaving, and then takes several days of weaving to make enough cloth for one full-length tunic. With the cloth for a single tunic taking around six weeks to make, clothing was a form of wealth. Each garment would have been made to last as long as possible, mended and patched and used by more than one wearer. It is doubtful that anyone would have owned spare clothing.

Little pottery is found on Mann from this time. Drinking and cooking vessels may have been made of wood or horn, while storage containers were probably various forms of baskets, or made of wood or hide; materials which often don't survive well. One unusual domestic find on Mann dates from around 450BC and is possibly the earliest human flea found in Britain! It was found beneath a buried wooden post from what had been a farming community on St Patrick's Isle.

Four Iron Age round houses, two of them well preserved, were excavated at Close ny Chollagh, west of Castletown, in 1953-6. They had square central hearths, paved entrances and elaborate drainage which makes them very similar to the houses in the Iron Age villages of Chysauster and Carn Euny in Cornwall. At Close ny Chollagh were found a semi-circular bone comb with twelve teeth, and a fibula brooch, i.e. one with a bar front and which fastens with a simple pin, like those on some modern badges. The brooch dates to around 80 BC and shows that the houses were still in use at that time.

Even more impressive are the three pale green glass beads which were excavated in 1985 from the site of an Iron Age dwelling at Braust, just west of the disused airfield at Andreas. Iron Age glass is extremely rare and very few glass beads have been discovered in Britain. Most glass was made in continental Europe, particularly in what is now northern France, and it has been suggested that glass beads were valuable trading items, acting as a kind of rudimentary currency. Coins first appeared in England and Wales during the middle Iron Age but weren't in use in Scotland and don't appear to have been acceptable on Mann as none has been found.

The usual form for Iron Age glass beads is a hoop or ring through which a cord can be passed. This arrangement would have been useful either when worn as decoration or for carrying as trading tokens. The Manx beads are very unusual in that they are shaped something like the buttons on a modern duffle coat. Each would have been worn hung from a cord secured by a knot tied round the thinner shank in the middle of the bead. They are extremely high status items and only two other similar beads have been found in Britain, at Torloisk, Isle of Mull and Balure, Knapdale, Argyll. Interestingly the sites could almost be on a trading route with Mann.

Chysauster, Cornwall, England. An Iron Age village. Note the quern stone for grinding corn into flour by hand

Escape from Rome

Most people know that the Romans never conquered Mann but this doesn't mean that the island was totally unaffected by the Empire looming just across the water. It also doesn't mean that Roman traders never came here.

Roman galleys patrolled the western coast of England and Wales, and Roman merchantmen ventured to Ireland – a Roman fort or trading centre has been discovered at Drumanagh, near Dublin – so Romans may well have called at a Manx port. Romans tended to look down on anything to do with the sea; Rome's navy was considered inferior to its army and under the latter's control. And the Romans loathed Britain. They considered the province cold, wet, infested by dangerous barbarians, and only worth tolerating because of its mineral wealth. They would probably have been even more condescending towards those living on a small island further north and west than the hated ends of empire. However it seems most unlikely that the skilled Manx seafarers didn't try to profit from the lucrative Roman trade conducted under their noses, whether that profit was legitimate or not.

The Romans used the term 'pirate' at sea much as they used the word 'barbarian' on land. To Romans a pirate was any sailor in their waters who was not Roman; Manx sailors would therefore all have been pirates and subject to Roman piracy law if caught. And Romans took the threat seriously. On Holyhead on the Isle of Anglesey beyond the north west coast of Wales is a heavily fortified signal tower at Caer Y Twr which might also have been a Pharos or early lighthouse. It commands a view west over the Irish Sea and seems to have been built to provide early warnings against raiders. Below the watchtower, in Holyhead itself, are the remains of a small Roman fort, Caer Gybi. Very unusually, it is three-sided, with the open side towards the harbour. It's unlikely therefore to have been built to defend the area against sea-bourne raiders, but might have been built to defend Roman merchant ships and their crews from local pilfering. In either case, it's unlikely that, when raiders came from the sea, the Romans would have stopped to enquire whether they were Irish or Manx.

Advent of Christianity

It was during the Iron Age that Christianity come to Mann. Pre-Christian religion on the island was probably Druidical, although Druids also had a semi-political role as law-givers and advisors. They sanctioned wars,

Above: Spooyt Vane (white spout), Glen Mooar
Left: Inneen Vooar (big girl), Dhoon Glen. Both sites may have been used by Druids

acted as keepers of knowledge, judged disputes, supervised sacrifices and religious ceremonies, and were often considered to be more important than the nominal leaders. Certainly Druids existed on Mann. An Ogham inscription on a stone found at Ballaqueeny refers to *dovaidona maqi droata* or 'Dovaidu son of the Druid'. Islands were considered to be places of special significance for Druidism, and Anglesey was a Druid stronghold until a particularly bloody Roman invasion and massacre in AD60. It seems likely that the surviving Druids fled across the Irish Sea to the Isle of Man and Ireland.

Druidism has been surrounded in mystique, partly because Druids themselves instructed their acolytes in secret and wrote nothing down, and partly because they left very few artefacts so we know little about them. The Druid religion was based on the natural world so they built no temples and therefore left no structural remains to be found. Instead Druids held their religious ceremonies in sacred groves of trees – oak for preference – or by hallowed springs or pools. Druidale, near Sulby Reservoir, is a relatively modern name for the glen traditionally called Eairyhorkell, but the new name does indicate the sort of place the Druids preferred for their worship.

Human sacrifice appears to have been practised in the Druidical religion although their very firm belief in an afterlife seems to have led some sacrificial victims to volunteer for the role; ancient texts written by Roman historians seem to suggest as much.

As well as sacrificing people and animals Druids also placed votive offerings of finely wrought swords, daggers, etc., into sacred pools. The two chief festival days when large

Gallarus Oratory, County Kerry, Ireland. Built between the sixth and ninth centuries, the oratory has a low door and one tiny window. Manx keeills may have been similar

tribal assemblies took place were Beltain and Samhain (in Manx *Laa Boaltinn/Boaldyn* and *Sauin* respectively). The former took place at the beginning of May to herald the start of summer, the latter at the beginning of November to usher in winter; the Manx festival of *Hop tu Naa* is a derivation of the *Sauin* celebrations. Druids were skilled

St Luke's, Baldwin, built on the site of an old keeill dedicated to St Abban

herbalists and used their knowledge to produce what would now be called hallucinogenic drugs to aid the celebration of the festivals.

Into the Druidical society came Christian missionaries from Ireland. Two of St Patrick's disciples, Romulus and Conindrus, are usually credited with establishing Christianity on Mann in AD447. Despite tales of warlike Celtic tribesmen, there was no race, as far as we know, who called themselves the Celts. The name has been given to a loosely-related group of tribes which probably shared a similar language, customs and religion. Celtic Christianity, which included much of Britain and Ireland, although agreeing liturgically with the Church of Rome, had slightly different traditions and practices. Monasteries could contain both men and women, monks and nuns could marry and raise children, while those seeking for a meditative spiritual life could become anchorites, living alone but still serving God within the local community.

Such solitary holy men – and they were almost always men – were known as Culdees. Each built a cabbal or tiny chapel, with a priest's cell attached. Cabbals are small, rectangular buildings sometimes no more than about five feet tall, built of sods, roofed with turf and with a floor dug away to a depth of between one and two feet. When built, the tiny structures looked a little like a Second World War Anderson shelter. Cabbals were situated at the eastern end of a small enclosure, the whole of which was set on top of a low mound. As the cabbals were so small, services would have been held out of doors.

Cabbals were probably introduced in the middle of the fifth century. Keeills, which took over from them, began to be developed in Ireland in the sixth century, although they seem not to have been introduced to the Isle of Man until around the ninth century. Keeills differ little in design from cabbals but are often slightly larger, have a single window in addition to a door and are generally built of stone. There are 174 recorded keeil sites on the Isle of Man many of which have been developed into the parish churches. St Luke's church in Baldwin, for example, is built on the site of an old keeill dedicated to St Abban, an Irish missionary and hermit. Because the Culdees were solitary and austere, cabbals and keeills were often in lonely or remote locations.

Maughold is unusually rich in keeills which are also placed unusually close together. Not only has the church been developed from a keeill, the remains of three others still exist in the churchyard, with the position of a fourth marked by a short granite pillar. Maughold churchyard is particularly large and occupies the site of an important Celtic monastery which enclosed and subsumed the earlier keeills. The arrangement of the buildings seems to demonstrate the transition from a Christianity based on isolated priests serving the spiritual needs of local families, to a Christianity based on specialist communities gathered at spiritual centres. The Maughold arrangement is confusing however, as the monastery has been dated to the sixth century which is before the time when keeills really got going on the island. Were the keeill system and monastic system rivals, perhaps representing two different interpretations of the Christian message? Or did the monastery and possibly others like it, act as something like base stations for the development of outlying keeills?

Each Manx keeill appears to have had its own burial ground, although, perhaps surprisingly, the graves appear to predate the keeill. The little churches seem to have been built on top of the burial grounds, perhaps to bring a more modern Christianity to sites which were already Christian burial places. Quite often white quartz pebbles were brought from the shore and placed within Christian burials. This is thought to be a reference to *The Bible*, Revelations 2:17 which says: '... I will give him a white stone, with a new name written on the stone which no one knows except him who receives it.' Could it be that each stone represents a different person buried at the site?

Stone-lined graves called lintel or cist graves dating from the sixth and seventh centuries are often found within the old burial grounds. Several were uncovered by the archaeologists from Channel 4's *Time Team* when they excavated Speke Keeill near Mount

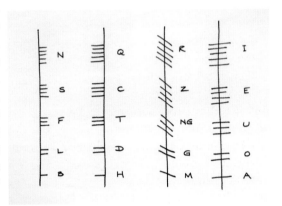

Ogham script. Ogham is read from bottom to top or left to right. The first twenty letters of the alphabet are generally agreed, although extra letters appear to have been added at a later date or might have had regional significance

Murray Hotel. One of the lintel graves contained the skeletal remains of a woman in her twenties, and included a plait of her hair. Carbon dating revealed that the burial took place between 530 and 650 AD. Lintel graves took a long time to fashion and it's likely that only the most important people – priests, leaders of the community, heads of households, etc. – would have been buried in them. During the Celtic period women were considered to hold virtually equal status with men and could be powerful individuals in their own right. As well as being lined with stone, the grave was covered by stone slabs possibly with another stone erected at its head. Such a slab may well have been incised with a cross and simple inscription.

The Manx crosses and Celtic art

The early Christians left unique evidence of their faith in the impressive number of carved stone slabs found on Mann, generally referred to as the Manx crosses. The earliest crosses date from around the fifth century, when Christianity first arrived on the island. Fittingly, as the faith first came from Ireland, some inscriptions on the Manx crosses are written in Ogham, a system of writing which was widely used in Ireland between the fourth and the eighth centuries.

The Ogham alphabet is based on a series of straight lines marked across a single unifying line, making it ideal for marking on anything with a straight edge. It is thought to have been developed from a tallying system which used notched sticks to indicate quantities. Although virtually all Ogham script survives as stone inscriptions, it was more commonly used on wooden rods, fence posts and trees. Ogham is read as the tree grows, i.e. from bottom to top, although when inscribed on a stone it can reach the top and go down the other side.

The Iron Age is noted for the richness of its decorative items and ornament was as important in the clothing and utensils of the time as it is now. It is during the Iron Age that decoration began to develop into the sophisticated patterns of what is now generally known as Celtic art or design. At first the decoration was of swirling lines which flowed but did not overlap or interlace. The intricate knotwork which appears magnificently on many of the Manx crosses was introduced in the sixth century almost certainly by Christian missionaries and probably from Ireland – the knotwork

Members of Wessex Archaeology, working for Channel 4's Time Team excavating the grave of a woman in her twenties (trench 3, grave 304) at Speke Keeill, Mount Murray. Looking on is Victor Ambrus artist and illustrator. Photograph © Wessex Archaeology

was at first used to illustrate religious texts. The new possibilities for overlapping and intertwining decoration were quickly incorporated into the older Celtic style of swirling patterns where the lines did not cross. A further layer was added to the decoration by the influence of the Norsemen. Many of the Scandinavian designs of the time were illustrative of Viking sagas, etc., and were populated with stylised representations of mythical beasts. Celtic designers again adopted new ideas without relinquishing their old templates. Consequently any knotwork which incorporates animal shapes shows the influence of three different traditions; early Celtic in the swirling patterns, Christian in the knotwork, Norse in the animals.

In England and Wales, the Iron Age is said to have ended abruptly at 43 BC when the Romans invaded. Of course the lives of most of the ordinary people continued much as they had been before, but natives of England and Wales couldn't escape the influence of the Roman conquerors. The Isle of Man, Scotland and Ireland were not subject to Roman invasion and so the Iron Age way of life lingered there until the next wave of invaders came, this time from the north. The Vikings.

INVADERS FROM THE NORTH

Unlike the gradual development which the Isle of Man experienced over the preceding millennia, the ninth century saw an abrupt change. The Vikings invaded. The first Viking raids on the British Isles were in 789 in Portland, Dorset, England, quickly followed by raids on Mercia, now part of Kent, England. The most famous account of those early raids comes from the *Anglo Saxon Chronicle*, where the scribe writes that on 8 January 793 'the harrying of the heathen miserably destroyed God's church in Lindisfarne by rapine and slaughter.' Two years later, in 795, the Vikings reached the Irish Sea, and another island monastery, this time on Rathlin off the north east coast of Ireland, was sacked. The *Annals of Ulster* noted '*loscadh Rechrainne o geinntib + Sci do choscradh + do lomradh*' (the burning of Rechru [Rathlin] by the heathens, and Scí [possibly a shrine] was overwhelmed and laid waste). Vikings reached the Isle of Man in 798.

The Viking Raiders Stone, Lindisfarne, England. Thought to be a memorial of the first Viking raids in 793, it marked a grave and shows a line of men holding swords and an axe

The Scandinavian invaders first attacked and burned the buildings on St Patrick's Isle, Peel, but quickly recognised the richness and strategic importance of Mann. They were superb seafarers and knew they'd found a base not only for future raids, but also as a trading centre for the neighbouring islands.

So who were the Vikings? Why did they come to Britain at all? And why now?

Raiders from the sea

With such a long coastline the Norsemen must have become excellent sailors very early in their history. Various suggestions including population expansion, global warming, and the need for younger sons to find a place of their own, have been made to explain why those living in Scandinavia started attacking their neighbours. The truth is that we don't know what prompted the Norsemen to start raiding.

Although the attackers called themselves Vikings, they weren't using the word to describe their clan or tribe, but rather their activity. In Old Norse a *vik* is a creek, bay or river estuary and therefore a place which provides access by boat; it is therefore vulnerable to attack from the water. *Viking* can be a noun meaning a sea-borne raid, or a verb meaning to raid from the sea, while a *vikingr* is a sea warrior. Vikings were therefore seafaring raiders, but very few of them were what could be called professionals, i.e. full-time warriors. Most were farmers looking to eke out their living. They might, for example, become a *vikingr* for a season or two before settling down, or return to raiding after a bad harvest. Only a few of the Norsemen were Vikings at any one time but most were or had been Vikings some of the time. Raiding was not only a way of increasing an individual or group's portable wealth, but also, according to Norse society's priorities, a praiseworthily heroic thing to do. Done once and successfully, rivalry and copy-cat activities would make sure that the number and severity of raids increased.

The fact that Vikings were only part-time raiders by no means meant that they were not effective. The Norse culture extolled the virtues of warfare and skill at arms, and prized courage and indifference to danger. Men carried a dagger but tended to fight with a spear or an axe. A spear was one of the cheapest of all weapons to make and was mainly used as a long-range stabbing implement, although they could also be thrown. Axes were popular because they were dual purpose – they could also be used to cut timber and brushwood on a farm. They were single-bladed and Viking boys were taught how to use them from a very early age. Specialist battleaxes – still single bladed; there is no historic evidence for double-edged axe heads – with longer handles and larger blades were only developed towards the end of the Viking Age. Swords were expensive and therefore rare, but showed that their owner was considered important.

Weapons were carried not only to be used but to show off with and so were often highly decorated. All free men were expected to own weapons, and tribal leaders were expected to provide them for their men.

From raiders to invaders

Around the ninth century a lot of solar activity caused the Earth to warm up; the ninth to the thirteenth centuries are often called the Mediaeval Warm Period (MWP). The Gulf Stream is the warm current of water which crosses the Atlantic ocean and makes Britain and the northern coastline of Europe much warmer than it ought to be for land that far north. Currents in the oceans change according to changing global temperatures, and the MWP had the knock-on effect

Viking ship Hugin, *Pegwell Bay, Kent, England*

of slowing down and diverting the Gulf Stream. This meant that, although the planet was warmer, Britain and northwest Europe were actually colder. With a less effective Gulf Stream, Norway's coastline iced up much more frequently, and its farmers struggled with more severe winters.

Britain's ambient temperature and relatively high rainfall makes its farming land richer and more fertile than most of the land east of it. Whether trading or raiding the Norsemen must have returned home extolling the virtues of the warmer climate and the productivity of the land. Most Vikings were farmers, and good farming land was probably a temptation. Having faced them in arms, the Norsemen also knew that the land's inhabitants were no match for their own military prowess. After only a few years of pillaging, the raiders became the invaders. It's odd to think that the activity of the sun thirteen hundred years ago might be the reason why the Isle of Man has so much Viking history.

The invading forces from Scandinavia seemed to divide into three groups. Invaders from what is now Norway settled in the Isle of Man, Ireland and south Wales, Swedes settled along the west coast of Scotland and Danes in north and west England. It appears that there was either some sort of prior agreement between the groups as to who had what, or they preferred to fight softer targets rather than each other.

Land, ownership and its organisation

Land in the Isle of Man was, and largely still is, organised into treens. Each treen is an area defined within natural borders such as streams and cliffs, plus boundaries developed by custom such as paths and stonewalls. The derivation of the word causes much debate, but it seems likely that 'treen' is connected with the Scottish Gaelic *tir-unga*, with *tir* being land and *unga* or *uinge* meaning an ingot of a particular weight, often an ounce. A *tir-unga* was a unit of land decided by the revenue it generated rather than by its size; a similar way of apportioning land occurred in the Hebrides and Orkney, also places invaded by Vikings. Like the *tir-unga* the Manx treen is also a fiscal unit. More can be produced from good agricultural land, so treens on good land are smaller than those on poor land. Treens therefore vary in size from less than 200 acres to more than 600 acres, with most around 400 acres, but, importantly, each treen produces about the same revenue – or at least they did once. It's a little like the modern rating system for houses. In the 1960s houses were assessed for how much rent would be needed to occupy them, and the rateable value drawn up based on the hypothetical rent. Over the years rents, houses and areas all changed so the rateable value has drifted away from the rent assessment.

Each treen was usually divided into four farms, known as quarterlands. Again the extent of the quarterland farm was determined by the revenue of the land and not its size. So, although most are around 90 acres, a quarterland is a division of the treen by the revenue it produces rather than an exact division of the size of the treen. There is also evidence to suggest that each treen contained its own keeill. If such be the case, it points to the treens being a Celtic organisation of land units and therefore predating the Viking invaders.

Vikings were not averse to taking over existing arrangements, however, so whether the treens already existed or not, the Norsemen certainly adopted them. Most treens have Norse names but about three out of four quarterlands are known by Gaelic names. The Manorial Roll states, for example, that the treen of Rauffe in Lonan has quarterlands Ballagawne, Ballabeg, Ballacannell and The Rae (or Rhaa). Rauffe and Rhaa are both from old Norse while *balla* is Manx for farm; the nomenclature underlines the dominance of the Viking invaders over the newly-conquered people.

Left: the remains of the Viking longhouse at The Braaid, Marown
Below: interior of Viking turf house reconstruction at Eiriksstaðir, Haukadalur, Iceland. Photograph supplied by Hurstwic, a group focussed on the research and practice of Viking-age fighting moves as explained in the Sagas of Iceland and elsewhere. Photograph © hurstwic.org

Above: site of Tynwald, Baldwin. In the distance is the roof of St Luke's church which would have formed part of the processional way
Left: Tynwald Hill, St John's. In the distance is St John's church, at the end of the modern processional way

Arrival of Tynwald

Most of the political and legal arrangements of the Isle of Man can be traced directly to the organisation of the Norsemen. Communities in Scandinavia lived in small groups isolated by forest and fjord. To ensure that harmony was maintained between the tribes, the free men of the community met periodically to discuss issues which affected them all, and to debate, affirm, amend or add to existing tribal laws. In Norse a meeting was known as a *thing*. Several communities coming together for a joint meeting on larger issues constituted an *all-thing*. The ancient tradition is echoed today in the names of the parliaments of Iceland (*Althingi*), Norway (*Storting*), Finland (*Lagting*), Denmark (*Folketing*), the Faroe Isles (*Løgting*), Greenland (*Landsting*) and the Åland Islands (*Lagting*). Even Shetland and Orkney had their parliaments, both at places called Tingwall. Only in the Isle of Man is the tradition unbroken in the oldest continuous parliament in the world – Tynwald. And, even today, the legal rather than political nature of the assembly is emphasised in its formal designation: The Court of Tynwald.

The assembly field where a thing took place was called the *thing-völlr*, which is where Tynwald gets its name; in Manx it is *Tinvaal*. The leaders of the assembly met on a low hill which was linked by a processional way stretching towards an area where courts met and which doubled as a place of worship. The whole was surrounded by banks. Traditionally the mound included a handful of earth brought from each tribal territory, so that all tribal representatives could think of themselves as being on their homeground and, perhaps more importantly, be governed by the laws of hospitality. It was considered bad form for Vikings to fight their guests! Tynwald Hill in St John's is said to contain earth drawn from every parish in the island and is still linked by a processional way to St John's Church. The church was consecrated in 1849 and so is relatively modern, but replaced a much older series of religious buildings, which were also used as court rooms. The Royal Chapel in St John's is unique for two reasons. Not only is it the only Christian church where a government meets (albeit only once a year on Tynwald Day), but it is also the only Christian church with an area which is unconsecrated. The area where members of the House of Keys sit is not consecrated so that any non-Christian members of the house can be accommodated (see appendix 3).

Midsummer was a time for celebration and it saved much travelling if a *thing* was held at the same time. Tynwald still meets on 5 July, Old Midsummer's Day. No record exists stating when Tynwald first began although, as an established part of Norse culture, it's likely that local *things* would have been introduced almost as soon as the Norsemen established settlements. In 1979 the Isle of Man celebrated 1,000 years of Tynwald, which suggests that the national *thing* was established by 979 when the island owed allegiance to Earl Haakan Sigurdsson, King of Norway (see appendix 1). A Tynwald didn't always need to meet in the same venue and two other Tynwald sites have been identified. One is near West Baldwin reservoir north of St Luke's church, while the other is at Cronk Urley upstream from Glen Wyllin on a small hill to the east of the current A3.

Millennium of Tynwald — Tynwald Hill and St. John's Church — ISLE OF MAN — J H NICHOLSON R I — 1979

Millennium of Tynwald — 10th Century Meeting of Tynwald — 7p ISLE OF MAN — J H NICHOLSON R I — 1979 — WADDINGTON

Viking way of life

Unlike Celtic round houses, Norse houses were rectangular with pitched roofs made of thatch or turf, although they too sheltered several families. The base of the walls was stone, with the rest of the walls built out of whatever was available – more stone, wood, wattle and daub, or turf. A circle of stones in the centre of the beaten earth floor made up the hearth, and smoke escaped through a vent hole in the roof.

When they weren't out raiding, Vikings were farmers, specialising in raising animals, although they also grew small amounts of barley and oats, and lots and lots of hay to see their animals through the winter. To protect their hay fields Vikings built walls around them made out of turf bricks laid on a stone base. Manx sod hedges are still built using a variation of the Viking technique. Parallel outer walls of turf bricks on a stone are built and then the core is filled with stone and compacted soil. Plants and even trees such as hawthorn or gorse can then either grow naturally or be planted on top of the hedge. When complete the sod hedge provides a long-lasting sturdy windbreak and attractive barrier for livestock.

Cosy domestic harmony clashes with the popular image of Vikings as wild-haired, quarrelsome savages. Quarrelsome they were but they were also fastidious when it came to personal grooming. Accounts from the time state that Vikings regularly washed and combed their hair, washed their faces and hands daily, and usually bathed about once a week. Hair for both men and women was worn shoulder length or longer – short hair was a sign of thraldom or slavery – and unwashed hair was only tolerated as a sign of mourning. Excavations of grave goods in Scandinavia suggest that both sexes carried personal combs, and men also usually had a rigid comb case made from bone or antler to protect their comb from damage. Women are thought to have carried their combs inside a cloth pouch.

Clothing was mostly made of wool, although shoes and belts would have been leather. Leather or toughened hide was used for shields and scabbards, and also for close-fitting hats to protect the head in combat. Fighters preferred iron skull-cap helmets which would deflect the blades of opponents, but many couldn't afford them. And forget the picturesque idea of horned helmets. Vikings were ruthlessly practical and if Wagner did not invent such headgear then the Scandinavian tourist industry probably did. Horned helmets would be heavy, unwieldy and prone to catch on things. They would also snag an opponent's sword blade.

Ornamentation was as important to people then as it is now. Both sexes wore armlets and torcs, cloaks were held in place by large penannular (combined ring and pin) brooches, and women fastened their overdresses with ornate oval shoulder brooches. Beads were particularly prized and women hung them between the oval brooches. One of the richest tenth-century female graves outside Scandinavia was found in 1984 during an archaeological excavation on St Patrick's Isle. Now known as The Pagan Lady, the grave's occupant had with her seventy-three high-quality beads, in a variety of shapes, the largest almost 4 cms (1.5 ins) in diameter. Most are of different coloured glass, but a few are of amber and jet. The amber would have come from the shores of either the Baltic or the North Sea, but the only source of jet open to the people of the time was Whitby, North Yorkshire, on the east coast of England.

THE MANX MUSEUM 1886-1986

VIKING NECKLACE, PEEL CASTLE

12p 1986

ISLE OF MAN

QUESTA

The larger beads might even have been spindle whorls, which are weights fixed to the end of a rod (spindle), which form a 'drop spindle' used for spinning yarn; you can make something similar (although less efficient) by pushing a disc of cardboard onto a pencil.

Spindle whorls help the rod to spin more easily and quickly, and their weight means that the spin lasts longer, making the manufacture of yarn quicker and more even. Drop spindles are highly portable and easy to use, even by children. Making cloth and clothing was a hugely time-consuming job and every Viking lady would have had spindle whorls ready for use by herself and her daughters. She may well have displayed them among her beads, rather as a wrist watch today can be both useful and decorative.

Skills at sea

Vikings were expert seafarers and skilled boatbuilders. Strictly speaking the Viking longship was used only for raiding; trading vessels tended to be wider in relation to their length. In practice the actual design of the boat was probably decided by regional variations, the local boatbuilders' efficiency, personal preference and even fashion, as much as the boat's intended use. What they did all share is exceptional seaworthiness.

Viking ships are clinker built, which means that the planking forms a hollow shell, rather than being attached to a rigid framework. The structure thus formed is rather like an egg shell; very strong for its weight. Clinker-built ships are more difficult to build, but are light and flexible. They are easier for a relatively small crew to manoeuvre, but can yet withstand ocean storms. Viking longships had sails which swivelled to catch the prevailing wind, complementing oars for extra speed – cargo ships often lacked oars. Ships were steered not by a rudder, but by a single oar mounted on the right near the stern (see the picture of *Hugin* on page 31). Decks were open with the fifty or so crew sleeping on or under the rowing benches. Fierce figureheads looked out from bow and stern and the warriors' circular shields could be mounted along the sides for defence; they would be removed while at sea. The whole was a light, fast, flexible ship equally capable of carrying cargo across the Atlantic to Greenland, or raiders up the Neb River to St John's.

The stones mark the Viking ship burial at Balladoole, near Castletown

The size and shape of one Viking ship was clearly indicated when a ship burial was excavated at Balladoole just west of Castletown. The timbers had rotted away, but the 300 or so clenched boat nails which had originally held them together indicated where the boat had lain. From that the vessel's original length was calculated at about 11 m long (36 ft) and 3m (nearly 10 ft) wide. The shape of the boat indicates that it was a cargo ship – a warship of that width would probably be twice as long – and could have carried an estimated load of around four tons with probably a minimum crew of five.

Who was he?

A finely-dressed man was buried in the Balladoole ship, surrounded by the luxury items he valued in life. Horses appeared to be very important to him, as his grave goods included a decorated bronze and iron bridle, stirrups and spurs. Owning horses conveyed status among Vikings, rather like owning an expensive car today, so the horse equipment means that he was considered important. On the other hand, and unusually, no weaponry other than a shield appears to have been included in the grave. As the vessel was a cargo ship, could its contents indicate that its occupant was a high-ranking merchant? Or possibly even a horse breeder?

Vikings owned slaves, but distinguished between unfree servants of their own tribes which they called *þræll* or thralls, and slaves or *anauð* which were captured in raids. Both thralls and slaves did the hard and dirty jobs which no-one else wanted, but slaves were also considered valuable trading items, constituting much of their master's portable property. As property, slaves were also considered valid grave goods to be buried with their master when he died. In the Balladoole ship burial, the remains of an adult woman lie at the dead man's feet. Her position indicates her inferior status.

Another high-status Viking burial was discovered at Ballateare, just south of Jurby, and again a slave woman was buried with her master. Excavation revealed that she had been killed by a blow from a sharp weapon across the back of her skull. Ahmad ibn Fadlan, a 10th century Arab traveller, writes of being in Russia and witnessing a female slave volunteering to accompany her Viking master in death. The Russian burial is about 2,000 miles from the Isle of Man, and perhaps 100 years later, but the Viking culture is similar, so such ritual killings may not have been without consent.

The Ballateare Viking was also buried with his treasures, including several weapons and an iron sword which had been deliberately broken in two places. The breaks might be a symbol that the living hand of its former master could no longer wield it, or even to deprive the dead man of the use of his sword if he returned as one of the *draugr* or walking dead. According to Viking belief, *draugr* were corpses who wanted to return and interfere with the living they had left behind. Today they might be called zombies.

Multicultural

Some of the Viking invaders may have brought their wives with them but many married native Celtic women, possibly the daughters of the families they conquered. Children would then have been brought up in a mix of two cultures and perhaps also a mix of two religions, Christianity and paganism. As the years went by and the children of the Norsemen became part of the island's indigenous people, so aspects of Viking culture merged with the older Celtic culture. The amalgamation of the two is obvious even today in the names given to various places around Mann.

Many, such as Niarbyl, meaning 'a tail', are Gaelic and have no Norse influence. A number, such as Snaefell or 'snow mountain', are pure Norse. Some names appear in both languages, for example Ballaglass (Gaelic) and Grenaby (Norse). *Balla*, sometimes *Balley*, is the equivalent of the Norse *byr* and means farm or homestead. *Glass* is Gaelic for the green of plants, while the Norse *grön* means green, and comes into English as 'gren'. Ballaglass and Grenaby both therefore mean Green Farm.

Perhaps most revealing are those names which combine elements of both Gaelic and Norse. 'By' the Norse for 'farm', for example, was usually used at the end of a word, but if the place was considered very important, it could be used at the beginning. 'By' appears, slightly transmuted to 'Be', at the beginning of Bemahague in Onchan. The name combines Gaelic and Norse elements which could mean that it was a place important to both Celts and Vikings. The original wording could be, roughly, 'By-Mac-Thaidhg', or 'important farm of the son of

Thurith's cross, Onchan. The runes on the left at the bottom say 'Thurith carved the runes'

Taig'. It was considered an important place over a thousand years ago and is still considered such today. Now it's more commonly known as Government House. It is the official residence of the Lieutenant Governor of the island.

Sagas and Runes

The Vikings, unlike the Celtic Irish, placed little reliance on written records, preferring instead to rely on oral tradition to pass on stories and history. Listening to a bard recite sagas was the Viking equivalent of television or the internet, and a good saga teller was highly respected both as a library of knowledge and as an entertainer. Despite their preference for spoken as opposed to written records, Vikings were not however illiterate. They used runes. In Old Norse the word 'rune' simply means letter or text. Runes gained their aura of slight mysticism as the word was taken to mean secret in some of the Old Germanic languages.

Just as the word 'alphabet' comes from the first two Greek letters, alpha and beta, so the runic equivalent is known as the futhark from its first six runes, F, U, Th, A, R and K. Runes can be difficult to read because there are many different variations depending on age and country. Just before the Viking Age the number of characters in the futhark had been reduced from twenty four to sixteen; towards the end of the Viking Age, around 1100, it was expanded again. From around 800, Denmark, Sweden and Norway each had a slightly different variation of runes, while the futhark of what was to become Germany differed again. The two main systems are called 'long branch' and 'short twig' because the straight lines used to create the letters are shorter in short twig. Long branch was used in Denmark and Iceland, short twig in Norway, Sweden and the Isle of Man.

Reading runes is made even more challenging as they might legitimately be carved back-to-front or upside down; the early inscriptions were even occasionally made to be read from right to left. Like ogham (see chapter 2) most runes were made up of straight lines which made letters easier to carve into stone, wood, bone or metal, and rune writing was obviously a skilled craft. Like craftsmen today, some of the rune carvers signed their work. In St Peter's church, Onchan, Thurith's cross has seven inscriptions in runes. The one running down the left side at the back says: *Þúríð reist rúna* (Thurith carved the runes).

Runic futhark. The futhark of different countries and times differs; this is the Norwegian version of what is known as the Younger Futhark and was used from about 800-1200

Religion

Not a great deal is known about Viking religious practices, although we do know that they believed in an afterlife, specified different destinations for the dead depending on how they died, and had a whole pantheon of gods. They don't however seem to have had priests, in the sense of full-time holy men as their leaders seem to have been responsible for conducting ritual or religious ceremonies.

The Viking belief in many gods might have made their acceptance of Christianity easier – the Christian God was just one more. The Vikings arrived on Mann as pagans, but soon adopted the faith of their new land. There must have been considerable pressure

Right: Irish round tower, Dunkineely, Donegal, Ireland
Below: Round tower in Peel Castle

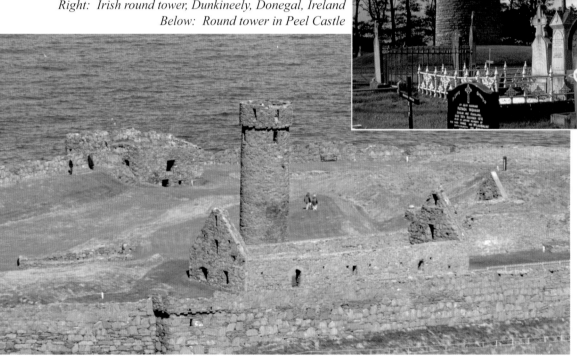

on the invaders to do so as, apart from the faith of the conquered people, rulers and traders across the water in England and Ireland were also predominantly Christian. A shared faith made transactions less problematic. Pagan funerary customs of ship burials and barrows were replaced by Christian burial customs of graves and grave markers, yet the latter combine scenes from pagan myths and Christian stories. Particularly interesting is the burial ground on St Patrick's Isle. It started being used in the seventh century as a Christian burial ground, was used for pagan burials around the tenth century during the Viking incursion, before reverting again to containing Christian graves.

The tenth century was also when the oldest surviving building on St Patrick's Isle was built; the round tower. Built in the Irish style such towers were fairly common in Ireland, but only three exist elsewhere: the one on St Patrick's Isle on Mann, and one each at Brechin and Abernethy in Scotland. Towers similar in appearance exist on Douglas Head and Langness but are much more recent and were built at the beginning of the nineteenth century as a guide to shipping and to mark harbour entrances.

Why the round tower was built at all is still something of a mystery. Invariably such towers were part of a religious foundation, usually near the western end of the monastery's most important church, with entrances to church and tower facing each other. Most were about a hundred feet high and fifty in circumference, with a conical roof at first of wood and slate, but later of stone. In Irish Gaelic such towers are called *clog teach* or bell house (*clag* or *clagg* is Manx for bell), which suggests that part at least of their function was to house bells to call the faithful and sound the alarm.

The Manx and Irish Vikings were originally from Norway and, certainly in Ireland, occasionally fought off waves of incoming Vikings from Denmark who were taking over England and had their eye on anything else which might be profitable. The Isle of Man might have been caught in the middle. The tower on St Patrick's Isle obviously had some sort of defensive role, as the doorway is about ten feet above ground level, accessible originally by a ladder which was hauled up after the last defender had scrambled in. The refuge was effective against casual raids but could not withstand a deliberate and concerted attack from a force intending to take over the area, as, apart from being cramped, the tower lacked a water supply.

Local boy makes good

It is something of an understatement to say that the Viking period is not one which is noted for its peace. Fathers fought against sons, brothers against each other and, under the largely tribal organisation of the society at the time, ordinary men were dragged away from their farms to help with the fighting. Not that they'd probably have objected too much. As we've seen, fighting skills were highly valued and a good Viking would have grown bored with too much peace. The Isle of Man was often called on to supply men, arms and ships, but itself knew an uneasy peace for almost three hundred years after the Vikings first arrived. That all changed with the arrival of Godred Crovan.

No-one seems sure where Godred was born, but it's likely that he was of Viking descent, probably related to the kings of Ireland and possibly also to the king of Northumbria. Brought up on Mann, he may have been one of those called on to help with wars overseas. Godred was certainly one of Harald Sigurdson's (Harald III) fighting men in September 1066, when the King of Norway tried to invade England. Better known by his epithet *harðráði* (hard ruler) Harald Hardrada was killed in the Battle of Stamford Bridge in Yorkshire by the English army under Harold Godwinson. Godred Crovan escaped back to Mann.

Crovan seems to have lived fairly peaceably, although not necessarily on the Isle of Man, until 1079. But he was ambitious. He wanted to rule Mann and was quite prepared to take the island by force. He must have been fairly determined as he was twice defeated. Third time lucky, he planned a trap. During the night he sailed up the Sulby river from Ramsey, landed with three hundred men and hid them in the trees on the slopes of Sky Hill. The *Chronicles of the Kings of Man and the Isles*, were written by the monks of Rushen Abbey in the twelfth and thirteenth centuries and so are hardly eye-witness accounts. Nevertheless they explain what happened next:

'At dawn the Manxmen formed up in battle order and after a massive charge joined battle with Godred. When the battle was raging vehemently, the three hundred men rose from their

The site of the battle of Sky Hill. Godred Crovan defeated the Manx here in 1079

place of hiding at the rear of the Manxmen and began to weaken their resistance, and they compelled them to flee... those who were left begged Godred with pitiful cries to spare them their lives.'

The Manx form of the name Godred is Goree, and Godred Crovan is the King Gorree, or King Orry of Manx myth (see chapter 9). It is Godred who is credited with establishing much of island's legislature and governance. He confirmed the *thing* assembly – Tynwald – and is said to have divided the island into its six sheadings, although there is little evidence that it was Godred who did so. Under the Norse law of *leiðangr*, which was developed around the time that Godred took over Mann, a king could expect tribes, or groups of people living in areas of a certain size to provide warships and enough men to crew them. In Mann, this responsibility is thought to belong to the sheadings. The word sheading is most often thought to come from the Norse *skeið*, an ocean-going warship with thirty benches, which needed sixty rowers and therefore had a crew of about eighty. The *skeið* was an eleventh century design, much larger than the ships Vikings used when they first started raiding, and tended to be the ship of choice for nobility and royalty. It's likely therefore that *skeið* would be popular among Godred Crovan and his followers. Whatever the derivation of the word, the sheadings have formed the basis of the island's organisation and administration ever since the time of the Vikings. Even today, the modern constituency map is based on the ancient sheadings

As a reward to the loyal followers who won him victory at the Battle of Sky Hill, Godred granted plunder to those who wanted to leave, and land in the south of the island to those who preferred to settle. Then, as now, north and south refers to a division of the island north east to south west along the mountain range from North to South Barrule, rather than north of west to south of east along the Peel to Douglas valley.

The invaders' dispossession of the native Manx from their good agricultural land rebounded on them nineteen years later. Civil war was fought between northerners – the natives – and southerners – the come-overs – at Santwat. No-one knows for sure where the site of the battle was, but C.H. Cowley, writing for the Isle of Man Natural History and Antiquarian Society in 1927, thought it most likely to be near Kirk Patrick where Barnell Lane meets the A38.

The *Chronicles of the Kings of Man and the Isles* state categorically that the victory went to the north, but other sources put the south as victorious, which Manx tradition appears to endorse. Virtually everyone agrees, however, that the victors at Santwat won because they were helped by their women. Watching the battle from the hills and seeing it go badly with their menfolk, wives and daughters swept down to fight, and the extra numbers carried the day. However, it's Celtic women, the pre-Viking natives, who traditionally fight next to their men when needed, so perhaps the *Chronicles* were right after all.

A possible site for the battle of Santwat, at the junction of Barnell's Lane and the main road between Patrick Church and St John's

Barefoot victory

The battle at Santwat in 1098 had a lasting effect on Mann almost by accident. King Magnus III of Norway, recent conqueror of Orkney and future conqueror of Anglesey, landed on St Patrick's Isle shortly after the battle, when the bodies of the dead were still unburied. Divided and exhausted, no-one was in any state to defend themselves and Magnus proclaimed himself king. The fortunate timing sounds like the work of spies or even an *agent provocateur*, but nothing remains in the records of the time to indicate such.

Known as Magnus *Barfot*, the king of Norway's soubriquet means barefoot or barelegs and is thought to have come from his habit of wearing a tunic to the knees without the trews which would normally go underneath it. King Magnus built a hall on St Patrick's Isle – a forerunner to Peel Castle – insisting that the people from Galloway, the part of Scotland nearest to Mann, should supply the timber to build it. By similar means he stated that the Isle of Man should pay tribute money to Norway and acknowledge the Norwegian king as an overlord in perpetuity. It's always difficult to refuse someone who's shown he's quite capable of taking what he wants and a lot more besides. Magnus couldn't take Ireland though. Despite a treaty with Muirchertach II, King of Ireland, Magnus invaded. And was killed.

'On his [Magnus's] death the chieftains of the Isles sent for Olaf, son of Godred Crovan, of whom we have previously made mention, who was at that time living at the court of Henry, King of England…' The Manx *Chronicles* describe the succession of Olaf as peaceful and popular, and his long reign proved to be both.

Rushen Abbey

The growth of Christianity

It was during the reign of Olaf I that Rushen Abbey was founded. Stephen de Blois, Count of Mortain, Lord of Eye, Lord of Lancaster and later King of England was a devout man. He was also wealthy. In 1123, he founded St Mary's Abbey in Tulketh, Preston, Lancashire as part of the Benedictine Congregation of Savigny. In 1127 the monks upped sticks and moved to a site on the Furness peninsula.

On a good day the coast of Mann is visible from Furness. Stephen de Blois and King Olaf had both lived at the court of King Henry I of England, and could easily have known each other, possibly well. In 1134, the *Chronicles* say: 'King Olaf granted to Ivo, abbot of Furness, part of his land in Mann to establish an abbey in a place which is called Rushen.' It's at least possible that the granting of Manx land to a monastic foundation favoured by Stephen was partly to cement an alliance between two powerful men.

Rushen Abbey was the third of seven daughter houses established for Furness, the others being Calder and Swineshead in England, and Fermoy, Holy Cross, Corcumruadh and Inislaunaght in Ireland. Originally part of the Savigniac Order, Furness and its daughter houses became absorbed into the Cistercian Order when two congregations merged in 1147.

Other monastic foundations were also established on Mann, including Douglas Priory, now known as The Nunnery, a Franciscan Friary at Bemaken, Ballabeg near Castletown and Mirescog Monastery in Sulby. Grants of Manx land were also made to religious foundations in England and Ireland. No religious foundation was as influential as Rushen Abbey however, and King Olaf himself was, according to the Chronicles 'devout and enthusiastic in matters of religion and was welcome both to God and men.'

The establishment of Rushen Abbey must have been fraught with difficulty, even if the locals were co-operative – and there was no reason why they should be. For a start, newcomers and locals would probably have had no common language. The monks spoke Latin, possibly Norman French, and probably the Cumbrian Middle English dialect spoken around Furness. The Manx spoke Gaelic and Norse. Perhaps traders or one of the island's priests acted as interpreter?

The rule laid down by St Benedict stated that foundations such as Rushen Abbey must be self supporting, offer hospitality to all who needed it, care for the sick and the poor and be places for prayer and study. The first abbot and twelve monks arrived from Furness to deprive local farmers of all or part of their land to make room for the new abbey. Materials taken to build the abbey – at first of wood, but soon replaced by stone – fuel for its fires, and fish and produce to feed the monks would have left less for the original Manx inhabitants, even if they were allowed still to make use of them. The abbey would also have expected to recruit locally for help and new members. Abbey lands would usually be worked by lay brothers or tenant farmers, to allow the monks more time for their devotions. Monastic landholdings became extensive, as more and more were donated by various patrons. Rushen Abbey eventually came to own land in the area east of Sulby as well as around Peel, Port St Mary and Port Erin.

Abbots and archbishops

The monastic foundation formed one branch of Christianity, the bishoprics and parishes another. 'The first bishop before Godred Crovan began to rule was Roolwer who lies at St Maughold's church,' says the *Chronicles*. Roolwer – experts disagree over whether he was Scottish or Norwegian – appears to have been a suffragan bishop of York and was in post at around 1050, i.e. just after the Pagan Lady was buried in what would become Peel Castle. Later, when Godred Crovan took over Mann, his overlord was the King of Norway, so naturally Norway was interested in who became bishop. The Isle of Man was incorporated into one huge Norwegian see.

At various times during the Viking occupation of Mann, the Hebrides, Shetland, Orkney, Iceland, Greenland and the Faroe Islands also came under Scandinavian rule. The Norsemen knew the Hebrides as the Southern Islands, which in Norse is *Suðoer* (Orkney and Shetland were the Northern Islands or

Roolwer cross slab, Maughold. The bishop was supposed to have been buried at Maughold. This cross slab might have been his grave marker

Norðoer). It is probably from *Suðoer* that the newly-created diocese gets the first part of its name, as its head was given the title Bishop of Sodor and Man.

The creation of the see was something of a shotgun marriage, as two archbishops, York in England, and Nidaros (Trondheim) in Norway, both claimed the right to consecrate its bishop. Fifty years later the situation became even more confused when King Olaf I of Mann founded Rushen Abbey. Despite having absolutely no authority to do so, the king granted to the abbey the right to specify who became Bishop of Sodor and Man. Rushen's mother house Furness Abbey, and even the leaders of the Cistercian Order in France, seized the opportunity eagerly and, over the next hundred years or so, tried to appoint bishops, with greater or lesser success,. All this jockeying for position sometimes meant that Mann had two or more bishops, each appointed by a different power and all with different agendas.

Bishops were powerful men, second only to the island's ruler, and sometimes deputising for him. They needed a suitably impressive – and fortified – residence. John Donkan, bishop from 1374, is thought to have extended an existing building and built a tower house, similar to the pele or peel towers build along the border between Scotland and England. The tower still exists and remains very much as it was built; even parts of the moat can still be traced. Better known as Bishopscourt, until 1974, it still formed part of the official residence of the Bishop of Sodor and Man. It is possibly the only building on the island known to have been continuously occupied since the thirteenth century and believed to have been so for at least a century before that; the earliest record of the house states that Bishop Simon (bishop 1226-1247) was living there.

Consecrated by the Archbishop of Nidaros, Simon was the first bishop to be accepted by all branches of the church as the rightful Bishop of Sodor and Man. Famous for many religious

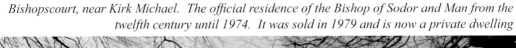

Bishopscourt, near Kirk Michael. The official residence of the Bishop of Sodor and Man from the twelfth century until 1974. It was sold in 1979 and is now a private dwelling

reforms and enterprises, he is particularly remembered for building St German's Cathedral on St. Patrick's Isle. Simon also ensured that the Bishop of Sodor and Man received revenue from the Manx estates granted to him, revenue which previously had usually disappeared into the pockets of stewards. Such lands became known as the Bishop's Barony (see chapter 4).

As well as income from property, Bishop Simon established the Bishop's Barony Courts and created laws and regulations to ensure that the bishop's revenue would be regularly collected. Two Barony Courts (see also chapter 4) dealing with all matters relating to the bishop's land were held each year in May and October, with at least a hundred people attending. Any changes of tenant had to be approved by the court and recorded, and rents and customs, i.e. payments in kind, were collected. The business was conducted in Manx and the records kept in Latin. Some courts were held at Bishopscourt, others at Peel, Braddan (at Ballaquirk, now Farmhill Manor just west of Douglas), Ballakilley, The Nunnery, Kirk Arbory and Castle Rushen. Barony Courts continued to be held until the mid-nineteenth century.

Back to politics

For about two hundred years from about 1070, Mann was a kingdom in its own right. The machinations of its rulers are extremely convoluted, rivalling a modern soap opera for complexity. Nevertheless, no history of the Isle of Man can really be complete without looking at its period of kingship. Readers unable to face even a simplified version of invasion, betrayal, power grabbing, blood, battles and sudden death should read the final two sentences of this chapter and turn, thankfully, to chapter 4.

Those of you who are prepared to canter through a brief retelling of the history of Manx kings, here goes.

The extent of the Kingdom of Mann and the Isles varied according to the various power struggles, but at different times encompassed Mann, the Hebrides, Orkney plus parts of Ireland and some of mainland Scotland. The Manx king was also never allowed to forget that the King of Norway expected homage as overlord. In 1153, therefore, King Olaf I sent his son Godred, as ambassador to King Inge 'the Hunchback' of Norway, grandson of Mann's previous king Magnus 'Barelegs'.

While Godred was paying his respects in Norway, his three cousins, who had been raised in Ireland, arrived in Mann with a large band of warriors and demanded to be given half the island. Prompted perhaps by family feeling or natural magnanimity (or perhaps lacking the support of the warriors who had accompanied his son) King Olaf didn't immediately send his nephews packing, but invited them to a parley. In the act of saluting the king with his axe, Reginald, the middle brother, cut off his uncle's head.

Dividing Mann between them, the three brothers immediately tried to emulate their grandfather Magnus Barelegs by subjugating Galloway, but the Scots were having none of it and drove them away. In the meantime Godred, on his way back from Norway, heard about his father's assassination, was understandably angry, and landed in Orkney to try to raise support and an army. 'All the chieftains of the Isles were overjoyed when they heard he had come, and at an assembly unanimously elected him their king.' It's interesting that the *Chronicles* use the Latin verb *elegere* (*eligere*), which means 'to choose'. The leaders of the island communities appear therefore to elect their king, rather than Godred becoming king by right of succession. Kings can of course gain a throne simply because they have more efficient fighters than anyone else but, that aside, in the eleventh century there were two routes to rule. English and Scottish Kings gained their throne by hereditary rights; Kings in Ireland were chosen by an assembly of leaders who at the same time appointed the king's heir apparent, or tanist, in case of his sudden death. It sounds as though the kingship of Mann and the Isles was decided using a system similar to that of the Irish.

Once confirmed in post, Godred lost no time in sailing to Mann and putting his father's killers to death. He seems, at least at first, to have been popular as the people of Dublin sent an envoy to Mann requesting that Godred become their king also. Dublin was supposed to be under the rule of Muirchertach III, High King of Ireland, who tried to oust Godred from his kingship, but was unable to do so, backed as Godred was by those who lived in the city.

Godred's success seems to have gone to his head, however, as, after less than two years, 'he began exercising tyranny against his chieftains, for some of them he disinherited, while others he deprived of their positions' – or so the *Chronicles* say. Those chieftains were the ones who had elected Godred as king, remember, and probably expected more in the way of gratitude. Godred's father, Olaf, had had a number of illegitimate children, one of whom was married to Somerled, King of Argyll. Thorfin, one of the disaffected chieftains, decided to do the twelfth century equivalent of giving Godred the sack. Thorfin went to Somerled and asked that his son Dougal, i.e. Godred's nephew, come and rule Mann. The *Chronicles* explain what happened next:

'Somerled was very much pleased to hear this request and handed his son Dougal over to him [Thorfin], who took and conducted him through all the Isles. He subjected them all to his sway and received hostages from each island. But one chieftain called Paul made a secret escape to Godred and told him everything that had taken place. Godred was alarmed to hear this and straightway ordered his men to prepare ships and to hasten to meet them. Somerled with his men collected a fleet of eighty ships and hastened to meet Godred.

'In the year 1156 a naval battle was fought on the night of the Epiphany between Godred and Somerled and there was much slaughter on both sides. When the day dawned they made peace and divided the kingdom of the Isles between them.' On 6 January 1156 therefore, Somerled took control of the islands Mull and Islay, which were closest to the rest of his kingdom of Argyll, while Godred retained control of Mann, Lewis and Skye. Somerled's acquisitions were right in the middle of Godred's kingdom and probably a thorn in his flesh.

The sea battle of 1156 wasn't the last encounter between the brothers-in-law. Two years later Somerled attacked, defeated Godred, and sacked Mann. Godred fled to Norway leaving the King of Argyll in possession. Somerled left the island, some say because of the intervention of St Maughold (see chapter 9), but also appears to have left a power vacuum, although it's possible that his son Dougal governed the island on behalf of his father. That, after all, was what the leaders of the island peoples had asked for in the first place.

In 1164, after Somerled had died in battle at Renfrew on the Scottish mainland, Godred's illegitimate brother Reginald opportunely seized the Manx throne. He didn't have it long. Four days later Godred appeared with an army borrowed from Magnus V of Norway. By this time Godred appears to have become fed up with the scheming of his relations as he blinded and castrated Reginald before taking back the throne. Godred ruled for another twenty-three years before dying on St Patrick's Isle on 10 November 1187. He is buried at the traditional burying place of the Kings of Mann and the Isles, at St Oran's Shrine on Iona.

Godred left three sons, Reginald, Olaf and Ivar, the first of whom was technically illegitimate, although his parents, Godred and Fionnula, granddaughter of a King of Ireland, had subsequently married. Godred had always intended that his heir should be Olaf, his second son, but the boy was only ten when his father died. Concerned that a regent would usurp the boy's powers, the Manx leaders established Reginald as king. To put such fears into context, the previous year, Ruaidri, the last High King of Ireland had been deposed by the English;

rival kings Magnus V and Sverre were fighting a lengthy civil war in Norway; and Gwynedd in Wales was divided between David I, Rhodri II and Gruffydd III, two brothers and a nephew. The Manx were aiming to get an adult leader capable of keeping peace in the realm. Fine in theory, the decision unfortunately didn't work in practice.

Reginald had problems right from the start. Not only did his brother Olaf want what he considered his rightful place as King of Mann, but the kings of Norway and England were both pressurising Reginald to help them with their separate designs on Ireland. Reginald kept his brother quiet for several years by giving him Lewis on which to live, but in 1208 when Olaf, now aged 31, complained that farming was poor, Reginald had him arrested and asked William 'the Lion', King of Scotland to keep him locked up. Only when William died, seven years later, did Olaf return to Lewis. He and Reginald also returned to squabbling over the kingdom, occasionally supported or otherwise by such opportunists as Henry III of England, Alan, Lord of Galloway and Thomas, Earl of Athol. After fighting his brother's troops at Ronaldsway in 1226, Olaf, aged 47, finally ousted Reginald from the kingship of Mann in fact, if not in law. Two years later, at the Battle of Tynwald – a real battle, not a legal or political one – Olaf and the northern Manx fought Reginald and the southern Manx and Reginald was killed. Monks from Rushen Abbey conveyed the king's body to their mother church in Furness where, as the *Chronicles* say: 'he was buried in the place he chose for himself while he was alive.'

Olaf II's reign was much more peaceful than that of his brother, not least because he had no rival brother contending with him; Ivar appears to have faded out of history somewhere in the previous forty years. Olaf did, however, have to exercise some political sleight of hand in order to reconcile various expedient allegiances. The Norwegian civil war was finally over and Norway's sea strength growing again, so Olaf had to be mindful of the old tribute. Against that, England, which had become much more powerful in the region, now held much of Ireland. As Olaf was having to defend Mann from pirate raids, the English King Henry III thought he could also help defend the English and Irish coastline around the Irish Sea. Nevertheless, despite being squeezed by his powerful neighbours, Olaf II's eleven-year reign was the closest thing to peace the Isle of Man had known for many years. He died on St Patrick's Isle in 1237 and was buried in Rushen Abbey.

Harald, Olaf's son, was only fourteen when he came to the throne, but, born at the height of Olaf's strife with his brother Reginald, Harald seems to have remembered and learned from the political chicanery going on during his formative years. Apart from a violent spat at a meeting of Tynwald in 1237, during which representatives of the king were killed, Harald's reign was largely peaceful. Once again the question of acknowledging Norway's supremacy came up and Harald was inclined to ignore it. Since the end of the Norwegian civil war, however, co-regents Haaken IV 'the Elder' and his son Haaken 'the Younger' were stronger and less preoccupied. The year after Harald's succession the two Haakens sent Gospatrick and Gilchrist to Mann to remind the young king of his manners. As the *Chronicles* say: 'They expelled Harald from the kingdom of Mann, because he refused to go to the court of the king of Norway. They took over the governorship of the whole country and collected the king's dues for the use of the king of Norway.' It was four more years before the Norwegian king ratified Harald as King of Mann and the Isles. The young king, now nineteen, was only allowed to return to Mann in 1242.

In 1247 Harald again left Mann, visited England where he was knighted by King Henry, and travelled to Norway, this time to marry the Norwegian king's daughter. Either the nuptial celebrations were particularly extensive, or there was much to discuss, as Harald spent more than a year in Norway, only sailing for Mann in the autumn of 1249. He never arrived. A violent storm blew up off the coast of Shetland and he, his new family, Laurence the new Bishop of Sodor and Mann, and his entire retinue were drowned.

The loss at the same time of so many of the nobility of Mann and the Isles created another power vacuum, and the kingdom suffered four kings in three years, none of whom had the backing of the Norwegian king. Eventually, in 1252, Magnus, the youngest son of Olaf II, was crowned Magnus IV on the island. Incidentally, it was probably Magnus who founded Castle Rushen at around this time. One year later, he was confirmed as King of Mann and the Isles by Haaken IV of Norway. There was trouble in the wings however.

Magnus was King of Mann and the Isles, and it was the 'isles' part of his kingdom which rankled with his neighbours. Almost exactly one hundred years earlier, Somerled, King of Argyll had divided the kingdom when he took control of Mull and Islay, leaving Lewis and Skye to the King of Mann. The Manx kings had never got them back and Mull and Islay had descended to the Scottish kings. They were eager to take over the whole of the Hebrides and felt that they had a good chance of keeping them, as the islands were

A version of the Viking ship used as the Isle of Man's emblem as it appears in the north window in Lonan Old Church

closer to the Scottish mainland than they were to Mann. Alexander II of Scotland had first mooted the idea to Haaken IV of Norway, the overlord of the King of Mann, but died before the issue could be resolved. His son, Alexander III, continued with the negotiations but wearied of them and opted instead for open hostilities.

In 1263 the kings of Norway and Scotland fought for possession of Lewis and Skye. The Norwegians were defeated more by the weather than the Scots, and Haaken IV died on his way home. Without his overlord Magnus had no chance of keeping the isles part of his kingdom, and without the good will of the king of Scotland, not much of retaining the throne of Mann itself. The allegiance formerly owed to Norway was hastily transferred to Scotland, and Magnus also promised to supply his new overlord with ten war galleys as often as he needed them. In return, Magnus was allowed to keep his crown, but had to drop the 'and the Isles' part of his title, becoming King of Mann only. Two years later he was dead. In 1265 Magnus IV died at Castle Rushen and was buried in the Abbey of St Mary at Rushen.

The following year another Magnus, Magnus VI 'the Law Mender', King of Norway effectively withdrew any claim to Mann, by selling the entire kingdom of Mann and the Isles to Alexander III of Scotland for four thousand marks down and one hundred marks per year in perpetuity. The annual fee soon lapsed and nearly five hundred years after the Vikings first invaded, the Manx independent kingdom, and the island's long allegiance to Norway was over.

THE SCOTS, THE ENGLISH AND THE LORDS OF MANN

During the period of Norse rule, the island's symbol, not surprisingly, was a Viking ship. The three legs of Mann seem to have replaced the ship after 1266 when Alexander III of Scotland gained control of the island, although both symbols may have been used earlier and continued to be used concurrently for a while. The Three Legs of Mann is a variation of the triskele or triskelion, the name usually given to a pattern consisting of three lines or legs identically bent or curved and joined at one end, and usually representing the sun. Such patterns have existed for around 5,000 years and appear in many cultures including those of Greece, Mycenae and North America. Its most obvious similarity is with the flag of Sicily which has a triskelion of three three naked legs with a face superimposed where the legs join.

Why then was the emblem adopted for the Isle of Man? No-one really knows, but it's possible that it has something to do with Alexander III's wife, Margaret. She was the daughter of Henry III of England who campaigned for a long time and largely unsuccessfully to make

The Sicilian flag flying in a back garden in Ramsey

her brother Edward King of Sicily. Edward was actually in Sicily when he learned of his father's death and his own succession to the crown. That was in 1272. The connexions are all rather tentative, but the two flags are undoubtedly alike, while being quite dissimilar from most others. It seems likely therefore that there must be some connexion although we no longer know what it is.

New rulers, new rules

Much of the next 150 years is marked by wars between Scotland and England into which Mann, under its new ruler, was inevitably dragged. The island's strategic importance in the middle of the Irish Sea, not only made it a useful springboard for invasion north or south, but also allowed its ruler to dominate trade routes to Ireland.

Three legs of Man in a shield on the Maughold cross inside the church. This and the Manx Sword of State are probably the earliest known Manx representations of the three legs emblem

Alexander III might have purchased the Isle of Man, but that didn't mean that the Manx people endorsed the change of management. Rather like the employees of a firm on the receiving end of a hostile takeover, the Manx felt that their new ruler didn't care about the way they did things. The Treaty of Perth signed on 2 July 1266 to ratify the transfer of the island to Scotland from Norway states: 'Mann, together with the other Sodor Isles, and all other islands to the west or south of the Great Sea'. No distinction was made between the Hebrides and the Isle of Man, and Alexander III was known to want to consolidate all the disparate regions of his kingdom under one law and one language. He didn't understand or appreciate the Manx laws, social organisation, or way of life, and almost certainly didn't want Manx rights or customs complicating his administration. Almost the first thing he did was to appoint bailiffs to tax the Manx people. Although very little is known about actual events, it is reasonable to suppose that the foreign bailiffs of a successful king who had paid good money for a new territory, would have little compunction about making harsh demands on the indigenous population to try to get some of the money back.

St Michael's Chapel, St Michael's Island. Built in the twelfth century, this chapel would have been about a hundred years old when the Scots put down the Manx rebellion

All this upset his new subjects. The natural focus for the growing discontent was Godred, illegitimate son of Magnus IV, the last King of Mann. After ten years of probably escalating unrest the Manx openly rebelled so, on 7 October 1275, Alexander sent troops to quash the recalcitrant islanders. Led by John de Vesci, a disaffected Englishman from Alnwick but working as what amounted to a mercenary for the Scottish King, a Scottish force landed on St Michael's Island, now linked to Langness but then a separate small island.

Vesci sent an embassy to the rebels to sue for peace, but Godred defied it, so the Scottish troops crossed to Ronaldsway. The *Chronicles of the Kings of Man and the Isles* tell what happened next: 'a battle was fought between the Manxmen and the Scots, but the Scots were victorious and they cut down five hundred and thirty seven of the Manxmen in that conflict'.

537 Manx dead or badly injured. It's a huge number bearing in mind that the population of the entire island was probably only around 6,000 at the time. And most of the dead would have been men capable of doing heavy work and providing for families. If they were going to survive, the women, children, sick, injured and elderly who were left would have had little choice but to knuckle down under their Scottish overlords.

Eleven years later Alexander III died and was succeeded by his three-year-old granddaughter Margaret. She was known as the Maid of Norway as her father was the Norwegian king Eirik II.

As was usual in mediaeval courts when a successor was a minor – and a girl at that – other leaders, not necessarily only those in Scotland, began to consider how much a crown would suit them. Sure enough, when Margaret died after only four years, thirteen claimants to the Scottish throne eagerly stepped forward. The adjudicator between them was to be the most powerful ruler in the surrounding islands, Edward I of England.

The Isle of Man, further away and more difficult to defend but yet of strategic importance, was again considered a prize for whoever could take and hold it. Edward had always regarded the Isle of Man as properly belonging to England but had not yet had time to make good his claim. He did so now.

England v Scotland

English rule in Mann at the end of the thirteenth century was patchy at best. The island was a long way from the centre of power in England and, with the English monarch also laying claim to large areas of France, English kings typically looked south to Europe for the expansion of their kingdom. On the other hand, the small island almost off the edge of the map was of great strategic value. Edward II appointed Piers Gaveston governor of the Isle of Man in 1307, but changed his mind a year later and made Bishop of Durham, Antony Bek, the island's governor; Piers Gaveston became Lord Lieutenant of Ireland. It would be interesting to speculate what the Bishop of Sodor and Man thought about being effectively ruled by his spiritual brother of Durham, but either the Manx see was vacant at about that time, or Bishop Alan from Scotland was in the chair. As a member of a nation generally hostile to England (nothing changes) and whose king thought that the Isle of Man should be part of his kingdom anyway, perhaps the English King Edward didn't care too much about upsetting Bishop Alan. Antony Bek died in 1311 but control of the island had already been transferred to Henry de Beaumont the year before. Henry's sister was the wife of the John de Vesci who had taken the Isle of Man for the Scottish king thirty-five years earlier. Henry and his family were therefore very involved – on both sides – in the political machinations between England and Scotland.

And what about the Manx? They were divided in their loyalties, or, more likely, were canny enough to exploit rulers on both sides, none of whom was of their choosing. While some of the Manx were sailors on Edward II's ships, others supported Robert I ('the Bruce'), King of Scotland, in his attacks against England.

On 18 May 1313 Robert landed at Ramsey and spent the night at Douglas Priory, now known as The Nunnery, before laying siege to Castle Rushen. Five weeks later the castle fell. Mann reverted to Scottish rule and Robert gave the governorship to his nephew Thomas Randolph Earl of Moray in return for six ships and one hundred silver marks. Although nominally ruled by Scotland, many of the Bruce's invading army seem to have been Irish, as many of the Scottish nobility had moved to Ireland; Irishman Murtagh MacKennedy, for example, appears to have been left in charge of the garrison at Castle Rushen. The informal rule by Scotland of parts of Ireland may be why the Manx *Chronicles* write of an Irish invasion; the troops may have been Irish but their officers were probably Scots.

The Isle of Man remained in Scottish (or Irish) hands for under two years and, in February 1315, was retaken for the English by John of Argyll, a Scotsman who was nevertheless in charge of the English fleet. Like today, fourteenth century alliances were complicated by personal loyalty, nationality – and money. Over the next thirteen years the Scottish and English kings both claimed the island and invaded it in turn. The ordinary Manx people must have become adept at hiding their goods or there would have been nothing left for them to live on. The

Above: Douglas Priory, now The Nunnery. Formerly the home of the Goldie-Taubman family.
Right: Robert the Bruce stayed at Douglas Priory when he invaded Mann

question of the island's ruler was not settled until the English King Edward III ordered the invasion and capture of Mann in 1329. From then on Mann was inextricably tied to England.

Isolated or cosmopolitan?

The political musical chairs made life difficult for ordinary Manx people, as each new ruler tended to want to squeeze the island for all they could get. But there was a problem. Unlike its near neighbours, Mann had no rigid feudal system, which meant that new rulers had much less of a hold on the independent Manx. Constant invasion had made the island a mix of various cultures, not least among which were remnants of the Viking organisation and way of life. For five hundred years *things* (see chapter 3) had regulated the laws of the land. Literally the land as, in the thirteenth century, even on an island with extensive fishing, land was what provided most people with the means to survive. The mediaeval England and Scotland of the island's squabbling rulers may have had a strip-field system worked by serfs and owing allegiance to the lord of the manor, but such was not Mann's experience.

Few ordinary people in Europe had the traditional independence and freedom of movement (via the sea) of the Manx. Today it's difficult to appreciate just how important the sea was as a means of communication. It's only very, very recently, almost within the last few decades and certainly within the last hundred years, that people wishing to move themselves or their goods tend to consider road, rail or air travel first. Up until as recently as the 1960s scheduled passenger ships circled the British Isles and were regularly used as the best means of getting from the south of England to Scotland. For centuries the sea has been busy with small ships bustling round the coastline between ports or butting across the Irish Sea, collecting and delivering cargoes and passengers.

The Isle of Man was at the hub of most of the major communication and trade routes between Ireland, Wales, and the west coasts of England and Scotland. Not only that but the Irish Sea was a major route for merchant vessels travelling from Bruges to Bristol and northwards, so ships from continental Europe also called in at Manx ports. Nothing which could go by water was carried by land. The ease of sea and river communication, as least compared with overland routes, meant that trade rather than land ownership began to be the main source of wealth. All sorts of cargos were carried, from French wine to Irish horses, from German salt and silver to Flemish armour, from Asian silk to English wool. Merchants grew richer and, in growing richer, grew more powerful and the island offered a convenient stopping-off point in the centre of a sea criss-crossed by trading vessels. Peasants from the larger islands surrounding Mann would not have had such experience of other peoples and so were far more isolated by comparison. In the fourteenth century, Mann was about as isolated as Gatwick Airport.

The geography of Mann doesn't lend itself easily to the creation of roads, and wheeled traffic was unknown until the eighteenth century (see chapter 5). Wherever possible, trade goods or other bulky items were transported by sea or river, which is why the older towns are either on the coast or near a good watercourse. Occasionally water transport was not possible and, in these cases, goods were carried by chapman (a man carrying a pack) or pack animal on trackways created by feet and custom. Some mediaeval pack horse roads still exist, such as the one which passes near Cornaa Mill in Maughold, a continuation of the road which runs down Old Laxey Hill crosses the river near Laxey harbour and climbs away from old Laxey up Puncheon Road.

For those loads which were too large to carry, but where water was not available, the Manx may have used sledges which ran on grass. They were fairly common in Ireland, where they were known in Irish Gaelic as carrs. Designed to run well on turf and peat, carrs may have been used to transport loads inland on the Isle of Man, particularly on the grassy, unwooded slopes of the island's uplands.

Above: mediaeval trackway near Cornaa Mill
Left: old postcard of Ireland showing carr. Similar sledge-like vehicles were used on Mann

Multi-skilled

The ordinary Manx people were farmers, fishermen, traders and miners from choice, warriors from necessity. The various rulers who claimed Mann usually backed up their claim by invasion, pillage and/or taxation, and so robbed the Manx people of food and stores. Partly from the depredations of their changing overlords and partly because of the size of the property, farms would not often support an entire family. Some of the men would spend part of their time working elsewhere to bolster the family income while the women kept things going at home and did much of the work on the farm. Seafaring – either fishing or working on trading vessels – and mining were the two most common sources of extra income.

Mining became more prevalent when technology made deep mining possible using shafts, but extracting ore from the ground had been a feature of island life and something of a cottage industry since the Iron Age (see chapter 2). The Abbot of Furness Abbey, the mother house of Rushen Abbey, had been granted mineral rights on Mann in 1246 by King Harald. Remains dating from the thirteenth or fourteenth century of what was probably a bowl hearth for smelting or refining iron have been found at Kirk Braddan, and Edward I of England granted John Comyn, 3rd Earl or Mormaer (a regional or provincial ruler in mediaeval Scotland) of Buchan a licence to dig lead on the Calf of Man. The earl wanted the lead to make a new roof for his castle at Cruggleton in Galloway. He might have been granted the licence, but it was Manxmen who did the digging.

Up until the middle of the fourteenth century the official language of England was… French! English was growing in ascendancy, however, and was widely spoken; it replaced French as the national language of England in 1362. Scotland also had two languages: Gaelic, which at this time was called Ersche, and Scots; very, very loosely the two can be divided respectively into the speech of the Highlands and Lowlands. Ireland went one better and used three languages, Irish Gaelic, French and English. The church used yet another language, conducting its services and keeping its records in Latin.

The Isle of Man's position, surrounded by larger often hostile countries, together with its fairly mobile population, meant that the Manx were to a certain extent multi-lingual, rather like the Dutch today. Manx, Irish and Scottish Gaelic are part of the goidelic group of Gaelic languages while Welsh, Cornish and Breton make up the brythonic group. The differences between the two groups stem from the relationship between the tribes of the original Viking invaders. Even so, anyone speaking Gaelic can usually communicate with other Gaelic speakers regardless of their nationality. It would have been even more true of the fourteenth century when the languages had had far less time to develop independently.

As well as their own language Manx merchants would probably have had smatterings of French and English plus Scots and Ersche and Irish Gaelic where it differed from Manx; they may also have been able to get by in Welsh and Cornish. They, or more probably their clerks, may also have been familiar with Latin. Manx fishermen would have been able to make themselves understood in the ports of most of the countries surrounding Mann and also probably those in Scandinavia, as bad weather would force them to take shelter in various harbours. Their wives would speak only Manx, and so would young children, taught at home by the women of the family.

Its seafaring contact with the wider world meant that Mann was not as quarantined from disease as might have been expected. Its ports offered shelter to traders not only from the neighbouring islands, but also to ships from the Hanseatic League, Scandinavia and occasionally the Mediterranean – and hence also to any pests or illnesses they might be carrying. Outside

The monastic church from Bemaken Friary. It survived as it was incorporated into the Friary Farm. As a registered building it can't be used to house animals or machinery so currently stores equipment used in the celebrations for Laa Columb Killey *(St Columbus' Day)*

the port areas, however, most of the Manx people lived in small agricultural communities, which, because they were both self-sufficient and relatively isolated, restricted the spread of epidemic. With spring water running off the hills, communities generally also had a clean water supply. From 1348 to 1350, between a third and half the population of Britain died of bubonic or pneumonic plague. Diseases such as plague and measles need high densities of population to spread quickly, as the bacteria, although virulent, are not long lived. Such bacteria also tend to need warmth to thrive. Summer temperatures on the Isle of Man are colder than is usual in larger land masses, and the sparse and widely-scattered Manx population would not have been a good breeding ground for disease. There is no record of plague reaching Mann, but it may have done so and yet not caused high numbers of deaths.

The quiet power

Amid the hurly burly of invasion and counter invasion, political wrangling and the search for fortunes, the church with its emphasis on a simple contemplative life might have been thought to have provided a sharp contrast with the secular world. Such was not the case.

Mann was home to several foundations. Among them, Rushen Abbey was founded in 1134 as a daughter house for the Savignac order in Furness (see chapter 3). It became Cistercian in 1147 when the two orders merged. Douglas Priory, founded in 1226, was also Cistercian and a house of nuns, while Bemaken Friary, founded in 1367, was Franciscan. All were dissolved in 1540 when Henry VIII of England became short of money (see chapter 5).

Without doubt, Rushen Abbey was the wealthiest monastic foundation on Mann. Unlike Benedictines who regularly built monasteries in or near towns, the phrase often quoted from the Cistercian rule is that their houses be founded 'far from the concourse of men'. Consequently Cistercian monasteries were usually built on an isolated site on low-lying land beside running water. Great importance was placed on self-sufficiency and therefore on manual, particularly agricultural, labour. However, monastic foundations required that monks take part in eight services of worship, plus a mass, per day, and also attend chapter meeting, chantry prayers, etc. There simply wasn't time also to do sufficient work to provide for the needs of the community. Cistercians therefore introduced the concept of lay-brothers who were primarily responsible for managing the land and animals, yet observed the rules of the order and took vows of obedience. They were often distinguished from choir monks – so called because they sat in the choir part of the church and usually sang the services – by wearing a different habit; Cistercian lay brothers wore a brown robe instead of the white one worn by choir monks; both were topped by a black scapular or tunic.

By the fourteenth century the Cistercians had what amounted to a two-tier membership. Lay brothers and monks not only formed separate but complementary communities within the abbey, but were seen as distinct vocations. Lay brothers were not trainee monks – and indeed were not allowed to be – but servants of the abbey in their own sphere. Both communities worked and prayed, but the monks' lives centred around learning and the church services, while those of the lay brothers were focused on practicalities. Monks were literate, lay brothers were not. Monks also tended to come from a much wider area, often from the mother house or other daughter houses. Lay brothers would almost always have been indigenous Manx.

Lay brothers were essential to Rushen Abbey and its economic success, as they did most of the manual work including farming. The abbey owned almost half the land in Malew parish where it was situated, about a fifth of that in German stretching from Peel eastwards, a large chunk of the middle of Lezayre west of Ramsey, and smaller parcels of land in Rushen, Lonan and Maughold. The amount of land owned by the various branches of the church grew hugely in the fourteenth and fifteenth centuries with Douglas Priory, Whithorn Priory, St Bees Priory, Bemaken Friary, Bangor Abbey and Sabal Abbey all holding land on Mann.

Whether driven by their aim to distance

themselves from the secular world, or because they owned too much land to work it all without help, the Cistercians developed a new way of managing their property. Rather than introduce to Mann the type of feudal relationship which existed in most of Britain they established self-contained grange farms, rented out to tenant farmers, which acted as centres of agriculture. Bellabbey Farm near Colby in Arbory is said to have been one of the grange farms for Rushen Abbey. The Cistercians were noted for operating the mediaeval equivalent of intensive farming. Even their critics acknowledged that they were excellent farmers and developed the most out of even unlikely sites.

Cistercians were particularly skilled at channelling and harnessing running water. The Isle of Man has no shortage of fast-flowing streams and early water mills using horizontal wheels were probably introduced to Mann from Ireland. The vertical wheel more common today is more powerful and was probably introduced to Mann by the monks of Rushen Abbey. Their craftsmanship, coupled with their new methods of farming, changed the landscape.

But it was for sheep farming that the Cistercians were particularly famous. Throughout Europe they were known not only for the quantity of wool they produced, but also for the innovative changes they made to the way the wool was farmed, sold and traded. The monks became merchants, and Furness Abbey became the second richest Cistercian house in England – the richest was Fountains Abbey in Yorkshire – with its own fleet of trading ships. As a daughter house, Rushen Abbey was part of a large-scale enterprise, regularly visited by the Furness Abbey ships to collect Manx goods for trading, and to bring whatever the monks needed or their neighbours could buy.

Baronial bravura

The history of the Isle of Man is very much tied up with who owns the land and how they own it (see chapter 5). During the middle ages, all land was considered ultimately to belong to the monarch, so anyone 'owning' land did so because the ruler permitted it. The title 'Baron' indicated someone who

Above: the high ground between Dhoon Glen and Port Cornaa once belonged to the Priory of St Bees, Cumbria. It is still called The Barony today

Right: the Monk's Bridge, near Rushen Abbey. The packhorse bridge was probably built by lay brothers in the fourteenth century

was responsible for a large amount of land and there are two types; baron by tenure and baron by writ. Baron by tenure is the older form and means that the landholder could become known as a baron simply because he (it would almost always be a he) had held his land for a long time. By the end of the thirteenth century, newer barons were granted their title by writ from the king. The church was a major landholder and so its leaders became ecclesiastical barons by writ.

There were eight ecclesiastical barons: the Abbot of Rushen Abbey, the Abbot of Furness and the Prior of St Bees both in Cumbria in England, the Prioress of the Nunnery at Douglas, the Prior of Whithorn in Galloway in Scotland, the Abbot of Bangor and the Abbot of Sabal both in Northern Ireland, and the Bishop of Sodor and Man.

A baron had manorial rights which included mineral and timber rights, the right to hunt animals and birds, the right to take fish from rivers, the right to insist that tenants used only the lord's mill, and the right to control the use of common and unenclosed land. To enforce his rights the baron could hold a manorial court at which infringements of manorial rights were punished and relations between tenants regulated. A steward usually presided over two main types of manor court, the Court Baron and the Court Leet. The former dealt largely with the estate and its regulation while the latter had a wider remit covering public order and minor criminality – major crimes were supposed to be tried by the king's travelling judges. The Abbot of Rushen Abbey and the Bishop of Sodor and Man each had both Courts Baron and Courts Leet.

Courts met regularly, at least every half year and sometimes as frequently as every three weeks. Many of the offences brought before the manorial court of Rushen Abbey were subject to a fine, but some carried the death penalty. The abbot's gallows were situated at Blackhill, north east of the abbey, and he may have had others in other parts of the island. When the monks built the packhorse bridge across the Silverburn River in around 1350 it not only provided easier access to abbey's estates on the other side of the river, but also to the abbot's gallows.

Courts Leet declined during the fourteenth century being largely replaced by county justices of the peace. Only the Court Leet for Laxton, Nottinghamshire in England still retains its full powers today. Barony Courts survived for longer and were held regularly until the mid-nineteenth century. Business was conducted in the vernacular, which meant Manx on the Isle of Man, although the records were kept in Latin. The last Barony Court on Mann was held in 1916 in the Barony of Bangor and Sabal, which is between Dalby and Glen Maye.

Parishes, prelates...

Monasteries didn't control how local churches were run and there was often much rivalry between the monastic and parochial arms of the church, particularly when it came to the collection of tithes. Parishes had been introduced to the Isle of Man probably around 1275 and probably from England via Scotland. Around the twelfth century in Scotland – earlier in England – it became usual for landholders to build a church for their tenants and to pay for a priest to look after their spiritual wellbeing. As the parish priest was appointed by the landholder he was to some extent expected to act in the landowner's interest, whether spiritually or administratively. Before long, cottages and a pub grew up around the parish church and formed the nucleus of a village with the whole hanging onto the skirts of a great house. The pattern is repeated all over England and much of Scotland. But Manx parishes are not like that.

On Mann, certain keeills (see chapter 3) were nominated as parish churches. However keeills had usually been built to provide for the spiritual wellbeing of isolated farming communities and were therefore almost invariably on isolated sites in farmland. On the Isle of Man a parish church is, more often than not, situated some distance from the village it serves. Ballaugh Old Church, for example, is the original parish church; parishioners decided to build a new parish church in 1830 precisely because the old church was so far away from the village.

Unless Mann was actually under threat of invasion its nominal rulers tended to have other things to think about, so little was done to check the might of the church on the island. Bishops made their own laws and, unlike the secular law of the time, wrote them down. Records from the synod held by Bishop Mark in 1291, for example, state that: 'Under pain of excommunication, we ordain that all persons in our diocese pay tithes of all their goods…namely, of every kind of blade, of pulse, of swine, and of fruits, whether growing in gardens or in fields.' Tithes were also to be paid on animals, fish, dairy produce, woven and metal goods and the profits of trade, whether made by Manxmen or those based elsewhere and merely offloading cargo in port.

Edward I of England and ruler of Mann was at war with Scotland and needed money to pay for it. He tried to tax church income and succeeded, until Pope Boniface VIII issued a papal bull (an official instruction from the pope) in 1296 forbidding the clergy to pay taxes to

Right: Ballaugh old church with its famous leaning gateposts, a mile and a half from the village
Below: Ballaugh new church, built in the village to save parishioners the walk!

a secular ruler without papal consent. Boniface was pressurised into rescinding his instruction at the end of the year, and Edward continued to tax the church. The pope was not pleased, not only because church money was being diverted to secular use, but also because his authority had been challenged and challenged successfully.

The Bishop of Sodor and Man, Bishop Mark, was from Galloway, an area supportive of Robert the Bruce who became King of Scotland in 1299. The bishop insisted that tithes be collected, but his enthusiasm might have had more to do with his political affiliations than with greed, as Edward I expelled him from Mann that same year. Pope Boniface promptly came to his bishop's aid. Irritated, Edward I wouldn't back down, so Boniface placed the diocese, which of course meant the whole of the island, under an interdict.

For a devout medieval churchman, an interdict was a disaster, only one step up from purgatory. An interdict prohibits those it censures from taking part in most church rites; only baptism and last rites were allowed. While king and pope argued, no one on the Isle of Man could marry, masses could not be held, no-one could be ordained, priests could not attend the sick and no-one could receive absolution. As priests were also teachers, the interdict would also have affected the education of those few able to pay for it.

After three years the king was forced to give in and, in 1302, Bishop Mark returned to Mann. To flaunt his authority the bishop imposed a tax of one penny per year on every house with a fireplace. A penny doesn't sound much, but it amounted to about two weeks' pay. The 'smoke penny' wasn't unique to Mann but was a recognised episcopal tax also levied in Wales, the English lake district and various English counties. It was said to be a payment in lieu of a tithe of the wood burned for warmth and cooking. Not surprisingly it was deeply unpopular. Bishop Mark died a year after imposing the smoke penny, but the Manx paid it for centuries.

...and priests

Ordinary people may have resented paying ecclesiastical taxes, but they did want their church to provide spiritual guidance and intercession. The trouble was that there was a shortage of priests. Political machinations between England and Scotland disrupted the training and availability of priests, and also affected where they would serve; a diocese would often be suspicious of employing clergy from a country with which their own country was at war. The few trained priests who were available tended to be directed to posts considered more important. It therefore became difficult for smaller, more rural, less wealthy congregations to find any priest at all. In 1350 or 1351 a worried Bishop William held a synod at Kirk Michael to try to solve the problem. Priests were recruited from Ireland, but not in sufficient quality or quantity. Ten years later the bishop was still perturbed when he appealed to Pope Urban V, stating that he was having problems finding churchmen who knew both Latin and Manx, the former to celebrate the church services, and the latter to communicate with their congregations. As a result the pope gave the bishop permission to appoint to the priesthood eight 'illiterates', i.e. men unable to read or speak Latin.

During the Kirk Michael synod, Bishop William is also thought to have instructed his priests to teach their congregations the Apostles' Creed in Manx. The creed is the oldest in the Christian church, written in the first or second century (although not by the apostles) and lays down the bedrock of the Christian faith. It still forms part of Morning and Evening prayer in Christian churches today. The creed begins 'I believe in God the Father Almighty, Maker of heaven and earth...' In Manx it is '*Ta mee credjal ayns Jee yn Ayr Ooilley-niartal, Chroo niau as thalloo...*' The Apostles' Creed is so important to Christians that it's very unlikely that the bishop did not himself provide the translation from Latin into Manx which he required his clergy to use. If he did so it would be the earliest recorded translation of part of the liturgy into Manx. It's a pity it no longer survives.

The island gets a king again

Five years after English King Edward III ordered the invasion and capture of Mann in 1329 (see above) he granted the right to rule it to one of his best supporters, William Montacute (or Montagu), 1st Earl of Salisbury. When the king did so he probably had little thought of restoring Mann to be an independent kingdom, particularly as he had just spent over a decade trying to gain and regain the island for the English throne. Edward was much more likely to be giving the troublesome island to a loyal supporter who had a fearsome reputation as a fighter and strategist. On 9 August 1334, the king himself penned the letter that granted Montacute the lordship of Mann: 'Know that…we have remitted and released, and entirely for us and for our heirs quitted claim, to our beloved and faithful William de Monte Acuto, all our right and claim which we have had, or in any manner can have, to the Island of Man, with its appurtenances whatsoever.' Montacute and his descendants were appointed absolute rulers of the island.

Manx National Heritage
Castle Rushen
The Agency Ltd.
Manx National Heritage   2004   BDT

Mann's new ruler spent little time on the island as his duties to Edward III, and his son's duties to Richard II kept them away from Mann. William the elder did however make at least one decision which influenced Mann for centuries to come. He rebuilt and expanded Castle Rushen, and it still remains one of the largest unruined buildings on the island. The castle had been destroyed by Robert the Bruce in 1313, but some of the original keep was left standing and Montacute, or rather his Manx workmen, possibly reinforced by labour from Wales, repaired it. He then built the curtain wall and most of the buildings inside it. Local carboniferous limestone was used, probably from Scarlett quarry, and the huge building must have shone white and imposing across the bay.

So extensive was the rebuilding that William Montacute, who died in 1344, may not have seen it finished. After his death – from bruises gained in a joust at Windsor, which sounds as though they disguised internal injuries – his son, also William, inherited the Manx crown. A fighter like his father, he appears to have had neither sensitivity nor finesse. In 1362, Bishop William of Sodor and Mann complained to the pope that St German's cathedral at Peel was being used as merely another building in the fortress which was St Patrick's Isle. In response Montacute vacated the cathedral, but seems to have taken umbrage. For well over one thousand years Peel, or more particularly St Patrick's Island, had been seen as the place of most importance on Mann. Montacute

Castle Rushen. After 800 years it's still one of the largest unruined buildings on the island

named his other castle, Castle Rushen, as his principal residence on the island, effectively moving his capital city east and south.

William Montacute, 2nd Earl of Salisbury reigned over Mann for forty-nine years and is the only non royal to be ruler of the Isles of both Man and Wight. He spent much of his time fighting for his king against France and Scotland and, in 1387, was made Admiral for all England. During William's reign Mann was at least relatively peaceful and could recover from the ravages of the constant invasions.

Island for sale – again!

Jousting was unlucky for the Montacute family. William's father had died from injuries received at a joust at Windsor. Nearly forty years later, on 6 August 1382, William accidentally killed his only son at a tilt on the same ground. Had the Salisbury lands and titles been to be handed down by direct succession William might have kept them together. Going to a nephew, and with the Isle of Man being so far from his main concerns, William decided to sell it. In 1393 Richard le Scrope of Bolton Castle in England bought Mann for his son, another William, for £10,000, an enormous sum. Capgrave in his Chronicles of England states: 'Sir William Scrop boute the ylde of Eubony, with the crowne, of Sir William Mountagu erl of Salesbury: for he that is Lord of this yle may were a crowne. This yle stant betwixt Yngland and Yiland. The name is now Ile of Man.' Early writers, particularly those from Ireland, occasionally referred to Mann as Eumonia or Eubonia after references calling it that in Nennius's *Historia Britonum* (History of the Britons) written in the ninth century.

William le Scope was a powerful man. As well as being King of Mann, he was governor of various castles, Knight of the Garter, Lord Chamberlain. effective ruler of England whenever King Richard was away and was eventually created 1st Earl of Wiltshire. He was absolutely loyal

Warwick Tower, Peel Castle. The Earl of Warwick and his lady were imprisoned here in 1398

to Richard II and was trusted in return. In 1398, when Thomas Beauchamp, Earl of Warwick, tried to restrain some of the king's favourites, Richard II banished him to the Isle of Man. The king knew that William le Scrope and his brother Stephen would ensure that Warwick stayed there. Beauchamp and his wife Margaret were imprisoned in Peel Castle, and the tower in which they are thought to have been held is still called the Warwick Tower in their honour.

Richard II might have banished the Warwicks for life, but they didn't stay banished. After only a year they were freed and reinstated by the new King of England, Henry IV. Richard was deposed in 1399 by Henry of Bolinbroke, another grandson of Edward III, and died in Pontefract Castle less than a year later, either from stab wounds or starvation (no-one really knows). His loyal servant William le Scrope also died, although rather sooner. Henry IV took over England at Bristol on 28 July 1399. William was beheaded the following day.

The death of le Scrope meant that the crown of Mann lacked a head to wear it. On the occasion of his coronation in October 1399, Henry IV granted the lordship of Mann to Henry Percy, 1st Earl of Northumberland under the splendidly titled 'Concession of the Isle of Man by Service of the Lancaster Sword'. Percy was from Alnwick and Alnwick was the place from which John de Vesci set out to put down the Manx rebellion (see above). Despite appearances, Alnwick's connexion with Mann proved tenuous. In 1405 Percy supported the rebellion

Alnwick Castle, Northumberland, England. Still the seat of the Dukes of Northumberland

organised by Richard de Scrope. Richard was Archbishop of York and a member of the family of the previous wearer of the Manx crown. When the rebellion failed Percy fled to Scotland.

Perhaps in poetic justice Henry IV decided to reward one of those instrumental in defeating the rebellion with the lordship of Mann lost by Percy as a result of it. In 1405, therefore, the English king granted the lordship of Mann to Sir John Stanley. A letter from Henry himself dated 4 October 1405 said: '...we lately, by our letters patent, entrusted to our beloved and faithful John Stanley, Chevalier, the Castle, Peel, and dominion of Man, and all Islands and Dominions belonging to the said Island of Man, together with the royalties, regalities, franchises, and all other profits and commodities specified in our said letters for our benefit, safety, and security to keep it during our pleasure.'

In delivering the island to Sir John, the king jumped the gun slightly as Percy was attainted on 4 December 1406, so technically had not been deprived of the lordship when the king awarded it elsewhere. That fact was to cause the Stanley family problems two centuries later. Even so, the Stanleys and their family connexions remained the Lords of Mann for the next three and a half centuries.

TWO AND A HALF CENTURIES OF STANLEYS

No one thought the Stanleys and their cousins the Murrays would rule Mann for nearly four centuries, least of all Henry IV when he granted Sir John lordship in 1405. The Stanley rule lasted until 1736 and was subject to only two interruptions. The first was a challenge levied by the Percy family and as much a result of political manoeuvrings and sharp practice as anything else. The second reflected the revolution in England and the introduction of the Commonwealth; if the King of England could be beheaded then it's hardly surprising that his subject Lord of Mann was similarly insecure in post.

Despite such interruptions however, the family's tenure on the island lasted from before the publication of John Wyclif's Bible in English (1408) to the establishment of the free press in New York (1735); from the invention of the screwdriver to that of the sextant; from the medieval belief that health arose from the balance of four humours to the first successful appendectomy (1736). On the Isle of Man the Stanleys came to power when the ordinary Manx people had suffered from constant invasion and were still largely peasant farmers and seafarers. When the Stanley lordship of Mann finally ended, the Manx people were prosperous, better educated than many in the neighbouring islands, and growing in political influence.

New rulers, new rules

Initially the grant of kingship of Mann had been for Sir John Stanley's lifetime only, but in 1406 the king granted him the title in perpetuity on payment of two falcons and his loyalty. The Calendar of Patent Rolls dated 6 April 1406 says: 'Grant to John Stanley, knight, and his heirs and assigns, in lieu of a grant to him for life… to hold with royal rights, royalties, franchises, liberties, etc. by service of rendering to the King two falcons immediately after doing homage and to the King's heirs two falcons on the days of their coronations…'

The conditions could be a wry comment both on the crest of the Stanleys and the hierarchy of hawks. In 1385 Sir John Stanley had married Isabella de Lathom, the only child of a family with no legitimate male heirs. The Lathom family crest of eagle and child came from the legend that Isabella's father's illegitimate son had been found in an eagle's nest. Stanley was a younger son, so when he married Isabella he used the Lathom crest over his own shield. By the rules of falconry at the time, only the king could hunt with an eagle; lords flew peregrine falcons. Viewed in this light, the gift

Manx heraldic achievement as it appears on the Isle of Man Government Office

Manx sword of state sundial in Millennium oak wood, Cronkbourne

of two falcons asked of Sir John by Henry IV made it clear that, although King of Mann, Stanley was still subservient to the King of England. The falcon is still used as one of the supporters of the Manx civil coat of arms today.

The first Sir John didn't visit Mann, being taken up with his duties for Henry IV in Ireland, but does appear to have sent his son, also John, to act in his stead. When the second Sir John succeeded to the lordship of Mann in 1414 he seemed determined to maintain his contact with the island. He visited Mann in 1417, 1422 and 1423; on the last two occasions he presided over a meeting of Tynwald. Unlike today, Tynwald did not always meet at St John's (see also chapter 3). The Manx statute books, for example, say about the 1422 Tynwald: 'The Courte of all the Country is houlders at Kirke Michell, upon the hill of Reneurling, before our most doubtfull Lorde, Sr John Standley, by the grace of God, King of Man and Isles, the Tewsdaye next after the Feaste of St Barthioamew the Apostle, in the year of our Lord Jesus Christ, 1422.' 'Doubtful', at this time, had nothing to do with improbability, but meant rather 'to be feared'; the meaning survives today in 'redoubtable'. Reneurling is thought to be near Barregarrow, south of Kirk Michael.

It's generally agreed that, although Manx laws existed long before the second Sir John took over the island, it was he who first had them written down. The earliest Manx statutes are dated from the 1422 Tynwald and the book which contains them goes on to inform Sir John about the Tynwald ceremonial. To take just one example: 'Upon the Hill of Tynwald sitt in a chaire covered with a royall cloath and cushions, and your visage unto the east, your swoard before you, houlden with the pointe upwards…' Six hundred years later very little has changed (see appendix 4). The seating is as stated and the Manx Sword of State is still carried upright in front of the Lord of Man or his/her representative the Lieutenant Governor.

The Manx Sword of State is thought to date from the early fifteenth century and may have been the sword borne before Sir John Stanley at the 1422 Tynwald. Ceremonial bearing-swords developed from longswords like the Scottish *claidheamh-mòr* (great sword or claymore). Longswords are long, not particularly because of the length of the blade, but because of the length of the hilt; they were designed to be swung two-handed. As the blade of the Manx Sword of State was replaced, probably in the late sixteenth or early seventeenth century, we cannot now be sure exactly how long it was originally. The ceremonial sword was a symbol of power and authority over those ruled, but also of the duty to protect them. The cruciform shape of the sword placed religion firmly in support of the secular authority.

As so much Manx land was under its control, the church had enormous power on the island and had various advantages which the state at the time lacked. The church levied tithes, had its own courts with recorded laws and penalties – secular rulers were only just beginning to write laws down – and, in the case of the monastic arm, had a huge number of unpaid workers labouring to increase its wealth. By comparison the state was badly funded and had only piecemeal organisation. Sir John seemed keener to rule the island than many of his descendants and understood that he would not truly be King in Mann until the power of the spiritual barons had been curtailed. He was also an able and experienced administrator in Ireland and England, and one who used his official duties to increase his own income – or so his detractors claimed.

Stanley identified that the church had three sources of power. It administered the sacraments, had its own laws, and was independently wealthy. Stanley could not interfere with the church's religious duties, but could and did stop canon law taking precedence over civil law. He is said to have introduced trial by jury, and abolished the right of sanctuary nearly a century earlier than occurred in England; the right of sanctuary for debt in Holyrood, Scotland has never been

Peel Castle, St German's cathedral looking north. Some churches were granted a charter to extend their sanctuary area beyond the church building and surround it by a wall. The two buttress-like sections of wall in the foreground are what remains of the sanctuary wall

repealed. Instead, Stanley made the spiritual barons responsible for returning the sanctuary seeker to face justice. The church was also prevented from welcoming important visitors without the knowledge of the ruler of Mann or his representative, and was discouraged from exporting Manx-created wealth, for example by sending it to religious establishments in other countries. Such regulations were intended to curb the power of the senior clerics who often acted as though they were secular lords. The parochial clergy, who tended to be just as poor as the flock they served, and who occasionally were subjected to unreasonable demands or levies from their superiors, benefited almost as much as the laity from the restriction of the church's autonomy and fiscal demands.

Keys, Captains and Deemsters

Even as early as 1417 the record of Manx laws refers to 'The Twenty Four', and for centuries Manx speakers referred to their parliamentary representatives by their number. Today they are called the Keys. There have been many suggestions as to the origin of the term 'Keys', varying from being a derivation of Norse for 'chosen', or Scottish Gaelic for 'tax', or Irish Gaelic for 'rent', to being the 'key personnel' on the island. At the end of the nineteenth century, historian and Speaker of the House of Keys A.W. Moore believed that the term probably derived from the Manx for 'Twenty Four', *kiare-as-feed*, clumsily pronounced by a non-Manx administrator and then transcribed phonetically and only in part by a fifteenth century English clerk.

Even the earliest records suggest that the Keys existed to represent the people of the island, although they, like parliamentary representatives worldwide, were probably more interested in representing their interests and those of their peers, than the peasant class. For centuries, membership of the House of Keys was for life unless they resigned or were dismissed by the King of Mann. New Keys were co-opted by the other Keys when a vacancy occurred. And, although they had to be ratified by the ruler, Keys were rarely if ever refused the post – which ruler would want to upset twenty four of the most powerful people in the country for no obvious gain? Anyone nominated to the House of Keys had to be male, over twenty-one, and the owner of landed property to a particular value. Interestingly, there was no stipulation about the Keys having to live on the island although almost all of them did. The rules about landed wealth not only disqualified ordinary people, but also prevented the new, rich merchant class from becoming Keys, as their wealth was in goods rather than land – and they of course resented the restriction. None of the Keys was paid, but they were exempt from certain services levied on their peers.

Probably the most senior office to which an ordinary Manxman could aspire was Captain of the Parish – and even that originally relied on the ownership of land. The Isle of Man has never had a standing army, at least not one which was not an invading force. Instead it relied for its protection on ordinary citizens forming themselves into a militia to defend themselves and their island, a little like the Swiss do today. A system of Watch and Ward had been introduced to the island by the Vikings, and a constant watch was kept in different areas in case of invasion. Once parishes had been introduced in the thirteenth century, the watches were organised on a parochial basis. A rota of men kept look-out in groups of four stationed during the day on high ground and at night overlooking likely landing places. The Captain of the Parish was in

Stained glass, St George's Church, Douglas

charge of the watch, and also of organising the militia in his parish. Even today the wording appointing the Captain of the Parish states that he or, since 1990, she is granted 'full power and authority to train up and exercise the said Militia in the best manner for the defence of the said Isle of any emergency, or in any time of danger…' Watch and Ward was enforced strictly until 1815 and revived in a modified form during both world wars. At the time of writing it is not an elected post and Captains are appointed by the Lieutenant Governor as advised by the parish concerned.

If Captain of the Parish is a title unique to the Isle of Man, Deemster is nearly so; only Jersey in the Channel Isles also has Deemsters. Although the Channel Island role differs from that on Mann, there are strong legal ties, so much so that, from 18 May 2015, David Doyle, First Deemster and Clerk of the Rolls to the Court of Tynwald was sworn in as a Judge of Appeal in the Bailiwick of Jersey. The Bailiffs of Jersey and of Guernsey are also able to sit in the Appeal division of the High Court of Justice of the Isle of Man from time to time.

The title Deemster is an anglicised term, probably stemming from the verb to deem, i.e. to judge. The Manx for Deemster is *briw*, which is similar to *Brehon*, the Irish Gaelic name for a high-ranking judge. Brehon Law or *Fénechas* (the law of the free landworkers) existed in a reduced form in Ireland until the beginning of the seventeenth century, so may have influenced legal procedures on Mann in the early fifteenth. Until the second Sir John Stanley started recording Manx laws, the Deemsters assessed each case by relying on their memory of previous decisions and their conscience as to what would be an appropriate punishment to make judgements. Such rulings were known as 'breast laws'. Today, of course, Deemsters, as the senior judges on Mann, uphold the laws passed by Tynwald. Historically there have usually been two Deemsters, but today there are three: First Deemster and Clerk of the Rolls, Second Deemster and Criminal Deemster. The Bailiffs of Jersey and of Guernsey are given the courtesy title of Deemster when they sit in the Manx court of appeal. As well as being chief judge, the First Deemster also acts as Deputy Governor whenever the Lieutenant Governor is away.

The Old Courthouse, formerly Oddfellows' Hall and then St George's Hall, Athol Street, Douglas

Left to get on with it!

The second Sir John's interest in the island was not continued by his heirs and neither of its next two rulers visited Mann. From 1437 to 1507 the island was under the effectual rule of a series of governors (see appendix 3) assisted by the local Manx administration. During that time, life for the ordinary people stabilised and in many respects was better than that in the rest of Britain.

The staple diet of the ordinary Manx people consisted of barley bread, lots of cheese, herring, oat cakes, vegetables such as turnips and, once introduced, potatoes, with water, milk or buttermilk to drink. A traditional Manx blessing is *palchey puddase as skeddan dy liooar* (potatoes in plenty and herring enough). Beer or ale tended to be reserved for special occasions, as hops were not grown on the island and most of the limited cereal crop was reserved for food

---

STANLEY FAMILY TREE

Sir John Stanley (1350-1414), King of Mann (1405-1414)

Sir John Stanley (1386-1437), King of Mann (1414-1437)

Sir Thomas Stanley (1405-1459), King of Mann (1437-1459), 1st Baron Stanley

Thomas Stanley (1435-1504), King of Mann (1459-1504), 1st Earl of Derby

George Stanley (1460-1503), Lord Strange

Thomas Stanley (1485-1521), Lord of Mann (1504-1521), 2nd Earl of Derby

Edward Stanley (1509-1572), Lord of Mann (1521-1572), 3rd Earl of Derby

Henry Stanley (1531-1593), Lord of Mann (1572-1593), 4th Earl of Derby

| Ferdinando Stanley (1559-1594) Lord of Mann (1593-1594) 5th Earl of Derby | William Stanley (1561-1642) Lord of Mann (1609-1612) (succession disputed, hence the delay) 6th Earl of Derby | *married* | Elizabeth de Vere (1575-1627) Lord of Mann (1612-1627) Countess of Derby |

James Stanley (1607-1651)
Lord of Mann (1627-1651)
7th Earl of Derby

English Civil War
Thomas Fairfax (1612-1671)
Lord of Mann (1651-1660)
3rd Lord Fairfax of Cameron

Charles Stanley (1628-1672)
Lord of Mann (1660-1672)
8th Earl of Derby

| William Stanley (1655-1702) Lord of Mann (1672-1702) 9th Earl of Derby | James Stanley (1664-1736) Lord of Mann (1702-1736) 10th Earl of Derby |

James Stanley's sons died before he did, so the Lordship of Mann went to a distant cousin, James Murray, 2nd Duke of Atholl. He was the great grandson of the 7th Earl of Derby and the grandson of the 7th Earl's daughter, Amelia who married John Murray, 1st Marquess of Atholl.

---

and fodder. Local beer, when it was brewed, was flavoured with herbs and known as *jough* although the word in modern Manx tends to be used generically to mean an unspecified drink. The Manx ate little in the way of meat, as agricultural animals were bred for their yields of wool and/or milk; what meat they did eat tended to be goat or pork from wild indigenous pigs called purrs, now extinct. Rabbits, although living on the island, were not yet common, mountain hare had not yet been introduced and there were no wild deer. Amateur hunting was largely restricted to sea birds; either the birds themselves or their eggs. Fish however, particularly herring, was readily obtainable. Luxury goods such as honey, eggs, surplus fruit etc., were often bartered with traders and shopkeepers for items such as soap which people needed but couldn't easily make themselves.

Manx employment laws often mirrored much of what happens today, and were far less severe than the conditions of service across the water. Servants who fell sick had to be cared for by their employers for one month, after which, if not recovered, the cost of their care fell on their friends and family, presumably with someone else being employed in their stead. Employees were not permitted to seek work with an alternative employer without giving a proper period of notice. Employers could tell staff to leave with immediate effect, but Deemsters ensured any wages owing were paid; in England wages owed could be withheld if the worker were sacked. Wages tended to be fixed by statute, which was a mixed blessing as, while an employer could not cheat his workers, neither could he easily reward them for good service. No Manxman could be arrested for debt without a special warrant from the lord or governor, and none could be imprisoned without sentence being passed by a Deemster.

'Yarding' was a peculiarly Manx form of hiring servants for the Lord of Man, deemsters, mooars (bailiffs who collected money due to the Lord), coroners (who enforced the judgement of the court) and serjeants of baronies. Anyone chosen would have to serve the officer named for one year – and not necessarily on the island. Those yarded were paid, although not generously, but had no right of appeal against their co-option. Only servants who worked for the clergy or the Keys were exempt. Yarding was detested both by the smaller Manx employer and those he employed, as it meant that labourers could be requisitioned at any time.

Women were much better treated on Mann than their sisters in England, possibly as a result of Irish influence on Manx law. In Ireland women were considered the equal of men, could train in the legal or medical profession, and own property in their own right. In England and Scotland, high-born women were considered the property of their nearest kin or overlord and useful only for making marriage alliances; lowly-born women could occasionally be independent but were usually subject to husband, father or brother. On Mann a widow inherited half her husband's property on his death and, if her husband committed a crime, did not lose her half of the property in forfeits for him. The rape of a married woman carried the death penalty, but that of a single woman left the man's fate in his victim's hands. The Deemster called to pass sentence would offer the woman a rope, a sword and a ring. Her choice determined whether the man was hanged with the rope, beheaded with the sword or married her with the ring

Such laws make life on Mann sound much easier than across the water but, although Manx laws were often less harsh, living conditions were more so. Small, dark houses usually sheltered both people and animals, the latter helping to heat the home. Temperatures in Britain were generally more extreme during the late fifteenth century. A series of severe winters and the occasional sea freeze were punctuated by the occasional hot drought-ridden summer. Life must have been harsh on Mann, as island residents needed a licence to leave.

Demoted?

After an absence of seventy years, the ruler of Mann again visited his island when, in 1507 Thomas Stanley arrived to deal with local trouble. The island had not been entirely forgotten in the meantime but, apart from being heavily taxed, seems to have been used mainly as a dumping ground for noble undesirables. Presumably the powers that be thought the island remote enough for exiles not to pose a continuing threat, but near enough for their return not to take too long if required. It was also reassuringly far from the hotbed of plotting which was continental Europe.

From 1504, when he inherited the title, Thomas Stanley, the 2nd Earl of Derby preferred, perhaps tactfully, the title Lord of Mann to that of King. Henry VII of England was his overlord and notoriously suspicious of any apparent threat to his power. Nineteen years earlier, Henry had defeated and killed Richard III at the Battle of Bosworth to take the English throne. Richard had inherited the crown from his brother Edward IV and only lost it because the King of Man's younger brother, William, defected to Henry. It was partly to reward the Stanleys for their help that Henry VII granted them their earldom, the only earldom he created in the whole of his twenty-four year reign. That and the fact that the 1st Earl of Derby, as the fourth husband of Henry's mother, was the king's stepfather.

By threatened Acts of Attainder and an active network of spies, Henry VII exercised far more control over his nobles than previous English kings. The 2nd Earl of Derby, also Thomas, was the head of one of the most powerful families in England, with huge land holdings in Cheshire and Lancashire as well as being King of Mann. Thomas Stanley's decision nominally to downgrade himself from king to lord seems likely therefore to have been a graceful gesture of submission while in reality relinquishing none of his privileges. In any case both titles still continued to be in use for some years.

Visit of THOMAS, 2nd EARL of DERBY, to the ISLE of MAN in 1507 landing at DERBYHAVEN

ISLE OF

19½P

A.D. THEOBALD

1982

Thomas Stanley first visited the Isle of Man in 1507, three years after he became its lord, when he landed at Ronaldsway 'and ended a public tumult'. The fact of his visit seems to be generally accepted, but all the information we have comes from a traditional Manx ballad. The appropriate verse is:

'*Ayns un thousane queig cheead as shiaght* (In fifteen hundred and seven)
She ayns mee ny Boaldiney ve (And in the month of May)
Ghow eh thalloo ayns Roonsyssvie, (He came on shore at Ronaldsway)
Er boirey'n theay hug eh slane fea.' (And ended a public tumult)

As part of the rest of the ballad praises Stanley's person, wealth, display and military prowess it seems reasonable to conclude that he ended the public tumult to protect his Manx people rather than subjugate them. The bay where Stanley landed was named Derbyhaven in his honour, and still is.

The Derby name was also attached to the circular mediaeval fort on St Michael's Isle, but not to honour the same earl. The fort was built about 1540 to guard the entrance to Derbyhaven; the glacis or paved slope in front of Castle Rushen was built at around the same time. Both

Derbyhaven, named after the 2nd Earl of Derby who landed there in 1507

were created in response to English King Henry VIII's wish to build coastal defences around his domain which were capable of withstanding the growing threat posed by cannon fire. The fort's original name does not appear to have survived, but it became known as Derby Fort after James, the 7th Earl, who refurbished it in 1644 at the time of the English Civil War.

Changes in the church

The Tudors – that's Henry VII and his descendants – were keen to assert that they were in charge. Unthreatened by other countries and acknowledged by the nobility, only one group challenged the English king's supremacy: the church. As long as the church claimed to obey the Bishop of Rome, another country could interfere in the Tudors' domain. That changed in 1531 when Henry VIII made himself Supreme Head of the Church in England. Taking over the church had little to do with what Henry VIII believed and everything to do with the money and power he intended to gain.

With Henry VIII as head of the church, it was only a matter of time before he began casting covetous eyes at the wealth of the monasteries. Henry was hard up and wanted the monastic cash to finance his extravagant lifestyle. Like his father before him he was also eager to suppress any centres of power which might challenge his rule. In 1536 the First Suppression Act dissolving monasteries with fewer than twelve 'monks, canons and nuns' was passed by the English Parliament. A second Act was passed in 1539 dissolving those monasteries remaining.

Furness Abbey, of which Rushen Abbey was a daughter house, was huge and therefore was not included in the First Suppression Act. Its abbot could see which way the wind was blowing, however. On 9 April 1537, Abbot Robert of Furness 'with complete consent and

St Bridget's chapel. No longer used as a chapel but the only monastic building remaining at The Nunnery

assent conceded and surrendered the Monastery of Furness and all its inheritance in the Isle of Man' to Henry VIII, making it the first of the large houses to be dissolved. The mother house might have been the first of the larger monasteries to go, but the daughter house was one of the last. It took another three years to close Rushen Abbey.

The dissolution of the religious houses in the Isle of Man was undertaken by Robert Calcott, Receiver to Edward, 3rd Earl of Derby, Lord of Man. The religious foundations had stood for centuries; it took a mere five months to close them all, between 15 April and 29 September 1540. Robert did alright out of it though; he married the former prioress of Douglas Priory, Margaret Goodman. The estate, now called The Nunnery, remained in the family of the Calcotts and their descendants for the next 200 years. In March 1543, Bemaken Friory and Rushen Abbey were rented to Thomas Hungate. He was from Yorkshire, England, a lieutenant on the Isle of Man, and former keeper of the king's stables. Rents from the abbeylands were in fact collected for the next seventy-one years until James I granted all the property to the 6th Earl of Derby in 1611.

Rather like the difficulty of absorbing refugees today, the sixteenth century had trouble absorbing the sudden huge influx of former monks and nuns. In England over 800 monasteries were closed in four years, with over 20,000 people made homeless. The problem was exacerbated by the fact that homeless people had previously been helped by the monasteries.

The Isle of Man, with its large religious foundations, must have experienced – and struggled to cope with – a similar tide of 'spare' people.

Once Rushen Abbey had been vacated, many of the monastic buildings were demolished and used as a source of building materials – much of Ballasalla is built out of the spare parts of Rushen Abbey – while the abbey's livestock and other moveables were sold off. The silver from the abbey was purchased by Edward Stanley for between £34 8s 5d to £37 8s 8d; reports vary about the exact amount. Perhaps the abbey silver ended up gracing the Earl's private chapel at the family seat of Knowsley Hall, Merseyside.

Edward Stanley, 3rd Earl of Derby and Lord of Mann at the time of the dissolution of the monasteries, was staunchly Catholic, as was the island. By contrast the Bishop of Sodor and Man, Dr Thomas Stanley, could not be said to be a man of great spiritual worth. Bishop Thomas was probably Edward's illegitimate second cousin and the family presented him to several livings, probably in order to avoid paying for his keep themselves. Even so, in 1545, the bishop objected to the diocese of Sodor and Man being transferred from the Province of Canterbury to that of York. Why he objected doesn't seem to be clear. It may be that, as a Stanley, he viewed York as second best, or it may be something as simple as that he liked Thomas Cranmer, Archbishop of Canterbury, and didn't like Robert Holgate, Archbishop of York. Whatever the reason, he lost his job. He was reinstated twelve years later.

A hiccough in the Stanley succession

Born in 1531, Henry Stanley the future 4th Earl of Derby was only nine when the monasteries disappeared from England. Succeeding to the title in 1572 Henry ruled Mann quietly for the next twenty-one years. He did visit the island three times, in 1577, 1583 and 1585 to attend to various legal and financial matters, and was generally accounted a fair and even generous Lord. About the only exciting thing which seems to have happened to him is the name he gave his heir, born in 1559. Ferdinando was not an obvious choice of name for the son of an English earl, but the boy's mother, Lady Margaret Clifford, was related to King Ferdinand of Aragon, so it seems likely that the Stanley heir was named after him. If so the choice was not a tactful one at a time when the relationship between England and Spain was declining rapidly.

Ferdinando inherited the Earldom and Lordship of Mann on 25 September 1593, but died less than a year later, in April 1594. The victim of suspected poisoning, his death caused a problem for the Stanley succession to the Lordship of Man as he left three daughters and a brother, William, but no son. The daughters and their uncle, the 6th Earl, all felt they had a right to rule the island, so Elizabeth I of England as feudal overlord, was left to adjudicate.

During the deliberations, a rival claim was raised by the Percy family, Earls of Northumberland. Back in 1405, Henry Percy, then King of Mann, had supported the rebellion against King Henry IV of England. The Stanleys had fought in support of Henry, helped suppress the rebellion, and gained Mann as a result (see chapter 4). The Northumberland family now argued that their ancestor had not been deprived of his titles until convicted of treason in absentia in 1406. As a result, King Henry IV could not legally have granted Mann to the Stanleys in 1405 as its ownership by the Percys had not yet been rescinded. The Earl of Northumberland wanted the island back.

Such an argument might have had weight with anyone but a monarch. Queen Elizabeth I was notoriously touchy about the rights of monarchs and was never likely to bow to a clever argument which upset the status quo and overturned the decisions of an anointed king in favour of the descendants of an attainted traitor. The Privy Council pointed out that the Percys did appear to be right about the date of the attainder, tactfully decided that Mann belonged to the monarch anyway and carefully overlooked the Stanleys' near two-hundred-year reign. Queen Elizabeth, however, was too astute at political manoeuvring to decide for herself the claims of two of the most powerful families in her kingdom and probably alienate one of them by her judgement. She gave up her right to Mann and batted the contending claimants back to the Privy Council.

The Law Lords on the Privy Council decided that 'the grant being by letters patent under the Great Seal of England, such right would descend according to the Common Law of England to the heirs general, and not to the heirs male'. Translated this meant that Ferdinando's eldest daughter Anne, rather than his brother William, had the right to rule the Isle of Man. Anne was fourteen when her father died, twenty three when Queen Elizabeth I died in 1603 and twenty seven when the Privy Council granted her the right to the Lordship of Mann. The four-year delay might have been due to the complication that, under the will of Henry VIII and the Third Act of Succession, Anne Stanley was heir presumptive to the English throne. In other words, as the great, great granddaughter of Mary Tudor, Henry's sister, and after the death of Elizabeth, Anne Stanley should have been queen. Not being granted the crown of England, the Privy Council might have given Anne the crown of Mann as a consolation prize.

All this wrangling took some time and James VI (of Scotland) and I (of England) had occupied the English throne since Elizabeth's death. William, who had become the 6th Earl of Derby thirteen years previously, agreed to purchase the Lordship of Mann, together with its rights, from his niece. For some reason, however, he had to wait a further two years, until 1609. Many historians state that William had to wait until his niece came of age, but this seems unlikely as, in 1609, she would have been twenty nine. The delay may have been due to Anne's marriage in 1607 to Grey Brydges, the 5th Baron Chandos. He might have had something to say about giving up the lucrative rights to Mann.

William Stanley 6th Earl of Derby was confirmed in office in 1610 by an English act of parliament which stated: 'The said William Earle of Derbie [Ferdinando's brother] hath paid dyvers somes of money for their clayme, right, and title to the said isle, castle, peele, and lordship of Mann...' and confirmed '...forasmuch as the said isle and lordship of Mann hath long continued in the name and bloud of the said Earle [of Derbie], and to the end the same may continewe still by your Highness princely favour and gracious allowance...'

The rule of the Stanleys resumed.

The first book in Manx

William Stanley purchased the Lordship of Mann from his niece, but doesn't seem to have cared much for the island he went to such trouble to procure. The 6th Earl may have been the titular head but firstly his wife and later his son showed far more interest in the island. Probably the most important single event in William's reign was the publication in 1610 of the first book to be written in Manx. Even that was largely finished before he took over.

John Phillips, Bishop of Sodor and Man, was from North Wales and so had something of a headstart when it came to understanding Gaelic. He also took the trouble to learn Manx in order to be able to preach to his flock in a language he could be sure they understood; the men might have had a smattering of other languages, but the women and children would not, and Phillips knew that. The bishop not only wanted the Manx people to understand his words, but also to understand the words of the church. *The Book of Common Prayer* in English had been first published in 1549 and contained in one volume all the services most often used. It had

Church of St Adamnan, better known as Lonan Old Church. Adamnan was a seventh century Irish saint noted for celebrating Mass in Gaelic and translating religious works into the vernacular. Nine centuries later Bishop Phillips wanted to do something similar

gone through a couple of revisions, reflecting the Tudor swings from Protestant to Catholic and back again, before a compromise was accepted by all church factions in 1559. A few more minor changes were made in 1604, after James came to the English throne, to lengthen the catechism by adding sections on the sacraments, and the book was then used in Anglican churches for the next fifty years. Bishop Phillips wanted a similar prayer book in Manx. He decided to translate the English one.

It is difficult now to realise just how big a job the bishop had taken on. Until the mid sixteenth century, with the exception of the odd place name, Manx was purely an oral language. It was the language of the country, everyone spoke it, but nothing was written down. The administration of the island, the Manx statute books, the Tynwald records, etc., all were recorded in French or English. Church records, which went back further, had traditionally been in Latin. Irish Gaelic (*Gaeilge* in Irish) and Scottish Gaelic (*Gàidhlig* in Scottish), with which Manx Gaelic (*Gaelg* in Manx) has the closest links, had both been transcribed since about the eighth century, but there was nothing in Manx at all.

As written languages, the Gaelic of Ireland and Scotland already possessed accepted orthographies which were similar to each other. The third member of the goidelic group of Celtic languages, Manx, could have fitted into a similar pattern relatively easily. Bishop Phillips either didn't know that or didn't care to use it. He therefore not only had to translate the English words and phrases into Manx equivalents, but had to invent phonetic and consistent spellings for the Manx words, using English pronunciation as a base. It's as if French had never been written down and someone today wrote the French phrase *tête-à-tête* as *tet atet*, with the latter becoming the accepted spelling. Phillips' efforts were further complicated by the fact that the English of his time was changing unusually rapidly. Known to linguistics experts as 'the great vowel shift', it means that words such as 'life' (modern spelling) were pronounced 'leef' in the thirteenth century, 'lafe' in the sixteenth century and 'life' today. Bishop Phillips' translation occurred at about the 'lafe' stage, so his spelling of Manx doesn't work as phonetic English pronunciation today. It also makes written Manx appear very different from other Gaelic languages, although in sound and structure Irish and Scots in particular are actually quite similar.

Phillips must have begun the translation after 1604 after *The Book of Common Prayer* was finalised, and it was completed in 1610, the same year that the Manx clergy were first permitted to marry (their English brethren had been allowed to do so since 1549). Translation was not made easier by the fact that there were two versions of Manx depending on whether speakers lived north or south of the island's spine of hills, but the bishop was helped in his work by the Rev Hugh Cannell. Rev Cannell was made vicar of Kirk Michael in 1609, possibly when the translation was as good as completed – and possibly even in recognition of his work on it. Obviously a clergyman, could Cannell have been the bishop's chaplain?

Everyone's a critic

The translation was completed and published in 1610 but does not appear to have been printed at the time. This doesn't necessarily mean that it wasn't used, however. In the early seventeenth century it was still very common practice for those wanting a copy of something, particularly something relatively short, to copy it out longhand.

It is one thing to produce a written translation of The Book of Common Prayer but quite another to get others to read it. If Manx had been a purely oral language before, then its transcription doesn't suddenly make Manx speakers literate in Manx even if they are so in English – and many wouldn't be. Bishop Phillips' letter to Robert Cecil says: 'The two Viccars Generall (Sr Wm Norres and Sr Wm Crowe) were asked by the Lieutennante whether they saw or knew of the Book of Common Prayer said to have been translated into the Manshe speech, they answered that they have seen the Book translated by the new Bishop of Sodor into Mannish. And Sr Wm Norres for his part further answereth that he could not read the same Book perfectly but here and there a word. And Sr Wm Crose for his part answereth that having the same Book a day or two before he could upon deliberate perusall thereof read some part upon it, and doth verily think that few else of the clergy can read that same Book for that it is spelled with vowels wherewith none of them are acquainted.'

Bishop Phillips died in 1633 but his co-translator remained vicar of Kirk Michael until his death in 1670 – he was in post for sixty one years. It was largely Rev. Cannell who taught Manx speakers to read their own language.

Although a later, and many would say greater, bishop, Bishop Wilson (see chapter 6) altered some of the Manx orthography so that the Manx of today appears slightly different, modern Manx versions of *The Book of Common Prayer* are still recognisably similar to that first book in Manx written by Phillips and Cannell. At the end of the nineteenth century, historian A.W. Moore provided an excellent comparative example in his *Historical Sketch of the Manx Language* of the first lines of the Lord's prayer (*padjer y Chiarn*):

Aer run ta ayns neau, kasserick gy row t'æn Ym. (Phillips' version)
Ayr am, t'ayns niau; Casherick dy row dt'Ennym. (1887 version)
Ayr ain, t'ayns niau, Casherick dy row dt'ennym. (Modern version)
Our Father which art in Heaven, hallowed be thy name. (English equivalent)

The Manx right to their own land

James Stanley represented his father on Mann for fifteen years before he himself inherited the title, and one of the first things he did was to invent a horse race! Mann had at this time its own native breed of pony, cow (Boaghan), pig (Purr) and sheep (Loaghtan), although only the sheep has escaped extinction. The Manx cat had probably not yet evolved (see chapter 6). James had the interests of a gentleman farmer and was keen to improve the native breeds, particularly the ponies, which were fine-boned and hardy. 'The Derby' founded in 1780 by the 12th Earl might be famous

as a race for three-year-olds at Epsom, but its precursor was the Manx Derby, founded in 1627 by the future 7th Earl and held on what is now the Castletown Golf and Country Club on Langness. It was the first regularly-held horse race in the world and ran annually for at least the next sixty years.

Above: 7th hole on the Castletown Golf and Country Club. Called the Racecourse, it marks the course of the first Derby horse race Right: Epsom racecourse, current home of the Derby

If James Stanley liked Mann, the Manx, in general, seemed to like him, calling him *Y Stanlagh Moare*, The Great Stanley. He had an odd contradictory relationship with the Manx people; Stanley as a person was generally liked, Stanley as a landlord was cordially detested.

The laws surrounding land tenure on Mann differed from those in the rest of Britain and were very complex, but put simply they meant that no-one apart from the land barons, i.e. the church and the Lord of Mann, actually owned any Manx land. The ordinary people were tenants, holding their land by custom on three kinds of payment. Firstly they had to provide food for the island's garrisons and the Lord's retinue, secondly they had to spend a certain number of days working on repairing public infrastructure such as the castles, roads, harbours, etc., and thirdly they had to pay a fixed rent in cash, kind and/or service.

Living on an island the farming population tended to be relatively static. Emigration – to escape poverty and/or starvation – was common, immigration far less so, as non-Manx were not allowed the same status and privileges as natives. Farmers and land workers were therefore in a stronger negotiating position than their peers across the water, as there were fewer potential tenants for farms. As a result and to ensure that farms continued to produce food, work and rent, farmers had been allowed more leeway, including being able to pass their land to sons and grandsons.

Gradually, therefore, tenants who had been working the same farm for generations came to consider the land as their own and, more seriously from the Lord's point of view, began treating it as such by selling or exchanging parcels of it. A custom had grown up called the 'tenure of the straw'. By it, a tenant parting with land delivered a straw grown on it to the manorial court to indicate that he had relinquished it, and the new tenant had the right to take charge of it. Under the tenure of the straw no approach was made to the Lord of Man and no account taken of his wishes, other than transferring to the new tenant the responsibility for paying the Lord his normal due.

Various laws had been passed to try and regulate the land question – in England and Scotland as well – but little had made much difference until James Stanley decided to sort things out on Mann. Considering himself as the official landowner, he naturally wanted to sort things out in his favour. He put together what would now be called a marketing campaign, emphasising that under the straw tenure the Lord had the right to evict families immediately, but with a lease, tenure was more secure as the Lord could still evict but had to give notice. Stanley also reduced the rent for certain terms of years for tenants who were changing to leaseholders in order to persuade them to do so. Many did, erroneously believing that they would be making their families more secure. In fact, by adopting the leases rather than continuing with the straw tenure farmers gave up their customary right of inheritance, and also enabled rents which had previously been fixed, to be changed (see chapter 6).

Matters were exacerbated by the influx of additional troops, and royalists looking for sanctuary. Under their laws of tenure, the Manx people had to feed those housed in Castle Rushen and the effort of providing provisions for protracted periods for so many extra mouths was considerable. To those struggling under the increasing demands for food, foreign fortification, and legalised theft of their livelihoods, news of the successful rebellion against the ruler of England must have encouraged the idea of a Manx rebellion against the ruler of Mann.

Stanley and Christian

When James Stanley first took over, matters were largely peaceful. He visited the island periodically – a thing many of the Stanleys had not bothered to do – and appointed Edward Christian, experienced sea captain and member of a large and influential Manx family, as governor. As Stanley himself wrote: 'Captain Christian had already made himself a good fortune in the Indies... he was a Manxman born... resolved to retire himself into that his own country... He is excellent good company; as rude as a sea captain should be, but refined as one that had civilised himself half a year at Court, where he served the Duke of Buckingham... While he governed here, some few years, he pleased me very well'.

The outside and inside of Derby Fort on St Michael's Island

For five years the two men rubbed along well until, in 1633, the captain of *HMS Lion's Whelp* accused Edward Christian of dealing with pirates. Then as now piracy was a grave threat to international trade so the allegation had to be taken seriously. Christian refuted it, claiming that the alleged pirate had a properly signed letter of marque. This was a government warrant which authorised the captain of a ship to seize the vessels and goods of a hostile nation. A letter of marque was considered just short of a declaration of war as it effectively nationalised piracy and turned pirates (brigands working for themselves) into privateers (guerrillas working for the good of their country). The difference is slight but important, and Christian would have been well aware of it; he had been a privateer.

The accusation is made more interesting as *Lion's Whelp* had been built at the expense of the Duke of Buckingham, who knew Edward Christian and had appointed him, while in his service, to another ship *Bonaventure*. Buckingham built ten ships, all called *Lion's Whelp* and all used as privateers for his own enrichment. When Buckingham was assassinated in 1628 they were taken over by the Royal Navy, although not until four years later, the year before the accusation was made against Christian. The ninth *Lion's Whelp* spent her service in Irish waters, so it seems likely that the accusation came from her captain. Unfortunately the accusation was apparently made by Thomas James, while the ninth *Whelp's* captain is listed as Dawtry Cooper, a man whose mental problems caused a series of near mutinies. It is not impossible that the captain of the *Lion's Whelp* and Edward Christian, both former servants of the Duke of Buckingham, knew each other, and the accusation of dealing with pirates arose out of personal animosity.

Whatever the truth of the situation, the charge was serious enough for Christian to be summoned to appear at Whitehall on 14 February 1634. He was too ill to go, a circumstance verified by a messenger despatched by James Stanley for the purpose. His illness may have been a convenience, as the Manxman would probably have had sympathy with seafarers who dodged the laws of England.

Smuggling was a case in point. Rife in England since the imposition of a tax on wool exports in 1275 (and carried on since Saxon times), smuggling was simply unknown on Mann (see chapter 6). Tynwald set the island's tariffs, and they were so low as to make it not worth ship captains and owners going to the trouble of avoiding paying them – not while ships could unload their cargo openly in a decent harbour and not secretly in a cove with amateur facilities. Smuggling is the illegal acquisition of goods by importation, while piracy is the illegal acquisition of goods by seizure. It is doubtful whether a good Manxman such as Edward Christian would consider them very different.

Although he backed Christian up, events such as the accusation of 'trucking with a pirate' seem to have made Stanley a little wary of him; Stanley replaced him as governor by appointing Sir Charles Gerard in 1634. However, matters really came to a head in 1642 when Christian was instrumental in stirring up the Manx to resist paying tithes. Tithes had long been a bone of contention (see chapter 4), largely because most of the funds raised went to senior churchmen such as the bishop, and ended up off island. Civil War had broken out across the water in England and Stanley was there raising men, arms and money for Charles I. Although the earl had deprived Christian of the post of governor, Stanley still apparently trusted him enough to place him in charge of the Manx militia, while he himself was away.

James succeeded to the title in September 1642, becoming the 7th Earl of Derby and Lord of Man. During most of that winter he was in England fighting in the royalist cause in the north west. In June 1643 rumours reached King Charles that the Isle of Man might be invaded by the Scots, and Stanley was ordered to fortify his realm for the king. Edward Christian had been training the militia at The Lhen in order to defend Mann if necessary, but many Manxmen were still unhappy about paying tithes. The discontent boiled over into a riot in Douglas, and Christian was involved. It was a serious threat to national order in a time of war.

The Earl arrested his former officer and, rather than bringing him before a jury for trial – the objection to paying tithes was widespread, so a jury drawn from the populace would be likely to acquit him – Stanley had Edward tried by the Keys, at least one of which, Ewan Christian, was a family connexion. Had Christian been accused solely of resistance to paying tithes then he might (just) have got away with a reprimand. However the charge included trying to take over Peel Castle and urging the Manx to rise against the Lord of Man. The Twenty Four found Christian guilty of 'great and manifest misdemeanours', fined him one thousand marks and imprisoned him until the Lord of Man thought he should be released. It wasn't the last the island was to hear of him.

Bearing in mind the bloodshed going on across the water, the moderation of the Manx verdict is surprising. Stanley undoubtedly manoeuvred to retain absolute authority on the island, and commented about the verdict that 'it was safer much to take men's lives than their estates', but even so did not suppress the disturbances with the vigour and violence which would have been normal for the time. He may have been pragmatic as well as humane. He could not afford the island to be rebellious while civil war was raging in England. If the royalist cause failed, the Stanley family needed a bolthole.

Opposing the English parliament

Stanley and the royalists wanted to make sure that the strategically-important Isle of Man remained in their hands, particularly as Ireland was royalist. The Earl recruited troops from among the Manx, and, in May 1644, Tynwald itself was called on to consider the best way to resist an invasion. Troops of cavalry and infantry were increased in size and seven camps were formed, one each at Knock y Doonee, Ramsey, Hanmerffould (which is probably somewhere between Sartfield and The Cronk), Knockaloe, Howstrake, Kirk Santan and Kirk Arbory (probably on a hill near Ballabeg). Two camps each week, one on each side of the island, were manned in rotation by the militia of each parish. In addition the old watch and ward lookout posts continued to be manned, and several forts were built largely to protect harbours.

During the seventeenth century, muskets and cannon finally ousted bows and armour from the battlefield. The high walls of mediaeval fortresses were vulnerable to cannon fire as they presented a large target through which shells could punch holes relatively easily. As cannon got heavier, older-style castles also lacked the weight and space to support them to return fire. By the seventeenth century, squat forts with solid earth bases had been developed which had projecting gun emplacements at the corners. The design, known as a sconce, allowed defending cannon fire to cover all the exterior walls, while attacking cannon fire was met by thick earth ramparts. Kerroogarroo Fort at Ballachurry is good example of a sconce fortification from the civil war. At the time much of the northern end of the island was marshy and Kerroogarroo Fort is situated on one of the few areas of slightly higher and slightly drier ground. It was therefore a good site for a defensive fort.

The most famous and most complete civil war fortification remaining on Mann is also the least typical; Derby Fort on St Michael's Island. It was adapted from one of Henry VIII's

Kerroogarroo Fort, Ballachurry. Photograph © Jon Wornham

coastal defences (see above), while other fortifications were built at Douglas (at the eastern end of what is now Fort Street, near the Victoria Pier), Ramsey and Point of Ayre as well as Ballachurry. From 1644 the Stanley family lived permanently in Castle Rushen. Loyal to the king, Stanley intended to hold the Isle of Man for the royalists come what may.

He failed of course, but only because the royalist cause failed. Country-rocking events were happening in 1649 not only on the Isle of Man but also the countries which surrounded it. To start with, in January, the English King Charles I was beheaded and government was taken over by parliament with an army headed by Oliver Cromwell. The new government, called The Commonwealth, placed the Isle of Man officially under the command of Thomas Fairfax. The change was only nominal, because the island was held by royalists, but it does show that The Commonwealth had Mann very much in mind.

After a couple of years of poor harvests, the island was running out of food. Tynwald noted that Stanley had sent to France for corn, and on 25 June decreed that '…considering the extraordinarie dearth and scarsitie of bread and all manner of victuall this present yeare…' all farmers and housekeepers should provide one meal every Wednesday and Friday for the local poor. Stanley's French corn might help relieve the food crisis – although some of the shortages were partly due to exiled royalists and military forces moving to Mann – but he was still adding to the Manx burden. Having lost his English holdings, Stanley's sole source of income was from the Isle of Man and he wasn't finding it enough. He not only expected the Manx to feed the royalists billeted among them, but also expected them to fund equipment for a war which was taking place in a different country and was nothing to do with them. He increased taxes.

In July, Henry Ireton, Cromwell's son in law, demanded that Stanley surrender the Isle of Man to the English parliament. The timing of the demand might have been influenced by the fact that Cromwell and Ireton were planning the subjugation of Ireland, and Mann was a useful base. Stanley refused. In a letter to Ireton dated 12 July 1649, and written from Castletown, Stanley says: '… you cannot but be sensible of my former actings in the late majesty's service, from which principles of loyalty I am no ways departed. I scorn your proffers, disdain your favor [sic], and abhor your treason; and am so far from delivering up this Island to your advantage, that I will keep it to the utmost of my power, and your destruction…'

In August Cromwell and Ireton began their invasion of Ireland. During September parliamentary troops stormed the Catholic, royalist town of Drogheda putting most of the garrison and a large number of civilians to the sword. Drogheda is north of Dublin and one of the nearest Irish towns to the Isle of Man. Undoubtedly the Manx would have known of the massacre and may even have had kin among the dead. They would have been aware of the dangers of tangling with the forces of the English parliament.

It was a danger which James Stanley failed fully to appreciate. In 1651 Charles Stuart, the uncrowned Charles II, attempted to regain his father's throne by invading England from Scotland. Few royalists responded to his call, but James Stanley was one of them. He and some of his Manx troops sailed to England in April, joined battle at Wigan in August and Worcester in September, and was defeated both times. After Worcester, Stanley was captured and was held in Chester Castle before being tried by court martial. The charge was one of high treason against the Commonwealth of England. As a royalist and opponent of parliamentary rule Stanley was guilty and was found so. He was beheaded at Bolton, Lancashire on 15 October 1651.

RETURN OF THE STANLEYS

James Stanley's eldest son, Charles, was around twenty three when his father died, and was living with many of the exiled English court in France. He inherited his father's titles, but, in practice, his mother, Charlotte dowager Countess of Derby, ruled the island. She had already successfully defended a four-month siege at Lathom House, the family's Lancastrian seat – contemporaries at the time thought her a tougher opponent than her husband – and probably felt that she was quite as capable of organising the defence of the Isle of Man.

Patriot? Traitor? ... Or pragmatist?

What the countess did not expect was a rebellion in her own backyard – almost literally. The official residence of the Stanley family was Castle Rushen and, across the bay in Ronaldsway under where the airport runways now are, was the farm of William Christian, known to his family as Illiam Dhone, Bill Brown. It was common practice to name babies after relatives, which meant that lots of people ended up with the same name, particularly in areas where most people were related. In the fishing communities of northern Scotland teenames often referred to a personal characteristic and were used to distinguish between people with the same name. Manx fishermen fishing in Scottish waters might have brought back the custom; contemporary paintings show Christian as dark-haired and swarthy.

William was the son of the Deemster Ewan Christian of Milntown, who was one of those who tried Edward Christian (see chapter 5). Ownership, or rather 'tenancy' as the Lord of Man would have it, of the Ronaldsway farm had long been in dispute between the Calcott and the Christian families. To pre-empt its resolution in favour of his son, Ewan Christian agreed that Illiam would hold the farm on the new terms advocated by the Lord of Mann, i.e. a lease for three lives rather than under the old custom of straw tenure.

A lease for three lives worked by the tenant purchasing the three-life leasehold for a lump sum called, confusingly, a fine. The three lives would be specified and would always include

Bust of Illiam Dhone, Kirk Malew

the tenant himself and then usually his wife and his eldest son or, occasionally, two of his children. Once the lease was purchased, the tenants would pay a small annual rent, sometimes called a head rent, until all three of the people named in the lease had died, when the process could begin again. Estimations vary about how long the three-life lease would usually last, but a reasonable average seems to be about thirty years. The advantage of the system is that the tenant gets a guaranteed home for himself and his immediate family and the landlord gets a lump sum. The disadvantage is that the landlord receives only small annual payments until the lease is up, and the tenant gets no guarantee that the lease will be renewed with his descendants.

As with many politicians, Ewan Christian was eager to promote his family's advancement. By falling in with James Stanley's known wishes, Illiam Dhone got his farm. In fact he got a lot more. In 1648, the Lord of Man made him Receiver General for the island. It was a position of huge power and influence, a little like Treasury Minister on the Isle of Man, or Chancellor of the Exchequer in the UK. It gave William Christian/Illiam Dhone, the power to collect all land revenues and many port dues, plus customs duties. He must have performed his duties conscientiously as, when Stanley left the island in 1651, he placed William in charge of the militia.

So, Illiam Dhone was a servant of the Stanleys. The problem was that, for all they had been co-existing for many years, the Stanley family and the Manx people did not trust each other. And with reason. On 18 October 1651 Colonel Duckenfield and an expeditionary force were despatched in parliamentary ships to conquer Mann. Charlotte, knowing that her husband had been captured, but unaware of his subsequent execution, secretly offered to surrender the Isle of Man to Duckenfield in return for Stanley's life. The countess viewed the island as merely another Stanley holding: Illiam Dhone and the Manx suspected the countess's actions and were concerned about their homeland. Naturally the two views clashed.

Mann for the Manx

People talk about a 'Manx rising' or 'Manx rebellion'. In fact there was almost no fighting as Manxmen already manned the Civil War forts built to defend the island, and recognised that the storming of the substantial castles of Rushen and Peel, garrisoned as they were by imported troops, was beyond them. It was a little like the passengers on a mystery tour disliking where their tour guide and driver were taking them, and deciding to plan the route themselves. The two opposing powers – the English king and the English parliament – were suddenly made to realise that there was a third power; the Manx. Formerly allied with the king, through Stanley, the Manx, led by Illiam Dhone, decided that the island would fare better under parliamentary rule and opened negotiations to switch allegiance.

Like the dowager countess, they also contacted Colonel Duckenfield. Illiam Dhone notified Duckenfield that English parliamentarian troops would be allowed to land unopposed, providing that he would guarantee the laws and liberties of the Manx as existed before James Stanley tried to impose leasehold tenancy on them. Duckenfield agreed to the terms – who wouldn't? – landed his troops with some difficulty in stormy weather, and immediately besieged both Peel and Rushen castles.

Castle Rushen was the stronger fortification and Charlotte Stanley, with experience gained from the Lathom House siege, was still defiant in it. On 29 October 1651, one day after the siege began, the Colonel wrote to the Countess inviting her to surrender Castle Rushen and, formally, the Isle of Man. His letter contained reference to 'the late Earl of Derby', and Charlotte didn't know that her husband was dead. Grief stricken, she at first promised resistance, but when she learned that the castle garrison was reluctant to fight, ceded victory. The terms of surrender specified that she, 'with her children, and servants, have liberty to transport themselves for England, there to make what application to the Parliament she shall think fit, and from thence to pass into Holland, or France, if she please'.

The English Parliament had already granted the Isle of Man to Thomas Fairfax, but also confirmed what Duckenfield had promised Illiam Dhone, namely that the Manx would retain their laws providing they be 'equitable and just'. William Christian (Illiam Dhone) retained his office as Receiver and, between 1656 and 1658, was also the island's governor. Deemsters John and William Christian (not Illiam Dhone) were summoned to London to represent Mann before the English parliament, while Edward Christian was released from his eight-year incarceration in Peel Castle (see chapter 5). If November 1651 was a terrible month for the Stanleys, it was an excellent one for the Christian family.

Not so friendly

The English parliament was formed largely of puritans, and they weren't noted for their fun-loving attitude, particularly when it came to religion. It had, for example, set up a Committee for the Demolition of Monuments of Superstition and Idolatry – which meant removing icons, religious carving, embroidered vestments and even candlesticks. Probably saved by its size and relative remoteness, the Isle of Man didn't suffer the iconoclasm suffered by the English churches, or it could well have lost its Celtic and Norse crosses (see chapter 3), but religious services did become simpler. However, on Mann, the religious group which suffered most through puritanism were the Quakers.

George Fox founded the Society of Friends in 1648. Two years later a judge in Derby disparagingly labelled the group Quakers from a sermon given by Fox when he told his followers to 'tremble at the word of the Lord'. Quakerism arrived in the Isle of Man in 1655, probably from Westmorland. Ballafayle farmer William Callow was one of the earliest and most prominent converts, so Quakerism in Mann centred in Maughold and Ramsey.

Persecution of the Manx Quakers began in 1657. Governor Illiam Dhone prohibited Quakers from meeting, and anyone else from receiving Quakers into their houses. Quakers

Quaker Burial Ground, Ruillic ny Quakeryn, Maughold. Note the single headstone marking William Callow's grave. Maughold lighthouse can be seen in the distance.

were also fined and imprisoned for refusing to attend church. It's possible that Illiam endorsed the persecution not so much out of personal conviction as to emphasise his new allegiance to the puritan parliament. Whatever his reason persecution continued after the return of the Stanleys, so much so that Callow appealed to the Duke of York (afterwards King James II) and his cousin Prince Rupert. The prince wrote to the Stanley: 'I…intreat with you for the said Callow… he is a quiet inoffensive person in everything save in the matter of his religion…if there be no more in it than being a Quaker I do presume your Lordship may be inclined to restore him and his family to their ancient possessions'. The earl replied that he: 'would not have that place [the Isle of Man] endangered to be infected with schism and heresy, which it might be liable to if Quakers should be permitted to reside there.' Charles Stanley was as good (or bad) as his word and in 1665 the Quakers were transported, very much against their will, to Dublin or Whitehaven.

Callow may have been forced off the island, but he did return. On 15 March 1672 Charles II of England issued his Royal Declaration of Indulgence in an attempt to extend religious liberty to nonconformists. Callow and the Quakers, took advantage of it, and returned to Mann. The king was forced by parliament to withdraw the Declaration the following year but by then the Manx Quakers had determined to stay. Their burial ground, *Ruillic ny Quakeryn*, was given out of his farmland by William Callow who is himself buried there. Only one headstone is visible and that was erected long after the event, but its inscription encapsulates the experience of the Manx Quakers: 'William Callow of Ballafayle 1629-1676 suffered long persecution, frequent imprisonment and finally banishment from his native island for his faith.'

Relief from persecution finally came in 1688 by the passing of 'An Act for Exempting their Majesties Protestant Subjects, Dissenting from the Church of England, from the Penalties of certain laws.' It is better known as the Toleration Act.

The question of Illiam Dhone

The Great Stanley's support for the royalist cause might have cost him his head, but it saved his inheritance for his heirs. When Charles II resumed the English throne on 29 May 1660, those who had supported him in adversity were suitably rewarded. James Stanley had been executed in the royalist cause, but his son Charles was confirmed as the 8th earl and all his titles and estates, including the Lordship of Man, returned to him.

Two topics needed addressing immediately: how to manage changes in land tenure, and what to do about Illiam Dhone. The former was a long-term project needing delicate handling, but the latter could be settled quickly. From Charles Stanley's point of view the question was simple: Illiam Dhone had betrayed the Stanley family. Charles' father had left Illiam in charge of the island with particular instruction to protect the countess. Illiam had made terms with the island's attackers and seen the countess defeated. Experts have argued about whether Charles was more interested in his estates than in his mother, but, regardless of which is true, Charles's anger at Illiam's actions was understandable.

William Christian (Illiam Dhone) had fallen out with Lord Fairfax, the parliamentary 'ruler' of the Isle of Man – Christian was removed from his dual role of Governor and Receiver in 1658 – and had been in England since 1659. King and earl were restored to throne and estates in 1660, Illiam Dhone returned to the Isle of Man in September 1661 and almost exactly a year later, in September 1662, Charles Stanley had him arrested.

The earl was taking a risk. At the prompting of the restored king and in an effort to heal factional rifts and prevent further violence, An Act of Free and General Pardon, Indemnity and Oblivion was passed on 29 August 1660. It offered general clemency stating: 'that noe crime whatsoever committed against His Majesty or His Royall Father [i.e. Charles II or I] shall hereafter rise in judgement or be brought in question against any of them.' Unfortunately the act mentioned only crimes against the kings of England. The Lordship of Mann was not mentioned, and the Stanley who held it was legally able to arrest William Christian aka Illiam Dhone. Christian was imprisoned in Castle Rushen and brought to trial on 26 November 1662.

The trial of Illiam Dhone causes high feeling even today. Those in favour of the Manx argue that jurors were ignorant, fearful of reprisals, or browbeaten into passing a guilty verdict. Those supportive of the Stanleys point out that Illiam Dhone had been accused of other crimes including embezzlement, and did actually surrender the island to parliament, which is what his trial accused him of doing. Without getting involved in political questions the trial has perhaps three points which are easily overlooked. Firstly, the trial of such a prominent Manxman and one who had held such high office, must have rocked the principal families of the small island community and caused a huge amount of worry about who might be next. Secondly, Illiam Dhone, a noted orator, refused to speak in his own defence. His brother was a Deemster, so Illiam must have known that staying silent meant that under Manx law he was at the mercy of the Lord of Mann for his life and property. Thirdly, Illiam appealed to the Earl of Derby, the Deputy Governor and the English King, the last on the grounds that he, William Christian,

Hango Hill where Illiam Dhone was executed. The ruins are of a later date.
In the background is Castle Rushen where Illiam Dhone was held and tried

owned estates in England, had lived there, and would be more fairly tried under English law.

The trial went ahead and Deemster Norris, was instructed to pronounce sentence. For treason – which is what Illiam Dhone was convicted of – the sentence could only be death. William Christian was duly sentenced to be hung, drawn and quartered. On 2 January 1663 at Hango Hill he was executed, the sentence commuted to death by firing squad to spare his wife distress. The instruction from Charles II that the Act of Indemnity also applied to the Isle of Man and its Lord arrived too late to save Christian. The ruling did however secure the Christian property, forfeited under attainder, to his sons.

Religious belief – and practice

England was protestant. The English parliament was (mostly) puritan, an extreme form of protestantism. The English king was a closet Catholic. The Lord of Mann tolerated Catholics and dissenters in Lancashire, but persecuted the Quakers on Mann, and wrote a pamphlet entitled *Protestant religion is a sure foundation and principle of a true Christian*. The Manx were protestant with puritan leanings. Religion was therefore a thorny issue. In an effort to avoid conflict, the Westminster parliament passed an Act of Uniformity in 1662, which meant that all religious worship should use the Book of Common Prayer in English. Put simply the act outlawed public worship for Catholics and non-conformists.

Religious worship on the Isle of Man was based on an earlier publication of the Book of Common Prayer, but in Manx (see chapter 5). Bishop Phillips, one of the translators, had died in 1633, but the other one, Rev. Hugh Cannell vicar of Kirk Michael, was still alive and in post. Fortunately the Isle of Man was not part of England and so English law did not apply. Rev Cannell could continue his ministry in the language of his congregation.

Leaders in learning

Before the seventeenth century, education was in the hands of the clergy who were paid to teach the sons of the wealthy; clerics might also offer free tuition to bright boys from poorer families. Girls were educated at home. One of the earliest plans to improve schooling on the

island was made by James Stanley, the 7th Earl of Derby. By 1646 he had established four grammar schools and had planned to set up a university, before the Civil War – and his death – intervened.

The puritans approved of learning, although, unsurprisingly, focused on religious education. Grammar schools were designed to coach boys for university, but one of the first schools for general education on

Stained glass window of Christ teaching in the temple, originally in the Clothworkers' School, now in the Leece Museum, Peel

Exterior and interior of the Old Grammar School, Castletown. Built in the thirteenth century as St Mary's Chapel it became a grammar school in 1701, and continued as a school until 1930

Mann is mentioned in the will of Philip Christian, a Manxman working in London as a clothworker. In his will, dated 1655, he stated: 'If it shall happen that there be not a Free School maintained for the teaching of children in the Towne of Peele, then my will is that the twenty pounds a year…be paid by the said Company of Clothworkers towards the maintenance of the said schools.' Christian wanted education in his home town to be available for all. Unusually he included girls in his plans, as he also gave one pound per year for five years 'for buying of small books, pen, ink and paper, or what shall be thought most fit by the minister and schoolemaster of the town of Peele… for the use of the poorest men's sons and daughters…'

Christian was not alone in wishing to improve the education of his countrymen; the Bishop of Sodor and Man agreed with him. Stanley's grammar schools had not survived the Civil War and Bishop Isaac Barrow, appointed in 1663, was appalled at the low standard of education in the island generally and among the clergy in particular. Bishop William Russell, three centuries earlier, would have sympathised, as he had similar problems and had to accept less well-educated men in order to be able to appoint priests who could speak Manx (see chapter 4). Bishop Barrow determined to improve matters and was in the position to do so; he was Governor as well as Bishop.

Barrow established a number of elementary schools, including a free school at Castletown, with much of the money needed to fund them being raised from benefactors. Charles II of

England gave £100, Charles Stanley, Lord of Mann made over certain tithes and, according to Bishop Wilson, a successor to the see about twenty-five years after Barrow, 'he collected amongst the English nobility and gentry six hundred pounds, the interest of which maintains an academic master'. Barrow's direct successor, Henry Bridgeman, also persuaded the Lord of Mann to insist that his tenants send their children to school or face a fine, effectively making education compulsory in 1672. Children in England and Wales had to wait until 1870, those in Scotland until 1872 and Irish children until 1892, for compulsory education.

As well as improving education for the ordinary Manx, Bishop Barrow arranged support for boys training for the ministry. He used his own funds to purchase the farms of Ballagilley and Hango Hill, with the intention of using the profit from the estates to support and maintain such boys. The tenant of Hango Hill, John Lace, objected to the purchase and the bishop resorted to rather un-ecclesiastical strong-arm tactics. As Barrow was head of both spiritual and temporal administrations on the island, Lace had no independent authority to whom to appeal.

The deed drawn up in 1668 explains that Barrow had given 'the profits of Ballagilly and Hango Hill...towards the maintenance and education of two Scholars at the University or Colledge of Dublin' and that, at the end of their training, they should 'returne if required by the Bishop or Trustees to serve their country or... to make full satisfaction for so much money as by them recd out of this gift during the said five years.' Not only was he improving the quality of his clergy, Bishop Barrow was also ensuring, what many of those ruling Mann had not, that profits made on the island should benefit the island.

The first Manx coins

Bishop Barrow in the deed setting up his trust, refers to money. He was writing in 1668, the year the Isle of Man first produced its own coinage. Money as coin had been known since antiquity, but had moved in and out of use according to what else was going on at the time. Gold coins, regardless of their country of origin and irrespective of their face value, were usually acceptable anywhere, purely for their value in precious metal. Low value coinage, the sort used by ordinary people, was both less common and less negotiable beyond national or sometimes local boundaries. In Ireland, for example, almost every town produced its own local penny and twopenny tokens, acceptable for goods locally, but derided elsewhere.

The Isle of Man had very little in the way of circulating currency and had in the past even used foreign coins, most notably ducatoons from the Netherlands, to make bartering easier. Even then, a ducatoon was a silver coin of quite large value. It was worth approximately six shillings, which would be about £36.00 today; one penny in the seventeenth century is roughly equivalent to about fifty-five pence today.

John Murrey was one of the most important – and wealthiest – merchants in Douglas and felt his business was suffering from the lack of Manx coinage, particularly of small denominations. He decided to issue his own. 'Murrey's pence' ('John Murrey His Penny' appeared on the reverse) were minted probably in Birmingham and were stated to be the equivalent of English pennies. It may well have been true. At the time the face value of the coin had to be the same as the value of the metal within it; the transition from a coin being a unit of weight to it being a unit of value had not yet taken place. As Murrey had a lease of all the Manx lead and copper mines he would have had no trouble getting the raw materials for his pennies.

Private banks were really only an extension of moneylending. Public banks, however, i.e. ones underwritten by a government, had only been set up to regulate the production of coinage since around the beginning of the seventeenth century. There can be few private individuals whose coinage is adopted as the national coinage of their country but such was the case with John Murrey. Murrey's pence were made legal tender in 1679 by the Court of Tynwald which also outlawed private tokens.

Coins were still in short supply however, as they left the island with traders when they were exchanged for purchased imported goods. Because of the difficulty in maintaining a supply of good coins on Mann, the coinage was debased slightly and consequently, in the 1690s, devalued. English Imperial coinage divided each shilling into twelve pennies. Tynwald decreed that fourteen Manx pennies were required for each English shilling. Such remained the case until 1839.

Murrey's pence remained the island's official currency for thirty years. Then, in 1708, the Isle of Man government approached the Royal Mint, housed at that time in the Tower of London, and asked that coinage be issued for the Isle of Man. The Master of the Mint, Sir Isaac Newton, refused, possibly because he had his hands full overseeing the silver re-coinage of both England and Scotland at the time. Not to be dissuaded, the Manx government went ahead on its own and, in 1709, issued £200 worth of halfpennies (112,000 halfpennies) and £300 worth of pennies (84,000 pennies). As it was not official coinage issued by the Royal Mint it did not have Queen Anne's head on the obverse. Neither did it have the head of the 10th Earl of Derby, the Lord of Mann. Instead the coins were issued with the Stanley crest of the eagle and child on one side and the three legs of Mann on the other.

How ordinary people lived

In the seventeenth century, houses for the ordinary Manx were small, single storey dwellings, often only two rooms with a beaten earth floor and a low loft in the roof space above. They were built of local stone and thatched with locally-produced straw, often wheat straw. High winds

Traditionally thatched cottage near Cranstal, en route *to Point of Ayre*

on the island led to the tradition of leaving stones jutting out just beneath the roof line to which twisted straw ropes could be anchored to secure the thatch. Many of the traditional cottages surviving in Cregneash, for example, were built at around the time the first government-issue Manx coinage was being produced.

Even as late as the mid eighteenth century there were virtually no wheeled vehicles on the Isle of Man. Bishop Wilson is credited with importing the first carriage, around 1749 when he was about 76. Even then he often travelled about the island by Manx pony. For centuries goods were moved by chapman (packman), pack horse or carr (a type of sledge, see chapter 4), but mainly round the coast by sea.

Wages for ordinary Manx people were in general lower than for similar work in England. True the cost of living was higher in England, but not so much so that the Manx were not poorly paid. Even so, the island population was generally healthy, apart from during times of great hardship. Farming, fishing and mining were still the main occupations, with farm work mainly taking place in the spring (planting) and autumn (harvesting), fishing in the summer (herring) and winter (cod), and mining whenever work was available. Women usually did more on the farm than their husbands, brothers, sons or fathers as the men were often away fishing or mining. There were also a number of cottage industries including spinning and weaving, particularly of flax and linen.

The question of land tenure, brought into prominence in 1630 by The Great Stanley, the future 7th earl, while looking after the island for his father (see chapter 5), had still not been resolved decades later. Uncertainly over tenure was not only bad for social harmony, it was bad for the land itself. With no guarantee that their children would be allowed to remain on the same property, farmers spent little on improving the land or maintaining the infrastructure. Consequently yields went down, buildings fell into disrepair, and farming children looked for jobs other than on the land. For a nation which relied heavily on farming, such agricultural neglect was a disaster. However the importance of good husbandry received promotion and emphasis from a rather unlikely source.

In 1698 Thomas Wilson was appointed Bishop of Sodor and Man. Even today, Bishop Wilson, with his unusual combination of practical common sense, deep faith and active

compassion, is considered the best bishop the island has ever had. He was also a very useful link between the Manx people and the ruling family. Bishop Wilson had been both the Stanley family chaplain and the current earl's tutor, and his obviously genuine interest in solving the problems of the Manx people gained their trust.

The bishop was the son of a farmer and knew the importance of good husbandry. He turned Bishopscourt farm into a model from which everyone could learn. James Stanley, the 10th Earl, was also much more sympathetic to the land question than his brother, father or grandfather had been (the 9th, 8th, and 7th Earls respectively), and indicated as much to his old tutor Bishop Wilson. In 1703 a small deputation assembled consisting of Bishop Wilson, John Stevenson of Balladoole, Ewan Christian of Lewaigue House, and the latter's relative another Ewan Christian who had inherited property in Milntown and also owned Ewanrigg Hall in Cumberland (see below). All held large tracts of Manx land, all were interested in keeping and improving it, and all went to see Stanley at his English home. The result of their negotiations was the Act of Settlement, sometimes called the Manx Magna Carta. By it, many of the rights of land ownership were effectively transferred to the farmers who worked it. Such farmers could buy and sell land or pass it on to their children as they chose, without an overlord's interference. Only the Lord of Mann's right to certain fines (the name given to leasehold payments, see above) was upheld. Even today the 1703 Act of Settlement is considered vitally important in the legal ownership of Manx land.

Tales of the tailless

The farmers gained their land just as their cats were losing their tails. The Manx cat's taillessness arose due to what is known in genetics as the founder effect, which is when a spontaneous difference arises in a limited gene pool. As the gene pool of cats on the Isle of Man was relatively small, short tails or none became much more common as the result of inbreeding.

We know that the Manx cats lost their tails around this time because of their name. 'Cat' in Manx is *kayt*, but a cat with a short tail or none at all is a *stubbin* from the English 'stubby'.

Farmland in Maughold. Lewaigue House is the white building among trees to the left of the right-hand page

Milntown, just outside Ramsey. Home of the Christian family since the early sixteenth century, although remodelled several times. Now open to the public

No-one invents a word for something which doesn't exist (although in the case of Manx cats perhaps they do!), and Manx speakers started using the word *stubbin* around 1740. Tailless cats had probably been around for some time before someone gave them a name, so they must have become far more common around then.

The beginning of the end

James Stanley, 10th Earl of Derby was a soldier and politician and, like most of his family, more interested in various appointments in England than in visiting the island of which he was lord. He succeeded to the title after the death of his brother William.

1707 saw the Act of Union which united England and Scotland. It was also a century which involved much of Britain in costly foreign wars. The British government was desperately short of funds (nothing new there) and so decided to increase taxation to raise more money (also not new). One of the easiest taxes to levy was on goods purchased. The tax was divided into two categories, customs duties levied on imported goods, and an excise tax levied on domestic consumption. Purchasers therefore not only had to pay tax twice on some goods, but also found that the tax was often more than half of the price they paid. Naturally people resented the extra cost and just as naturally tried to avoid paying it. Smuggling grew from a few fishermen bringing home the odd luxury for their family into a large-scale, well organised and highly profitable business.

There was however no smuggling into the Isle of Man, for the simple reason that it wasn't necessary. The small import duty levied by Tynwald was worth merchants paying as it meant that they could land their goods openly in safe harbours rather than clandestinely along the rocky and possibly dangerous coastline. Large trading vessels landed, paid the much-lower duties on Mann and then reorganised their cargo into smaller vessels. The little boats then slipped across the sea to waiting customers in England and Scotland. Somewhere out in the Irish Sea the honest little trading ships stopped being legal exporters out of Mann and started being smugglers heading for the UK.

The UK parliament was not happy. Its members protested strongly to Tynwald, which duly passed an act in 1711 prohibiting the shipment of foreign goods from Mann to Great Britain unless the correct duties were paid to the British government. It was a particularly cynical piece of legislative PR as many of the twenty four MHKs were from the Christian, Stevenson and Moore families, exactly the families which were most involved with the trade. If the Keys were not involved themselves they almost certainly knew who was.

George Moore, who became Speaker of the House of Keys and was eventually knighted, owned Ballamoore in Patrick and another house in Peel, both purchased using money obtained from smuggling. The Quayle family owned the estates of Crogga and Ballashamrock House, overlooking Port Soderick, and built Bridge House in Castletown on the profits of the running trade. The Christian family had gone one better and purchased Ewanrigg Hall in Cumbria, just up the hill from the small hamlet of Ellenfoot, a major centre of smuggling and handy for boats landing from the Isle of Man. Ellenfoot is now better known as Maryport.

The last of the Stanleys

It was the success of the Manx running trade, which led to the end of the island's independence from direct rule by the English crown. James Stanley, like his brother, died without male issue – his only son had died of smallpox in 1710 – and so was the last of the Stanley name to rule the Isle of Man. After James' death, in 1736, the lordship of Mann descended to James Murray, a Scottish cousin and the 2nd Duke of Atholl. James was the third son, but his only surviving elder brother William was a prisoner in the Tower of London for taking part in the Jacobite rebellions; a younger brother, George, was also fighting for the Jacobite cause. The Jacobites wanted to place the Scottish son and grandson of James II on the British throne in place of the Hanoverians currently sitting on it. Treason in favour of the 'Young Pretender' Bonnie Prince Charlie wasn't a good advertisement, but James Murray

Ballamoore, Patrick. Former residence of George Moore, smuggler and Speaker of the House of Keys

Crogga House, Port Soderick

avoided attainder by being a supporter of King George II; he later fought under the Duke of Cumberland to help defeat the Jacobite army, and his own brothers, at the Battle of Culloden in April 1746.

Visits from the Lord of Mann had become increasingly rare, but the new Lord did come to the island and was present at a meeting of Tynwald, despite some truly foul weather. In the twenty-eight years during which Murray was Lord of Mann the level of smuggling grew to epic proportions. The Lords of the Treasury of England tried to persuade Murray to sell the island back to the English crown but he refused. According to his heir he 'always declared that no temptation of gain could induce him to give up so ancient, so honourable, and so noble a birth-right such as no subject of the crown of England now has, or ever had'. As was the case of the last Stanley however, James Murray's sons predeceased him. When he died in 1764 his titles, including the lordship of Mann, passed to a nephew who was also his son-in-law.

Almost as soon as John Murray 3rd Duke of Atholl had inherited, he was contacted by the Lords of the Treasury about the sale of the island. Unlike his uncle, the Westminster government had a lever they could use against the 3rd Duke. John's father, was the George Murray who had been part of the Jacobite army twenty years earlier and had been attainted for it, which meant that he would not normally be able to leave anything he possessed to his son. On 7 February 1764 the House of Lords in Westminster agreed that Murray should inherit the title, possibly as a quid pro quo for parting with the lordship of Mann; Westminster was desperate to stop the haemorrhaging of tax revenue caused by the Manx smugglers. In 1765, the British parliament also passed the Smuggling Act, known on Mann as the Mischief Act, giving revenue men the right to stop and search every boat entering or leaving Manx ports. Murray bowed to what was fast becoming inevitable and agreed to sell the island.

In 1765 the British parliament passed the Isle of Man Purchase Act, known as the Act of Revestment, merging the lordship of Mann into the English crown and compensating the Murrays to the tune of £70,000. A proposal had been made to annex the island to the English county of Cumberland, but Sir George Moore, Speaker of the House of Keys and merchant (smuggler!), ensured that Mann was not absorbed into England's political machinery, much to the relief of the islanders. Even so Westminster thought it advisable to station troops on the island for a time, in order to keep the peace. The troops sent were Lord John Murray's

Ballashamrock House, Port Soderick. Like Crogga, it was owned by the Quayle family and used for smuggling

Highlanders, now known as The Black Watch; their colonel, Lord John, was the 3rd Duke of Atholl's uncle.

Interestingly John Christian, grandson of the Ewan Christian of Milntown who helped negotiate the Manx Magna Carta (see above) was High Sheriff for Cumberland in 1766. Could such a politically influential man have been one of those suggesting annexing Mann? Also interesting is the way Westminster seems to have used both carrots and sticks to manipulate John Murray. In 1764 he was permitted to inherit the title and becomes 3rd Duke of Atholl. In 1765 he was forced to sell the Isle of Man. However, the following year he became one of only sixteen Scottish peers allowed to sit in the Westminster House of Lords. And in 1767 he was invested in the Order of the Thistle, the highest honour in Scotland.

Under the Revestment Act the Duke of Atholl surrendered 'the Island, Castle, and Peel of Man, with all the Lordships thereto belonging, together with the royalties, regalities, franchises, liberties, and sea-ports appertaining to the same, and all other hereditaments and premises therein particularly described and mentioned as holden under the several grants thereof, or any other title whatsoever, reserving only their lands, inland waters, fisheries, mines, mills, minerals, and quarries according to their present right therein, felon goods, deodands, waifs, strays, and wrecks at sea, together with the patronage of the bishopric and of the other ecclesiastical benefices in the Island, to which they were entitled.'

For such privileges as he retained, Atholl had to pay £122 12s 2d per annum, plus the two coronation falcons (see chapters 5 and 8). The Revestment Act brought to an end over 350 years of family rule, although it did not end the Stanley/Atholl connexion with the island, which ceased only in 1828 (see chapter 7). For once the Manx people and their former ruler were in complete agreement. Both deeply resented the compulsory purchase of the island, although for very different reasons. Murray resented giving up an inheritance before he'd even had time to enjoy it, while his former subjects were dismayed by the end of their lucrative trade. A jingle often repeated at the time is:

> 'The babes unborn will rue the day
> The Isle of Man was sold away.'

For the third time in its history, the Isle of Man was sold. Almost exactly five hundred years earlier, Alexander III had purchased the island with the intention of making a profit from it. 350 years later the 6th Earl of Derby bought it from his niece. Now the island belonged to the British crown and the Manx people were rightly wary of a parliament whose sole interest in the island was the revenue to be made from it.

THE ENGLISH, EMIGRATION AND ENTREPRENEURS

The Manx were right to be concerned about their island's change of ownership. Within a very few years, customs men working for the UK parliament had recouped in revenue duty the £70,000 paid to the Atholls, and a lot more beside.

The administrative changes were far reaching and rapid. To begin with, executive power was removed from Tynwald, in fact if not explicitly. British administrators took over the organisation of the island. British rules were applied and the Westminster parliament began to make decisions which had previously been the prerogative of the Keys. The Manx felt it particularly keenly as they had no representation in Westminster. To be fair, in the mid-eighteenth century quite a lot of British people had no parliamentary representative either, but the Manx had been used to running their own island with a largely absentee ruler. They were now being micromanaged.

In many respects the Isle of Man was treated like the American colonies, but was not protected by the width of the Atlantic from detailed interference. The Revestment Act was passed in 1765; the Duties in American Colonies Act, better known as the Stamp Act, was passed the same year. When times were hard the Manx had frequently sought a new life in other countries, and many had sailed to the American colonies, including several from the Christian family. One of the most famous was William Christian of Virginia

Above: William Christian
Below: North American Manx Association plaque on Ramsey quay

who founded Fort William (the boundary moved and it's now in Kentucky). The American colonists weren't represented in the Westminster parliament either, got fed up with being taxed by a country which didn't understand their problems and cared less about solving them, and eventually declared independence in 1776. Citizens of the brand new United States of America fought for their independence and became self governing in 1783. That's fewer than twenty years since the passing of the Revestment and Stamp Acts, easily within the lifespan and memory of those smarting under the new British rule and looking back with nostalgia at the comparatively easier times of the Atholls. Distances were great and communication slow, but people did keep in touch. Did the Christian family still on Mann receive news, and ideas, from their cousins in the US?

Others take charge

A flurry of acts followed the Revestment Act, most of them designed to raise taxes and make sure people paid them. In 1765 alone, acts were passed to check smuggling; discontinue the pecuniary advantages granted to those exporting corn to Mann; ensure the correct taxes were paid on the sales of wines, spirits and salt; secure and raise customs and excise revenue; and – on the plus side – allow certain goods to be exported from Mann to the rest of Britain without the payment of duty. The 1765 Acts had concerned existing taxes, but in 1767 the Westminster parliament passed an act to levy new customs duties, the first time non-Tynwald legislation had imposed taxes on the people of the island.

Loss of executive power was not the only difficulty for Tynwald. With Westminster taking over legislation, the Manx could no longer raise money to maintain the harbours, repair the roads, deal with criminals and feed the poor. To get round the problem Tynwald created a number of committees or boards, each to deal with a different topic, and gave them the authority to raise funding through the rates.

As well as new non-Manx legislation there must also have been an influx of new non-Manx administrators. Westminster would not have trusted the locals to impose the new English laws and would have sent its own civil servants to ensure taxes were imposed, penalties paid, and the money collected sent to the British exchequer (and not disappear into the Manx one). The new administrators would have been highly unlikely to speak Manx, and would probably have seen no reason to learn it. All administration would have been conducted in English and any Manxman who wanted to query a decision, or gain a post in the new administration would have had to be familiar with that language. Locals would probably have maintained their Manx as a way of being able to discuss what was going on in front of comeovers without any danger of being understood (and irritating the comeovers in the process – probably deliberately!). However an unforeseen consequence of the Revestment Act was probably the beginning of the demise of Manx Gaelic as a first language.

With the seat of power now 300 miles away in Westminster, and little communication faster than by boat or horse (rudimentary telegraphs did exist in the south of England but were reserved for the use of the navy) the new officers relied on copious correspondence to raise problems, receive new instructions and keep up to date with what was happening in Whitehall. But there was a problem. Mann had no official means of handling mail. The royal mail had been opened to commoners in the UK by Charles I in 1635. Twenty-two years later Oliver Cromwell had established the General Post Office throughout Britain. A century after it was created in England, an official post office had not been thought necessary for Mann. Mail was carried to and from the island by friends doing a favour, or private carriers paid on delivery. For two years the new island administrators put up with such *ad hoc* mailing arrangements and complained vociferously about it. Then, in 1767, the Isle of Man Postage Act was passed in Westminster to establish post offices on the island, set a postal rate for mail going to and from Mann, and organise an official packet boat from Whitehaven to Douglas to carry it. Island post offices were, however, adjuncts of the British Royal Mail; the Isle of Man Post Office would have to wait another two hundred years to be created.

Growth of industry

One benefit the Isle of Man did gain from the Revestment Act was that it was treated as part of the rest of Britain, which meant that farmers and manufacturers could sell Manx-grown and Manx-made goods without being taxed on them.

Industry has been part of Manx life since at least the Iron Age and mining had long been one of the three main sources of work (farming and fishing being the other two). Possibly the oldest mines on Mann are the copper mines at Bradda Head and a lead mine on the Calf, but it was the eighteenth and nineteenth centuries which saw a huge growth in mining. All sorts of metals

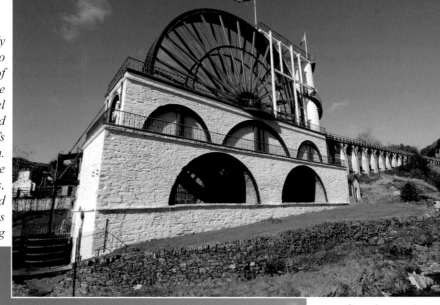

Right: Lady Isabella. Built to pump water out of the mine, she is the largest waterwheel in the world

Below: Beckwith's Mine, Glen Rushen. Part of the Foxdale group of mines, Beckwith's had constant problems with flooding

were found: copper at Glen Chass near Port St Mary and Langness, iron ore at Maughold, even small amounts of gold at Langness and Onchan, but it was for lead and zinc that the island mines were famous. At peak production the Laxey mines produced more zinc than all the other British zinc mines put together. Laxey also produced lead and copper, although the biggest source of lead on the island was in Foxdale.

The mines were hugely profitable. Zinc and copper together make brass, while lead was used in cosmetics, paint, bullets and plumbing – plumbing in fact gets its name from *plumbum*, the Latin for lead. Many lead mines also contain silver. If they contain enough silver, i.e. more than sixty ounces of silver per ton of lead, then, until 1688, they were nominated 'royal mines' and belonged to the crown. Even after that date the mine owners had to pay duties on any precious metal ore. Some of the Manx mines came close to being royal mines, but never produced enough silver to warrant the designation. Or so their owners claimed.

Perhaps surprisingly, the growth of the mining industry benefitted the fishing fleets too, as many harbours were improved in order to be able to load and transport the mineral ore. Laxey harbour was built around 1791 in response to a petition submitted to the commissioners for the construction of a short quay on the south side of the river (roughly where the promenade ends today). The community at Laxey considered a harbour essential not because twenty herring boats fished out of the bay – they launched from the beach – but because the mines needed to be able to import machinery and export ore. Even with the new harbours, some tasks were beyond standard harbour equipment. In the mid nineteenth century some of the castings for the new Lady Isabella waterwheel had to be brought into Laxey at high tide lowered over the side of the cargo ship into the sea and then retrieved from the beach after the tide had gone out.

Probably the least well known of the major Manx industries of the eighteenth and nineteenth centuries is that of linen production. It had been a small cottage industry in the early eighteenth century but had grown in importance as linen had grown to be a valuable export. The 3rd Duke of Atholl may have been forced to sell Mann, but he still held manorial and other rights on the island and was instrumental in encouraging the linen trade. Linen is made from flax and the duke paid much of the cost of the flax seed distributed by the Manx Society, and also gave wheels for spinning flax to the poor. As a result exports of linen rose by a staggering 733% in just two years, from 12,000 yards in 1765 to at least 100,000 yards in 1767. Flax is vital for making sailcloth and, in the eighteenth century, the few vessels powered by steam operated on rivers; sea-going boats relied on the wind and sails. The Tromode Sailcloth Works of W.F. Moore & Son opened in 1790. Owned by the same family for the whole of its existence the works eventually closed in 1906.

John Wood weaving at the Laxey woollen mill. In the background the dummy reflected in the mirror is wearing Manx tartan

Smaller industries also existed of course. They included boatbuilding at Castletown, Peel and Ramsey, brickworks at Castletown, Andreas and West Craig, starch making at Sulby, tanneries and bark mills including one behind Glentrammon House and papermaking at a number of sites including Laxey and Ballamillaghyn. Possibly the most famous of the smaller industries, and one of the few still remaining, is St George's Woollen Mill at Laxey, founded by the pre-Raphaelite sympathiser John Ruskin in 1881 and now the only commercial producer of hand-woven cloth on Mann.

The smuggling problem – again

Before 1765, trade goods could be legally brought into Mann on payment of the small import duty set by Tynwald. OK, goods were then smuggled into the UK to avoid the huge duties levied by Westminster, but the first half the process was entirely legal. After the Revestment Act, the Isle of Man was included within the British borders, and the much larger Westminster import levies applied. The British parliament needed the money and intended smuggling to cease. Not a chance! The Revestment Act might even have prompted more people to get involved to defy the laws imposed by their new rulers.

Uniquely, one of the vessels purpose-built for the Manx smuggling trade survives. *Peggy* was built for George Quayle in 1791 by W.S. Yarwood Ltd. of Northwich, and possibly named after Quayle's mother. She was fitted with a new invention, so new in fact that George's brother Thomas went to meet Captain (later Admiral) John Schank, the inventor: sliding or drop keels. At their simplest, such keels are

Peggy. Moved from her boathouse after more than 200 years, she is here undergoing preservation

one or more boards – *Peggy* had three – which slide down into the water to prevent sideways movement but which, when retracted, make the boat easy to bring close to shore. Sliding keels also have the advantage of enabling small boats to carry more sail and so travel faster. They were approved for use in the British navy in the same year that *Peggy* was built. George Quayle obviously didn't want to be at a disadvantage, particularly when, despite claims to the contrary, there's little doubt that *Peggy's* primary role was as a smuggling vessel.

In the five years 1789 to 1793 George Quayle had two other boats as well as the *Peggy* built; *Neptune* and, confusingly, a second *Peggy* referred to as *new Peggy*! Fewer than ten years later, in 1802, business was profitable enough for the family to open the Isle of Man's first bank. The bank was run from the family home of Bridge House in Castletown – but it had a secret. A cellar, previously walled in, was discovered in 1935, exactly one hundred years after George Quayle's death. In it, *Peggy* slept undisturbed. She even had some of her cargo of French brandy still on deck.

A black trade

Many Manx merchants were not only smugglers, they were also slavers. The two trades were very closely linked as some of the smuggled items landed on Mann were collected by slave ships leaving Liverpool and used to trade for slaves. The market in Africa wanted only items not obtainable locally, so brandy, gunpowder, tobacco, cloth and beads all formed part of the cargoes available for collection from Mann. The same cargoes were available in England, but, because the duties paid to import them into England were much higher, so was the cost of the cargoes. Using smuggled items as trade goods was a form of early tax evasion.

The slaving ships sailed a triangular route. Ramsey and Peel certainly had their share of slave trade, but the main Manx port used was also the biggest: Douglas. Leaving the Isle of Man with a cargo of trade goods, ships sailed down to Africa and bartered the cargo for slaves. From Africa they sailed to North or sometimes South America where the slaves were sold. Returning home to the Isle of Man and Britain, the ships would be carrying sugar, rum, tobacco and anything else which would fill up the corners. Because most slaves were transported from Africa to America, few slaves were seen on Mann, which obscured the Manx involvement.

Over sixty Manx captains were involved in the Atlantic slave trade, many of them in charge of slaving ships from the English ports of Liverpool, Bristol and London. The most famous was undoubtedly Hugh Crow who made thirteen voyages on slaving ships, seven of them as captain. Known as 'Mind your Eye' Crow because he'd lost his right eye in infancy, the captain had a reputation for treating his human cargo kindly, or at least kindly by comparison with other captains. He made little distinction between the captive Africans whom he called black slaves, and the press-ganged crew, whom he referred to as white slaves. A 'Song Made by the people of Colour in Jamaica on CAPTN HUGH CROW' which includes lines such as 'But we glad for see em now and den', seems to indicate that at least some of the slaves held Crow in high regard, or were at least politic enough to say so.

Crow took over from Thomas Nuttall as captain of the last British slaver, *Kitty's Amelia*, which left Liverpool on 25 July 1807, returning on 29 June 1808. The Slave Trade Act of March 1807 had abolished the trade (although not slavery itself) in British colonies, and came into effect on 1 May. Henry Clarke, the owner of *Kitty's Amelia*, had however received clearance for the voyage in late April. Outfitting took several months so the voyage was technically legal, although it took place after the law came into force.

Kitty's Amelia was to be Crow's last command. He retired to the Isle of Man and purchased a small farm at East Ballaterson in Maughold. He rebuilt the house in Georgian style and renamed the farm Crowville. For such a flamboyant figure it's a surprisingly hidden spot.

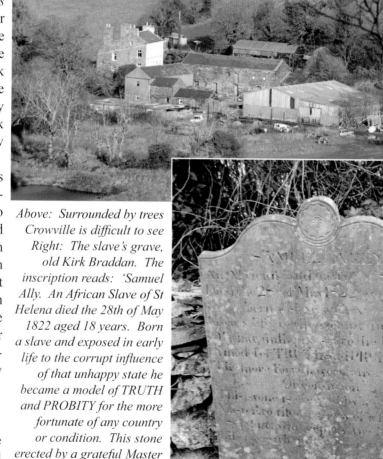

Above: Surrounded by trees Crowville is difficult to see
Right: The slave's grave, old Kirk Braddan. The inscription reads: 'Samuel Ally. An African Slave of St Helena died the 28th of May 1822 aged 18 years. Born a slave and exposed in early life to the corrupt influence of that unhappy state he became a model of TRUTH and PROBITY for the more fortunate of any country or condition. This stone erected by a grateful Master to the memory of a faithful servant who repaid the boon of Liberty with unbounded attachment'

Atholls return

John Murray the 3rd Duke of Atholl might have been induced to sell the island to the English crown, but his son didn't feel the matter ended there. The family had retained certain rights on Mann (see chapter 6) but the 4th Duke felt that the island had been sold too cheaply and wanted compensation. To that end he pestered both the British Government and King George III, and eventually nagged them into appointing a Royal Commission to enquire into his claims. In 1792 the Commission produced a detailed and very long report on the economic state of the island which eventually concluded that the Duke had a point. Since the Revestment Act, the Isle of Man had been under the administration of a series of governors appointed by Westminster. In an effort to reconcile the matter, in 1793 the British Government appointed John Murray, 4th Duke of Atholl as governor to the island his family once ruled.

The Manx reception of the Duke of Atholl appears to be mixed. On the one hand they deeply resented being ruled from Westminster where island concerns were swamped by Empire issues; on the other they were wary of their island becoming again the domain of a single (and foreign) ruler. The Manx were not reassured by the Duke building Castle Mona as his official residence, and he was not happy at the Westminster parliament's refusal to pay for it.

Another bone of contention was the lack of any permanent meeting place for the House of Keys. Elected members of the Westminster parliament used the chapel of St Stephen in the

Old House of Keys, Castletown, seen from Castle Rushen

Palace of Westminster as their 'house of commons' but the twenty-four Keys met in Castle Rushen or one of the member's houses. From 1710 they met in the lower storey of the library built in Castletown by Bishop Wilson, but by the end of the century the building had fallen into such a state of disrepair that the 1792 Royal Commission – the same one which reported in favour of additional compensation for the 4th Duke – stated it to be a 'mean, decayed building.' The Keys needed a new and permanent home but, by the Revestment Act, had no means of raising revenue to build one. After struggling on for another twenty-five years, in 1817 the Keys resolved that the building was 'not only unfit, but imminently unsafe for holding their meetings, and that they should forthwith adjourn to the George Inn'!

The Duke of Atholl was already in discussion with architect Thomas Brine about a building for the Keys, but there were arguments about who should pay for it. The Westminster parliament didn't see why it should pay for a meeting chamber for a body it would prefer to be without, while the Keys contended that the cost should be paid out of revenues gained from Mann. Eventually the two sides compromised with each paying part of the costs, and the go-ahead was finally given on 31 May 1819. The old library building was demolished and the new meeting house for the Keys built in its place. It was completed in 1821, twenty-nine years after it was first deemed necessary. Even so, the MHKs were ahead of the MPs. The Westminster parliament didn't get its purpose-built building until 1852. Both lagged behind the newly independent United States of America however, whose Capitol Building was completed in 1800, although later expanded to include the dome. Even the US Capitol Building was not the earliest. That distinction belongs to a near neighbour of the Isle of Man. The earliest purpose-built two-chamber parliament building in the world was *Tithe na Parlaiminte*, completed in 1739 and built to house the parliament of an independent Ireland.

Cutting the final ties

By the early nineteenth century, the island's administration was divided between the unelected Keys who tended to treat their office as a club to benefit the leading families, and the equally unelected governor and his staff who had been appointed by what many of the Manx considered a foreign power. There had been hope that the governor, the 4th Duke of Atholl, would assist the Manx as, even after the Revestment Act, he retained much patronage on Mann. Unfortunately his habit of nepotism made him increasingly unpopular as he filled vacant Manx posts with his own Scottish dependants. Meanwhile the Keys were more interested in maintaining their own profits than in looking after the wellbeing of the ordinary Manx.

Even so the *status quo* might have limped on for a while had it not been for the weather. The early nineteenth century was noted for harsh winters and cold, wet summers, particularly during the years 1812-20. Harvests were poor and herring scarce. Large landowners with a surplus of wheat were doing very well, however, as poor harvests meant that it commanded a high price. People in the UK could afford it, those on Mann could not, so Manx landowners, many of whom were from families with members in the House of Keys, continued to export wheat despite food shortages on the island.

To make matters still worse, in 1821 the Keys petitioned the Westminster parliament to place the Isle of Man in the same position as the UK regarding importing wheat from other countries. As landowners, the Keys were determined to protect their own profits. The island's lieutenant governor, Cornelius Smelt, objected to the petition but was ignored, and the result was the Isle of Man Corn Act. It meant that when the price of wheat fell below eighty shillings per quarter (a quarter is a measurement of grain equivalent to eight bushels or sixty-four gallons), the ports were closed to foreign wheat, wheat became scarce and the price was pushed back up.

The Duke had little time for the Keys but his sympathies ran parallel with theirs. He wanted to make money out of the Isle of Man and so did they. The Manx were already struggling to cope with high taxation when the Duke increased the island's custom duties and endorsed the 1825 attempt of the Bishop – who happened to be the Duke's nephew – to impose a tithe on green crops such as turnips and potatoes. Legally such crops were subject to tithes but payment had in fact not been collected for many years. Potatoes and herring were the staple food of the ordinary people and taxing them during such a time of shortage was insensitive in the extreme.

So: harvests were poor; people couldn't afford to buy Manx wheat, much of which was sent abroad anyway; they were not allowed to import wheat from elsewhere; potatoes were heavily

Summerhill Glen. Paths now wind where water used to be held behind and between the dams of the first reservoir

taxed; fish catches were small. The result was almost inevitable. Starving people rioted, first in Peel and then at Douglas and Ramsey, and it was only an embargo placed by Cornelius Smelt on the export of wheat which calmed matters down and kept people fed.

The Duke's attitude had exacerbated the civil unrest and he constantly complained that his parents had sold Mann too cheaply. The Westminster parliament had had enough and passed acts in 1824 and 1825 to purchase all Atholl's remaining manorial rights in the Isle of Man, and pay the Duke an annuity to compensate him for their loss. After much wrangling over the valuation, the 4th Duke of Atholl sold his remaining rights for £417,144. He left the island in 1826, payment was completed in 1829 and his governorship ceased with his death in 1830. The last tie with the family which had governed the Isle of Man almost without a break for four hundred and twenty five years was finally severed.

In sickness and in health...

The growth of industry during the eighteenth and nineteenth century led to people moving to towns to look for work. Laxey, for example, grew from a small fishing village to a mining town as the mines were developed and expanded. Douglas, Ramsey, Peel and Castletown also got slowly and steadily bigger. However, as towns grew the health of their inhabitants declined. Houses were built higgledy piggledy wherever seemed convenient and although by the beginning of the nineteenth century some effort was being made at urban planning, towns were still cramped and insanitary.

Living on farms and in relatively isolated rural communities acted as a natural quarantine and the Manx had largely escaped huge population losses caused by the major killer diseases such as plague and measles, although smallpox, brought to the island in 1685, was a regular killer. The insanitary and crowded living conditions of the developing towns were excellent breeding grounds for disease however, particularly when combined with near starvation, and epidemics were the result.

One of the worst killers was cholera which arrived on the island from Liverpool in 1832 and caused major outbreaks in that and the following year. Cholera is a bacterial water-born disease which, unless treated, kills around half of the people it infects. Its victims die of dehydration as the disease causes sufferers to lose bodily fluids very quickly. Cholera microbes are killed by heat or acid. Nurses burned soiled clothes and bedding, and used vinegar to clean vomit off their hands so killing the bacteria. Dwellings were usually disinfected with chloride of lime which, when mixed with water, releases chlorine; it killed the cholera and a lot more besides.

For clean water towns relied on wells or water carts bringing supplies in from the country. Wells could be contaminated by seepage from middens, while unscrupulous carters filled their barrels from rivers, which were not only used as a general sewer, but in which infected linen was sometimes washed. Douglas, the island's biggest commercial port, and Castletown, its capital city, suffered most. They were also where most of the wealthiest people on the island lived and/or worked. Their influence prompted Tynwald to pass the Waterworks Act in 1834. Douglas Waterworks Co. was authorised to provide the first public water supply on the island. Mann's first reservoir was at Summer Hill and supplied the growing town of Douglas

Safety from the Sea

At the beginning of the nineteenth century, the Isle of Man had no lighthouses apart from harbour lights of various qualities at Douglas, Ramsey, Derbyhaven, Castletown and possibly Peel. The harbour light built in 1812 at Port St Mary had ambitions above its station and was visible for nine miles. Lighthouses to protect shipping had been frequently requested but it was not until 1817 that the first true lighthouse on Mann was built at Point of Ayre, designed by Robert Stevenson and built by his employers, the Commissioners of Northern Lighthouses.

Lighthouses warned sailors of hazards near shore, but rescue at sea was still unknown. In 1808 William

Point of Ayre. The original lighthouse is furthest away, in the middle is the fog horn and, nearest the camera, is the secondary light known as 'Winkie'

The old sea wall, Douglas, now more than 100 yards from the sea

Hillary was thirty when he moved to Mann to escape creditors. He and his wife divorced under Scottish law in 1812, and the following year he married Manxwoman Emma Tobin, also in Scotland, although none of them had ever lived there. Under English and Manx law Hillary's second marriage might even have been considered bigamous. To allay gossip William and Emma remarried in Braddan church in 1829.

It's well known that Hillary lived in Fort Anne, a large house on Douglas headland, but when he arrived in Mann he rented a house at the top of Prospect Hill; he couldn't afford to buy Fort Anne until 1831, when he was sixty. Prospect Hill was much closer to the sea than it is today – what is now known as Strand Street was once called Sand Street as it was virtually on the beach – and William witnessed many shipwrecks. A particular hazard to shipping was St Mary's Isle, also called Conister Rock from the Manx *koine y sker* meaning 'head of the reef', situated in Douglas Bay and just submerged at high tide. There was no organised lifeboat service when the revenue cutter *HMS Vigilant*, only launched the previous year, struck the rock in a storm on 7 October 1822.

People thought differently about wrecks in the early nineteenth century. To local

Below: William Hillary watches over Douglas Bay from Douglas Head
Right: The wreck of St George
Far right: The Tower of Refuge

150th ANNIVERSARY ROYAL NATIONAL LIFEBOAT INSTITUTION

WRECK OF "ST. GEORGE" IN DOUGLAS BAY 1830

J H NICHOLSON R I

1974

COURVOISIER S.A.

3½

Ramsey lifeboat, Ann and James Ritchie, *practising at Port Mooar*

communities a wreck could be a source of additional income. The cargo could be used or sold, equipment recycled and even the timbers of the ship turned into building materials or firewood. And there were no rewards for rescuing the lives on board either. Those hurt or killed trying to do so could easily leave their families starving if they, the major breadwinner, were put out of action; in addition the recent corn shortages (see above) meant that no-one had anything 'put by'.

It was considered unusual therefore when William Hillary and three friends organised a rescue attempt for the crew of the *Vigilant*. All were important people and Hillary was considered elderly for the time. Fisherfolk were bribed and shamed into helping, and the crew of the stricken ship was saved. Over the two days the storm raged, Hillary went on to help save 106 lives in ten ships. If amateur efforts could do so much it seemed clear to him that a properly trained organisation could do much more. He launched 'an appeal to the British nation' and formed The National Institution for the Preservation of Life from Shipwreck. In 1854 the organisation changed its name to the Royal National Lifeboat Institution (RNLI).

In Douglas there was still the problem of St Mary's Isle. Hillary urged that a lighthouse or sanctuary be built on it so that shipping could be warned away, or at the very least sailors who came to grief would have a safe haven to wait out the storm. It took another wreck on Conister rocks, that of the *St George,* in 1830, before anything was done. Even today, saving the crew of *St George* is considered one of the finest lifeboat rescues in the proud history of the RNLI. It was astonishingly risky, and an early test for the new lifeboat coxed by Sir William who was badly injured in the attempt.

Still reluctant to do anything about the islet, the Harbour Commissioners mumbled about it being in private ownership, so Hillary acted on his own, launched an appeal for public funds and promised to fund any shortfall himself. Sixty-three subscribers donated cash and, in support of the project, the Manx Attorney General, John Quane, owner of St Mary's Isle, presented it to Hillary and future presidents of the Manx lifeboat movements to hold in trust – which is why it often flies the RNLI flag. So much for private ownership being a bar to building! Sir William himself ended up paying just under a third of the costs.

Completed in 1832 the Tower of Refuge offered stranded sailors rough shelter from storms, had a bell with which to summon help and, in its early years, was kept supplied with fresh food and water.

It was designed by John Welch and modelled on a romantic idea of a thirteenth century castle. Welch was busy during the first years of the 1830s. Not only did he design the Tower of Refuge but, as assistant to his brother, he'd been involved in turning Castle Mona, the former residence of the 4th Duke of Atholl, into a hotel. He also designed several churches including Holy Trinity, Lazayre and St Peter's, Onchan with its Sunday School.

The other Welch brother, Edward, was partner to Joseph Hansom – he who designed the Hansom cab – and had arrived in the island in 1830 to design a more important building even than the Tower of Refuge. King William's College.

Leaders in learning - still

Bishop Barrow began it all 150 years earlier when funds from the farming estates of Ballagilley and Hango Hill were put in trust to support two scholars training for the ministry at Trinity College Dublin (see chapter 6). Quite how a trust designed to train Manx boys for the priesthood came to be used to fund a public school whose students often have no connexion with Mann is debatable. The fact remains however that pupils of King William's College are known as Barrovians.

The sum accumulated in Bishop Barrow's Trust paid for about half the building work and the rest of the money was raised by an Act of Tynwald which mortgaged the estate. Funds for building the college chapel were raised in England by Bishop Ward; the same Bishop Ward led the opposition to merging the diocese of Sodor and Man with that of Carlisle in the 1830s. Some brave souls approached King William IV for help with funding the college and the king is reputed to have replied that he offered 'my most valuable possession, my name'.

The founders probably hoped for something a bit more tangible and may well have been intending to name the college after Bishop Barrow but it's always difficult to refuse royalty and King William's College the new school became. It opened on 1 August 1833 with forty-six pupils. One of its early pupils was young Thomas Brown, who joined the school in August 1846 and returned as vice-principal in 1855, aged only 25. He's better known as Manx poet, T.E. Brown.

The college building was designed by Welch and Hansom – that's E. not J. Welch – and work began in 1830. Edward Welch left the island before the college was completed, and his brother John always claimed to have remodelled the college tower. Whether he did or not the current tower is different again as much of the original building was destroyed by fire in 1844.

Turning the Keys to democracy

It needed an Act of Tynwald to make it possible for Bishop Barrow's Trust to be used to fund King William's College. Despite its emasculation by Westminster, Tynwald still held an important place in island affairs. The Manx deeply disliked being governed

Manx poet T.E. Brown, Prospect Hill, Douglas

James Brown (left), campaigner for the reform of the House of Keys

Fusion Design

'James Brown'

BDT 2007

by an organisation uninterested in their welfare, particularly one in another country – and who can blame them? They wanted more of a say in what happened on their island. However while the Keys were lobbying Westminster, many of the ordinary people were lobbying the Keys.

Democratic government was important to Vikings and a feature of the Viking things (see chapter 3). While nowhere near the 'one adult, one vote' system existing today in Britain, the Viking assemblies acknowledged that ordinary people had a right to say who was going to be in charge and what rules their community was to live by. Somewhere over the years Tynwald had lost that. The Keys were an unelected body, or at least unelected by anyone other than themselves. Vacancies could occur by a member dying, voluntarily giving up his office or, in extreme cases, being removed from his post by the other Keys, but there was no limit to the term of office and no popular elections. There was also nothing like constituency representation and no responsibility, other than a moral one, to take decisions which benefitted the ordinary Manx. The Keys were in fact an oligarchy of senior Manx families. For nearly 150 years from 1750 to 1898, for example, Speakers of the House of Keys were members by blood or marriage of either the Moore or Taubman families.

To qualify to be one of the Twenty Four a candidate had to be male, over twenty one and hold landed property to a certain value per annum (see also chapter 5). The leader of the Keys was called Chairman until 1758 when George Moore on his appointment as chairman preferred instead the title of Speaker in emulation of his colleague in Westminster. Vacancies among the Twenty Four were filled by the remaining Keys deciding on two suitable candidates, the names of whom the Speaker then presented to the island's governor for him to choose one of them. It was no surprise when, advised by the Speaker, the governor chose the candidate favoured by the Keys. Membership of the island's parliament was not even restricted to those who lived on the island. John Christian Curwen, for example, although descended from one of the leading Manx families – Fletcher Christian of *Bounty* fame was one of his cousins – lived at Workington Hall, Cumbria. He became a member of the House of Keys (MHK) in 1781 and, five years later, member of the Westminster parliament (MP) for Carlisle too; he was therefore a member of two parliaments at the same time.

In 1832 the parliament at Westminster passed the Reform Act which greatly increased the number of people in the UK who could vote and therefore made anyone who wanted to be a member of the UK parliament more directly answerable to those who elected them. The Manx, of course, had no representative at Westminster, and no say in who became one of the Twenty Four. Possibly influenced by the increased enfranchisement they saw happening across the water, the Manx grew more vociferous for a similar democratic process to be applied to the Keys.

The campaign was led by two newspaper editors, Robert Fargher of *Mona's Herald*, and James Brown of the *Isle of Man Times*. Fargher was a Manxman, Brown was not; Fargher a radical, Brown a member of the establishment, but they were united in their wish to see Members of the House of Keys democratically elected. At different times both were incarcerated in Castle Rushen for criticising the Keys as undemocratic. Fargher went to prison on libel charges in 1845, 1847 and 1857 having crossed swords with banker, lawyer, MHK and Secretary of the House of Keys, William Dumbell (see below).

Brown's libel was more obvious. He called the lower house Don-Keys and accused them of despotic government. Tynwald is a court as well as a parliament and Brown was summoned to answer charges of contempt. Instead of explaining or apologising, he said in person what he had previously said in print and, in 1864, was sentenced to six months imprisonment. Undaunted Brown continued to rail against the Keys from his cell. Released on Appeal after six weeks, he sued the twenty members of the Keys who had signed the warrant for his imprisonment and won! The disgruntled Keys had to pay him £519 plus damages and costs. An account at the time states: 'in less than seven weeks he was again free, and was brought down in triumph to Douglas by a large number of persons.' Unfortunately the account cannot be said to be objective as it was published, among other places, in *Brown's Popular Guide to the Isle of Man*. The publisher was the same James Brown.

Money talks

While the public war of words was raging, a new island governor had been appointed. Henry Brougham Loch arrived on Mann in 1863 and, like his predecessor Francis Stainsby-Conant-Pigott, dwelt in Douglas rather than in Castletown. In 1861, Pigott had leased Marina Lodge (the Sefton Hotel now occupies the site) from Samuel Harris, Chairman of Douglas Commissioners. Getting the Governor to live in 'his' town was a triumph for Harris and started the process of the island's capital moving from Castletown to Douglas. Pigott was welcomed enthusiastically and quickly recognised that Douglas Harbour defence needed serious work, but died suddenly two years later. His successor, Loch, preferred a house out of town and leased Bemahague from the trustees of Francis Daly, who was a minor, and therefore not permitted to enter legal agreements for himself. Bemahague never returned to the Daly family, being leased to successive governors for the next forty years. On 24 November 1903, Tynwald purchased the house with 112 acres of land adjoining for £12,000. Today it is known as Government House.

Governor Loch very quickly noticed that the island needed some way to raise funds to repair its own infrastructure and endorsed Pigott's concern about the protection of Douglas

Government House, residence of the Queen's representative, the Lieutenant Governor

Harbour. Even the UK parliament seemed to realise that the something needed to be done, as it passed several Acts during the decade or so preceding 1866, many of them concerned with refurbishing harbours. It held the purse strings, however, and Westminster made it clear that it was unwilling to hand the control of taxes paid by the people, to a body not chosen by the people. If the Keys wanted to control the budget, they themselves needed to be controlled through the ballot box. The James Brown debacle merely made more urgent the solution of a problem which the Governor was already considering.

Governor Loch undertook a series of delicate negotiations, on the one side with the Twenty Four urging them to vote themselves out of a job, and on the other with Westminster urging it to renounce control of much of the Manx revenue. 1866 was a momentous year for Manx government. Almost exactly a century after the Revestment Act ended Tynwald's control of Manx revenue, the Isle of Man, Customs, Harbours and Public Purposes Act was passed by Westminster. The Act raised Manx customs duties to match those in the UK, stated that the island would pay £10,000 per year to the British government for providing naval and military protection and keep everything left over to spend on infrastructure and repairs. The catch was that expenditure would be supervised by Westminster and could be vetoed by the Governor. In return, the House of Keys Election Act was passed on 20 December 1866 by Tynwald. It ended the oligarchic nature of the Keys and provided for public elections.

By the people, for the people

The Election Act divided the island into ten electoral districts. The sheadings of Glenfaba, Michael, Ayre, Garff, Middle and Rushen were to elect three members each, as was the town of Douglas. The towns of Peel, Ramsey and Castletown each elected one member. Men who owned real estate valued at not less than eight pounds, or tenants paying an annual rent of not less than twelve pounds, were allowed to vote. Only thirteen of the previous Twenty Four continued to serve in the first elected House of Keys, although some stood down rather than contest a seat.

ISLE OF MAN
Votes for Women 1881
9p
Miss EMMELINE GOULDEN 1858-1928
Mrs SOPHIA JANE GOULDEN 1835-1910
A. D. THEOBALD
1981
QUESTA

Some of the Keys might have been reluctant to make their position subject to democratic election, but within twenty years the Twenty Four went from an unelected body to pioneers of democracy. The Election Act passed by the Keys in 1881 extended the right to vote in various ways, not least opening the franchise to spinsters or widows who owned property. The Keys led the world in recognising that its members represented taxpayers regardless of their sex. New Zealand is usually quoted as the first country in the world to recognise female suffrage in its national elections of 1893. In fact the Isle of Man granted women the vote twelve years earlier.

The focus of the island was now in Douglas. By the last half of the nineteenth century, it was the island's biggest town by far, most of Mann's legitimate trade was conducted through Douglas's docks and harbour, and Governor Loch had elected to live there. It made no sense for the island parliament still to be situated in Castletown, ten miles away. The Keys needed to move, and they needed suitable premises to move to.

At first they took up residence in the Douglas Courthouse, but were searching for somewhere with more room when the Bank of Mona closed (see below). The Bank of Mona's building in

The Manx parliament building, affectionately known as 'the wedding cake'

Douglas had been built in 1855 to the design of John Robinson, who also designed what is now Falcon Cliff Court – the white building with the single turret which stands above the Central Promenade – for its manager. On 7 November 1879 the building looking down Prospect Hill was purchased by the Keys as their new home. Perhaps indicating that the only organisations with any money – and that mostly other people's – are governments and banks, the Keys former home in Castletown became a branch of Dumbell's Bank, of which more anon.

Holiday hot spot

The preoccupation of Governors Pigott and Loch with repairing the harbours wasn't only to benefit trade. During the 1800s, travel ceased to be limited to the wealthy and short leisure trips began to be enjoyed by groups of working people. By the last quarter of the nineteenth century the idea of a week-long holiday, albeit unpaid, was becoming the norm in the textile towns of the north of England. As it was more cost effective to close the mill rather than have serial absences, it also became usual for all the mills in one area to close at the same time in a holiday known as Wakes Week. Those who worked together often played together and whole communities travelled to the Isle of Man for fun and relaxation. Considered exotic, yet reasonably easy to get to, the island infrastructure was transformed by the need to cater for its visitors, and part them from their cash.

The most pressing requirement for the increasing numbers of visitors was of course somewhere to stay; at the beginning of the tourist boom, accommodation was in such short supply that some visitors slept in bathing huts on the beach. The rapid increase in the number of visitors caused a major building boom and accommodation to serve every need – and purse – quickly flourished. Gentlemen's residences such as Fort Anne were converted to top-grade hotels, but many more were purpose-built ranging from the Villiers, the largest hotel on the island with upwards of three hundred rooms, through to family-run boarding houses and the first holiday camp in the world.

Opened at Howstrake in 1894 by Joseph Cunningham a Liverpool flour trader, baker and staunch Presbyterian the holiday camp could accommodate 600 'clean living young men'. Ten years later the camp moved to Victoria Road, Douglas, just to the east of what is now Noble's Park, and the Howstrake site continued to operate under different hands. Living quarters on the new site were a mix of tents and wooden huts accommodating nearly 4,000. Cunningham camp had its own shops, swimming pool, playing fields, a bank and was virtually self sufficient in food; in 1898 Joseph Cunningham purchased Ellerslie Manor and developed it as a model farm supplying almost everything needed to feed his holidaymakers

It's not immediately obvious, but Douglas front is made up of four promenades all of which were built on reclaimed land. The first was, oddly, one in the middle. The Harris Promenade stretches from the Sefton Hotel to the foot of Broadway, and is named after High Bailiff of Douglas Samuel Harris who organised the public subscription which had it built. It opened in 1868. Loch Promenade was named after the Governor, opened in 1875 and was handed over to the town commissioners two years later. It runs from Victoria Pier to meet the southern end of Harris Promenade. Central Promenade runs from Harris to Queen's Promenade, named after Victoria and opened in 1890, and Strathallen Crescent completes the sweep around the bay. Victoria Pier (where the Manannan docks today) was built in 1872 so that boats could dock at low tide, while the horse tramway, built in 1876, took visitors and their luggage to hotels along the front.

Other Manx towns also expanded. Hotels and boarding houses were built at Ramsey and Peel and, after the steam railway connected them to Douglas in 1874, also at Port Erin and Port St Mary. Roads on Mann were generally poor, so railways offered a welcome possibility for inland travel. The first line to open was from Douglas to Peel in 1873, followed by the line from Douglas to Port Erin the following year. The Manx Northern line opened from St John's to Ramsey in 1879 and the line from St John's to Foxdale in 1886. Within less than fifteen years therefore, the Isle of Man went from having no railways at all, to lines serving all its main towns, and many of its smaller ones.

Electric traction was still in its infancy, with the first electric tramway operating in St Petersburg in 1880. The first passenger-carrying tramway to open in Britain was the Giant's

Snaefell Mountain Railway. Despite the legend on the side of the tram, the SMR is usualy referred to as a railway. And, yes, that is snow...

ISLE OF MAN 4P

A D THEOBALD

1991

DOUGLAS CABLE CAR
BDT

Causeway Tramway in Northern Ireland in January 1883. What was to become the Manx Electric Railway (it's had several changes of name) opened a mere ten years later using state-of-the-art technology imported from America. So new was the tramway, that almost all of its tramcars, many of which still run in service, were in use before the first motor car arrived on the island. Originally terminating at Groudle, the tramway's success led to it being extended to Laxey in 1894, while a through service to Ramsey was introduced for the 1899 season. The last of the Manx transport systems to be installed was the Upper Douglas Cable Tramway in 1896 to serve the hotels and their visitors up Prospect Hill and along Bucks Road, descending again along Broadway.

Top: Upper Douglas Cable
Tramway
Above: Remains of Peel swimming
pool for 'healthy sea bathing'
Right: Douglas Southern Electric
Tramway
None of these attractions is still in use

Service routes were one thing, fun another, and several Manx tramways were built purely for tourists. The most famous of these is undoubtedly the Snaefell Mountain Railway, which and provided tourists who were not opportunity to visit the highest point on opened in 1895 good walkers with the the island. The same year saw the opening of an even more spectacular tourist tramway, the Douglas Southern Electric Tramway, which transported tourists along the newly constructed Marine Drive around the coast south of Douglas to Port Soderick; it included three overbridges, two of them across sea coves.

Tourists began to visit in increasing numbers and needed to be entertained. Entrepreneurs were only too happy to oblige. Cunningham supplied entertainments for his holiday-camp guests; Derby Castle had pavilions and pleasure grounds; Port Erin and Peel swimming pools. Glen Helen had its Swiss Cottage, and Injebreck House a dancing pavilion and switchback railway. Not to be outdone Groudle Glen was lit by electric light in the trees – astonishing for 1896 when electric light had been patented less than twenty years earlier – and had its own small zoo and miniature steam railway. Many of the attractions, including most of the glens, were owned by the railway companies, an entrepreneurial business venture unusual in British railways at the time.

The appearance of the island was changing radically and quickly. Within just twenty-two years, from 1868 to 1890, Douglas changed from a mishmash of cramped buildings and streets huddled round its harbour, to the imposing sweep of architecture visible today. The whole of the Manx railway system was installed in the twenty-three years between 1873 and 1896. In less than thirty years – easily within living memory – the island had changed from a largely rural community, receiving relatively few visitors, travelling little and that by sea, horse or foot, to a society bustling with tourists, hotels and attractions, and with one of the most modern transport systems in the world.

All this development needed start-up capital and investors willing to risk money at the beginning in return for a much bigger financial gain later. One of the main people supporting and funding new ventures was Alexander Bruce, entrepreneur, and, more significantly, general manager of Dumbell's Bank.

Farrago in finance

Two names stand out in Manx financial circles of the nineteenth century: Henry Bloom Noble and George William Dumbell. The former is the island's most notable philanthropist, the latter associated with its most infamous financial chicanery, and neither were Manxmen. Noble had come to Mann with nothing, had made a fortune by trade and money lending, and when he died childless left most of his wealth, including his house, in trust to benefit those of the Manx who were poor, sick or old. Noble left his name to a hospital, park, library and numerous smaller projects all of them financed either by him in his lifetime or by his legacy after his death. Dumbell left his name to a row of miners' cottages in Laxey, a lamp in Douglas and the biggest financial scandal known on the island.

John and Jonathan Dumbell, George's uncle and father, together with Messrs Day, Barton and Robinson founded the short-lived Stockport Bank in 1793. It lasted a mere two years and its failure was blamed mainly on mismanagement and sharp practice by the partners. In 1815, when George was eleven, Jonathan Dumbell moved his family to Mann. In time Jonathan went into business with his elder son Hugh while his younger son George entered the legal profession.

According to contemporaries George Dumbell was ambitious and ruthless. He became a Manx advocate, purchased several properties on the island and, from 1840 to 1858, was a Member of the House of Keys in its unelected days. Within a few months of his appointment he was Secretary of the House. Like his father he seemed to be particularly attracted to banking and was a major shareholder in the Isle of Man Joint Stock Bank established in 1837. It lasted longer than the Stockport Bank but failed for much the same reason in 1843.

Undaunted by the risk to other people's savings Dumbell tried again. The Douglas and Isle of Man Bank had been run by the Holmes brothers since 1815. When the final brother died in 1853 its assets were taken over by a partnership of George Dumbell, his son of the same name, and his brother in law Louis Geneste Howard. In law the bank might have been Dumbell, Son and Howard but it was known always as Dumbell's, and officially so after it became a limited liability company in 1874. It experienced its first problems only three years after it opened, suspending business in August and only reopening in November.

Dumbell was helped out of the crisis by his persuasive skills and the temporary closure on 1 November for a few days of his great rival the Bank of Mona. There was a third major bank on the island, the Isle of Man Banking Company Ltd., founded in 1865. 'The Limited' as it became known tended to be favoured by the monied upper classes, while Dumbell's dealt more with trade. The Limited was considered staid, Dumbell's, under its autocratic leader, much more agile in investments and speculation. By the time Dumbell's Bank floated in 1874, its chairman was or had been involved in many of the most significant Manx businesses, including the Manx Telegraph Company, the Great Laxey Mine and the Isle of Man Railway Company and was on the board of directors of most new companies. He also owned over 870 acres of land.

When the Bank of Mona's parent organisation, the City of Glasgow Bank, failed in 1878, the Manx division, although solvent, had also to close. Manager of the Ramsey branch of the Bank of Mona was Alexander Bruce and, when the Bank of Mona closed, Dumbell, now aged 74, offered Bruce a job. Within ten years and, just before the old man's death in 1887, Bruce became General Manager.

Bruce had the instincts of a venture capitalist without the judgement. He continued the bank's policy of investment, particularly in tourism, often without either sufficient security for loans, or the funds to underwrite them. He loaned to boarding houses, shops and pubs, and helped fund the Palace and Derby Castle Company Limited, the Isle of Man Tramways and Electric Power Company Limited, and the Isle of Man Breweries Limited. Such were the apparent profits that Bruce seemed metaphorically to be printing money. Unfortunately Dumbell's bank really did have a licence to print its own notes but had grossly insufficient assets to back them up.

The general public were taken in but other banks had been suspicious for some time. In September 1890 the Douglas Town Commissioners purchased the town's water supply from the Douglas Water Company for around £146,000. The commissioners banked with Dumbell's and Bruce was Town Treasurer. The Water Company however, whose chairman was Henry Bloom Noble, banked with The Limited and refused to accept a cheque drawn on Dumbell's as payment. Douglas Water Company demanded cash, and cash it was paid.

On 30 November 1899, John Curphey, head cashier of Dumbell's, resigned his position. The following day he wrote a personal letter to the Chairman stating: 'a most dangerous and critical state of the bank's affairs, brought about by years of gross neglect on the part of the managers…it is well-known to the managers themselves, the auditors and every member of the staff.' He was rewarded for his honesty by being appointed manager of a branch of the Isle of Man Banking Company Ltd.

Two months later Dumbell's bank crashed. Its obituary was written in the Manx Sun, which had long been criticising its soundness: 'The 3rd of February, 1900, will be a day of evil memory in "Our Island Story" for generations to come. It was on that day Dumbell's Bank, virtually the Manx National Bank, tottered to its fall, and, in its fall, spread ruin and misery far and wide.' Purple prose it might be, but the Manx Sun was right. Today many remember the financial crash of 2008 and the recession which followed. The crash of Dumbell's Bank was far, far worse. Its effects continued to be felt more than a century later. Some Manx organisations never recovered.

CHAPTER 8

CHANGING EMPHASIS

O nly one month into the new century, and the fall of Dumbell's Bank was a disaster not only to most people on the Isle of Man, but also to a goodly number beyond it. Directly affected, because they had mortgages with the bank or were part owned by it, were hotels, the brewing concern with its public houses, tourist entertainment complexes such as The Palace and Derby Castle, and the railways, particularly the electric railways which had been the brainchild of Bruce. Indirectly affected were hundreds of small businesses such boarding houses, eateries and shops which saw their capital disappear.

Money may not make the world go around but it certainly oils the wheels. A bank looks after other people's money so if it crashes they lose their working capital and their savings. Not having any money ex Dumbell customers couldn't buy food or fuel or pay staff. That meant that the food producers – farmers, bakers, market gardeners, etc. – couldn't sell their goods, so they in turn couldn't buy fuel or pay staff. The staff all these people were not paying therefore lost their jobs and in turn didn't have any money to buy the things they needed. Buying and selling… stopped. Not only that but, unable to buy food or pay staff, many small private hotels had to turn away tourists whose cash might otherwise have helped them out of the mire. Even the Isle of Man Steam Packet lost thousands. Its company account was with Dumbell's so that disappeared, and, like many, the company also found its profits affected. In 1900 it carried fewer passengers to the island and about half the freight of the previous year. The Steam Packet did however make a small profit from those taking one-way tickets to Liverpool to try to escape the mess.

A new king and a new start

The new century had started badly and did not improve immediately. On 29 January 1901 Queen Victoria died. Public mourning was decently observed, but of more immediate concern to the island was the liquidation of The Isle of Man Tramways and Electric Power Company (IoMT and EP Co Ltd). The demise of the company affected not only public transport and tourist rides, but also part of the public electricity supply – the tramway provided it. As well as the electric tramway from Douglas to Ramsey (what is now the Manx Electric Railway) the company also owned the Snaefell Mountain Railway, the Douglas Bay Tramway (the horse trams), the Upper Douglas Cable Tramway and several commercial activities, including the Howstrake Estate, Strathallan Hotel, Laxey Station Hotel, Ramsey Palace concert hall (later The Plaza), quarries at Dhoon and Ballajora and refreshment rooms at Bungalow, Snaefell Summit, Tholt-y-Will, Dhoon and Ballaglass. The company also owned Ballaglass Glen, but, contrary to popular belief only rented Garwick and Dhoon. Groudle had been privately developed, but the tramway had entry agreements (and fees) with R.M. Broadbent its owner. IoMT and EP Co Ltd was an enormous conglomerate.

With no working capital the IoMT and EP Co Ltd had to be sold off. Douglas Corporation purchased the horse and cable tramways and the newly-formed Manx Electric Railway Co. Ltd. (MER) took over everything else. That sale is the reason why those wishing to travel on the MER today have to go to the wrong end of Douglas promenade to do so. The plans to run the electric railway to the Victoria Pier and thus near to the business heart of Douglas were shelved when Dumbell's crashed. Despite lobbying, they have never been seriously reconsidered.

The MER took over on 18 August 1902. Just over a week earlier, on 9 August 1902, Victoria's son Albert Edward, was crowned King Edward VII. Mann no longer belonged to the Derby/

Manx Electric Railway car 2 leaves Dhoon Glen bound for Douglas towing royal trailer 59

Atholl families, but the ancient tie was still acknowledged by feudal tribute. On 28 August 1902 the *Manchester Guardian* stated: 'Among the feudal services the two falcons from the Isle of Man were conspicuous... the beautiful Peregrine Falcons... sat perfectly tame on the arm of his Grace, completely hooded and furnished with bells. The King descended from his chair of state, and the ladies of the Court pressed round to caress and examine the noble birds.'

On 25 August, the new King, who was convalescing after illness, paid a surprise visit to the Isle of Man aboard the royal yacht. It was his second surprise visit. He was five when his parents, Queen Victoria and Prince Albert, called in on 20 September 1847 *en route* from Scotland to London. In the mid nineteenth century there was no continuous railway line between London and Scotland so the royal party went by boat to Fleetwood and caught the train to London from there. Passing the island they moored in Ramsey Bay although only Prince Albert came ashore. He landed on the beach below Ballure Glen, and was greeted by Mr Anson and Captains Gordon and Crippin. In their company Prince Albert walked to the top of Lhergy Frissell and admired the view. The Albert Tower was built to mark the spot.

After several royal visitors the town became known as Royal Ramsey and flourished under the fortuitous civic one-upmanship. Unlike during his first visit, King Edward came ashore – perhaps his mother had not allowed him to do so as a boy. With Queen Alexandra, he visited Bishopscourt, Peel Castle and Cronkbourne House, home of A.W. Moore, historian and Speaker of the House of Keys, before returning to Ramsey on the MER. The Royal Saloon (trailer 59) in which the king and queen travelled still exists and is still occasionally used.

The value of heritage

Nor was the king the only tourist. The last quarter of the nineteenth century had seen a huge growth in visitors to the island and, although interrupted by the financial crisis caused by the crash of Dumbell's Bank, visitor numbers increased further. The need to preserve the island's heritage was acknowledged by the Manx Museum and Ancient Monument Act passed in 1886. It was largely due to this Act that the Manx crosses were protected from further damage by the weather or people. Recognised internationally as an expert on Celtic and Viking antiquities, Philip Kermode was the first to realise that the Manx crosses carry some of the earliest known illustrations of scenes from the Icelandic sagas. So important was his discovery that the Government of Iceland made him a Knight (*Riddari*) of the Order of the Falcon (*Hin íslenzka fálkaorða*). The news of the high honour arrived on 5 September 1932. It was the day he died.

Ten years earlier Kermode had become director of the newly-founded Manx Museum. Housed at first in Castle Rushen, it moved into its present more spacious accommodation on Crellin's Hill, Douglas in 1922. The building was the first Noble's Hospital (not the first island hospital; that was in Fort Street from 1850 to 1888) and was used as a hospital from 1888 to 1912. The new museum – old hospital – at last gave Manx heritage the recognition it deserved and encouraged several important sites to be preserved.

In 1938, for example, local builder E.C. Kneale obtained a fifteen-year lease on the Lady Isabella, derelict since the mine closed in 1929, restored it, and finally purchased it in 1946. The same year that Kneale took over the Lady Isabella, Harry Kelly's cottage was donated to the Manx Museum by members of his family. Harry had lived all his life in Cregneash and is often referred to as the last Manx speaker, i.e. the last person known to speak only Manx; he had no English. He died in 1935. His cottage formed the nucleus of what was to be one of the earliest living museums in Britain and was the first building in it to be open to the public.

The Manx language society (*Yn Cheshaght Ghailechagh*) had been founded in 1899 and then as now was dedicated to preserving and promoting Manx Gaelic. During the 1950s, the Manx Museum, at first with the help of the Irish

Right: the Manx Museum, formerly Noble's hospital
Below: Harry Kelly's cottage (right), Cregneash

Folklore Commission, recorded the reminiscences and Manx speech of as many of the older generation of islanders as they could. The museum also corresponded with the descendants of Manx ex-pats to learn the oral history which helps make up the story of Mann.

In 1950 also, the Castletown Town Commissioners gave the grammar school, built in the mid-thirteenth century as a chapel, to the Manx Museum. The following year the Manx National Trust was established. Like *Yn Cheshaght Ghailechagh*, the National Trust in the UK had been going since the end of the nineteenth century, and the Calf, the small island off the south west end of the Isle of Man, was given into its care in 1939. The Manx National Trust, established in 1951, soon obtained a long lease on the Calf from its older peer.

Two decades later, in 1974, the last member of the Gibb family, Janet, died aged 96. The home she'd lived in unchanged for eighty-eight years became the Grove Museum of Victorian Life. Today artefacts, archives and architecture all over the island are cared for by Manx National Heritage (*Eiraght Ashoonagh Vannin*).

The need for speed

The event most associated with the Isle of Man is undoubtedly the TT (Tourist Trophy) races. Now purely for motorcycles, the first races took place in cars. James Gordon-Bennett (he of the surprised expression) owned the *New York Herald* and was a notable sports promoter. He established various sporting trophies including the Gordon-Bennett Cup for the long-distance balloon race which is held annually in August, and, in 1900, the Gordon-Bennett Cup for car racing. Planned as an annual race for national teams, the British did not attend the first race, had only one car in the second and, by a fluke, won the third race in 1902; their man Selwyn Edge driving a Napier was the only one to finish. The rules were that the winning country had to host the following year's event, but no purpose-built stadia existed at the time and the Westminster parliament was reluctant to close the necessary roads. The Automobile Club of Great Britain and Ireland therefore remembered the final part of its name and took the race to Ireland for 1903.

National teams had to drive cars designed and built in their country and British-made cars were inferior to those of their rivals. The problem was one of testing; the British team had nowhere to trial vehicles and see how they performed. The secretary of the Automobile Club, Julian Orde, thought of the Isle of Man. Its parliament was small – fewer people to convince – it was trying to extract itself from a major financial crisis so was looking for ways to make money, and its people were already used to welcoming myriad visitors from across the water. And of course Orde's cousin, Lord Raglan, was Governor. That helped.

The necessary legislation was rushed through on 15 March 1904, the royal assent necessary for all Acts of Parliament was granted on 28 March, and the trials were scheduled for 10 May. But there was a problem. For a thousand years no Manx law has taken effect before its promulgation on Tynwald Hill, and Tynwald Day is 5 July, *after* the date set for the trials. Nevertheless the legislature was determined that the trials should come to Mann so decided to hold a special Tynwald Day on 5 May to make everything legal. All necessary personnel were transported to St John's, appropriately enough in cars specially organised by Julian Orde, and the Highways (Light Locomotive) Act 1904 duly promulgated on Tynwald Hill. Most of the Keys and Legislative Council had not travelled in a motorised road vehicle before.

The roads were hardly ideal for racing. Often unfenced, with poor surfaces and liable to be invaded by straying animals without warning, the trials course was much longer than the current TT course, going through St Jude's and reaching as far south as Castletown. Nevertheless the trials were run, the British team selected, and the precedent set for road racing on the island.

2016 Junior Manx Grand Prix. Matt Mylchreest (53) and Lee Hembury (54) race through Ramsey

The car trials were repeated in 1905, with the addition of motorbike trials for a forthcoming series of international motor cycle races. That September also saw touring cars take part in a new race called the Tourist Trophy. The Gordon-Bennett car road-racing event was replaced by the first Grand Prix motor racing event in 1906 but by that time the island was hooked. 28 May 1907 saw the first Tourist Trophy race for motorbikes on the island, held the day before the car TT. It was another fifteen years before the current circuit became the accepted course, but the annual TT event was an accepted fact.

War

Always eager to bring extra revenue to the Isle of Man, in the early twentieth century, local committees from Ramsey and Peel lobbied the UK War Office and brigade headquarters in the north of England, suggesting that they bring troops to the island for training. In the days before central provision of food for the forces, troops on manoeuvres purchased their supplies locally, and visiting soldiers meant lots of sales of food and beer. The representation was largely successful and, from 1899, troops had visited most years to camp and train on various sites around the north of the island. The most frequented camp was probably Milntown, but the largest was, without doubt, Knockaloe.

1913 was a record season for tourists to the Isle of Man with nearly 616,000 people landing at Douglas and Ramsey during the summer. The entire population of the island was only around 52,000 at the time, and a large proportion worked in the holiday trade. When Britain declared war on Germany on 4 August 1914 that year's season was in full swing and few thought that the war would last more than a few months. Even so Mann, like everywhere else, was put on a war footing.

As was the case throughout most of Britain and its Empire, many Manxmen volunteered to fight, but, unlike most other places in the First World War, their families and homeland were also immediately affected by the conflict. The Manx holiday trade ceased abruptly and the island prepared for a different sort of visitor. The day after war was declared the Westminster government passed the Aliens Restriction Act requiring non-British citizens to register with the police. The Act also enabled the British government to decide where such citizens would be allowed to live. The remoteness of the Isle of Man, its distance from Germany, and the fact that

Kirk Patrick churchyard. Graves of two Jewish and seven Turkish internees who died during the First World War.

it was surrounded by water led the British government to consider it an ideal place to intern those living in Britain but who had strong connexions with Germany: so-called enemy aliens. It might even have been Cunningham's Holiday Camp (see chapter 7) which was the deciding factor. Chairman of the UK parliament's Civilian Internment Camps Committee was Sir William Byrne. He remembered seeing Cunningham's Camp on a pre-war visit to the Isle of Man and thought it might do…

Cunningham's Holiday Camp in Victoria Road, Douglas was taken over as the first internment camp, with the first group of internees arriving on 22 September 1914. Many of the tents had been replaced by wooden huts for holidaymakers and more were replaced by chalets built by the internees. The numbers interned increased rapidly and soon filled the room available for them at Douglas. Two months later the old territorial army camp at Knockaloe was transformed into an internment camp which grew and grew. Originally intended to house 5,000 internees, by the end of the war it contained around 23,000 prisoners, equivalent to almost half the normal civilian population of the island. Twenty-three compounds each capable of taking one thousand men were divided between four camps sharing the same site. Largely thanks to the organisation of the Society of Friends, Knockaloe had its own post office, bakery, schools for adults, workshops, theatres and sports events, and the central administration even had its own railway delivering coal and supplies from Peel on specially-laid tracks.

The Westminster government might have thought the Isle of Man a long way from Germany, but it soon had even more direct contact with the war than being host to internees. Atlantic trade was threatened by German submarines and Liverpool was Britain's largest port; the Irish Sea soon became known as U-Boat Alley. Manx fishermen were at risk, either of attack from U-Boats themselves, or from collision with German mines. Some also had a more active role. On 7 May 1915 Royal Mail Ship *RMS Lusitania* was torpedoed by German submarine U-20 off southern Ireland. The ship sank in less than twenty minutes, drowning 1,198 of her 1,962 passengers and crew. The Manx fishing fleet frequently fished those waters and the first boat to answer *Lusitania's* distress signal was Manx fishing vessel *Wanderer*. Skipper William Ball and his six crew took more than a hundred people on board as well as taking two of *Lusitania's* lifeboats in tow. Nearly half the survivors owed their lives to the Peel boat *Wanderer*.

The British government needed boats for the war effort and eleven of the Isle of Man Steam Packet's fleet of fifteen were chartered or purchased for war work. Probably the most unusual use of a Manx ship was the 1915 conversion of *Ben-my-Chree* to a seaplane carrier. Most, such as *Mona's Queen* were used as troop carriers. She carried a thousand men but no arms and, on 6 February 1917, was attacked by a torpedo fired by German submarine *UC 26*. The ship's captain, William Cain, feared *UC 26* would try again and therefore set a course directly for the offending U-Boat. *Mona's Queen* has the distinction of being probably the only paddle steamer to have disabled a German submarine by hitting it with one of her paddles. *UC 26* was forced to dive and then limped back to port. *Mona's Queen* survived, but seven Manx ships were lost during the war; only *Peel Castle, King Orry, Viking* (rechristened *HMS Vindex* for war service, as the Royal Navy already had a *Viking*) and *Mona's Queen* returned.

Nationalism and home rule

Despite housing enemy aliens and enlisting with British troops, the Manx had long wanted their independence to be recognised. They wanted it still. The Manx National Reform League was founded in 1903 to lobby for the island's right to decide its own internal affairs. The League also proposed that two thirds of the Legislative Council should be elected, that taxation should be decided by Tynwald, and that the justice system should be reformed. Rather oddly, the League's elected president was not a Manxman. Thomas Henry Hall Caine was born in Runcorn, Cheshire and, although his father was Manx and Hall Caine had often stayed on the Isle of Man, he was forty-one before he moved to the island permanently. MHK for Ramsey and probably one of the most highly paid novelists in the late nineteenth and early twentieth century, Hall Caine made it clear after Lord Raglan retired that he'd like the job of Lieutenant Governor, but was considered unsuitable. Many of the Manx disliked him as a patronising poseur.

In 1907 the island not only got motorbike racing, it also got its national anthem (see appendix 5). The words of *Arrane Ashoonagh* (National Anthem) were written by William Henry Gill and set by him to a tune adapted from the traditional Manx air *Mylecharane*. Gill was not a fluent Manx speaker and so wrote in English, his words being translated into Manx by linguist and lexicographer John Joseph Kneen. The anthem was sung for the first time at the 1907 Manx Music Festival in Peel, but it took nearly a century before it was adopted as the official national anthem of the Isle of Man. Tynwald did so on 22 January 2003, nominating *God Save the Queen* as the Royal Anthem, and using it only when the queen or her representatives are present.

In 1907 the Manx might have sung about home rule, but they didn't enjoy it. The Westminster government still made or ratified all policy decisions, local taxation and expenditure were controlled by the UK Treasury, and officials were appointed by Westminster. Most importantly, although the twenty-four Keys in the lower house were elected by the Manx people, the Legislative Council, which formed the upper chamber of Tynwald, consisted of the Lieutenant Governor, Clerk of the Rolls, Attorney General, Receiver General, two Deemsters, the Bishop, Archdeacon and Vicar General. All were appointed by Westminster, except the Archdeacon and Vicar General who were appointed by the Bishop. What is even more surprising is that the Lieutenant Governor held most of the real power. He had the right to decide almost everything not already decided by Westminster, and he could do so without calling together the Legislative

Council and without heeding the wishes of the Keys. What's more, the Lieutenant Governor was not appointed for a term of five years as now, but for as long as he wanted the job.

George Fitzroy Henry Somerset, 3rd Baron Raglan, was appointed Lieutenant Governor in 1902, some said at the direct request of the king. The Manx attitude towards him was curiously similar to their attitude towards The Great Stanley 300 years before (see chapter 5). As a private individual Lord Raglan was much liked, and his efforts and those of his wife for numerous charities were much appreciated. As the *de facto* ruler of the island however, he was resented as frustratingly hidebound. Only 61 at the end of the First World War, Raglan's decision to resign as Lieutenant Governor came as a surprise but not an unwelcome one. There was hope that his successor, Major General Sir William Fry, would be more sympathetic to the Manx wish for administrative and political reform. His wife was daughter to Sir John Goldie-Taubman, a former Speaker of the House of Keys and there was probably some thought that Sir William might be henpecked! Even before he arrived a curb had already been applied to the power of the new Lieutenant Governor. For the first time the appointment was for seven years rather than for life.

Pence and pensions

Tynwald had no authority to raise money to support the needy and so the Isle of Man lagged behind much of the rest of Great Britain in providing help for the old, unemployed, poor and sick. In the rest of Britain rudimentary support was introduced in 1909 for old-age pensions, 1911 for unemployment insurance and 1601 – the Elizabethan Poor Law – for the care of the poor and sick. The 300-year-old law survived as the basis for helping the destitute by raising money on a parish by parish basis to support the workhouse. The institution might have been feared and hated and have become a by-word for misery, but it did at least exist as a final resort. The Isle of Man had no official provision at all. Help for the Manx poor remained in the hands of private philanthropists or they went without.

That had to change and the new Lieutenant Governor was willing to co-operate with Tynwald in its search for greater independence from Westminster control, not least to manage its own budget. The argument used so effectively by Governor Loch in 1866 when seeking to transform the Keys into an elected body (see chapter 7) was now applied the other way round, and the Keys declared themselves unwilling to vote for additional taxes if Tynwald's second chamber, the Legislative Council, was not answerable to the Manx people. The argument didn't stop Tynwald introducing income tax to the island for the first time in 1918, however. The money was intended to subsidise the production of bread, a staple food which had risen hugely in price because of shortages caused by the war.

In 1919 the Constitution Amendment Act was passed. Like the Keys in 1866 some members of the Legislative Council were effectively voting themselves out of a job. Ex-officio membership of the Council by the Vicar-General, the Archdeacon, and the Receiver General ceased. In future the Legislative Council was to be made up of the President of Tynwald (up until 1990 that meant the Lieutenant Governor), the Bishop, Attorney General and eight members elected by the House of Keys, either from within their number or from elsewhere.

The beneficial effects of the new order were felt in some quarters almost immediately. On 18 May 1920 the Old Age Pension and National Insurance Acts were passed in Tynwald. In March of that year, anticipating the Act, more than 1,000 people aged seventy and over received an old-age pension for the first time. Rather less importantly, but perhaps more noticeably, in 1920 the Speaker of the House of Keys – at the time he was George Frederick Clucas – began wearing a black gown and bell bottom wig. In 1966, to mark the 100th anniversary of the introduction of democratic voting, the Speaker of the House of Commons in Westminster gave the Speaker of the House of Keys a ceremonial robe, black with gold braid. It's still worn on ceremonial occasions.

Wings over the island

After the First World War the Manx tourist trade increased quickly and was soon back to pre-war levels. The first aeroplane to arrive on the island came – by boat! – in August 1912, but pleasure flying began in earnest after the war. In 1919 two Avro biplanes crossed from Blackpool and, for a couple of seasons gave rides around Douglas Bay using the strip of grass between the Queens' Promenade and the beach as their airfield.

It was June 1925 before an aeroplane visited the island again, this time bringing thousands of *The Motor Cycle* magazines for visitors to the TT races. The first public flight on the island took place on 5 August 1929 when a DH 61 Giant Moth flew from Ronaldsway on 5 August 1929 with two passengers: R.C. Stephen and Tom Sheard. Passenger services began in earnest in 1931 when the British Amphibious Air Lines Ltd. began a service from Blackpool. The following year William Cunningham of Holiday Camp fame became the first Manxman to own and fly his own plane.

Flying visits by Prince George, youngest son of George V and Queen Mary, and Amy Johnson followed, encouraging travel by air. A regular service between Mann, Blackpool and Liverpool operated by Blackpool and West Coast Air Services Ltd (B&WCAS) was inaugurated for the summer season of 1933. The following year, flights linked the island with Manchester and Belfast. While B&WCAS were landing their passengers in a field in Ronaldsway, passengers from the north of the island had the choice of travelling from a second airfield near Ramsey on land belonging to Close Lake Farm. Opened in 1935 it was named the Hall Caine Airport in memory of the writer who died in 1931.

Site of Hall Caine Airport, near Ramsey. The field to the right behind the gate was the landing strip

Despite all this activity, airfields were little more than exactly that. Fields. Passed by the Westminster parliament, the Air Navigation Act had come into force in 1921. It was applied throughout the British Empire and was designed to make flying safer. It provided for the licensing of aerodromes and personnel, registration and maintenance of aircraft, as well as laying down some basic rules of the air. Even today there is no legal reason why a private pilot can't land on his own airstrip in his own field. However there is also nothing to prevent that field from being next to an inconvenient hill, crossed by pylons or surrounded by tall trees, any of which might be a danger to take-off or landing. Licensed aerodromes guarantee a certain measure of safety.

Three different sites were considered for an official airfield: Ballagilley Farm near King William's College, Red Gap on the area north and west of Scarlett Point, and Ronaldsway. It was generally agreed that the aerodrome should be near both the new capital and the old one, and Ballagilley was preferred. The college objected, however, that it would be too close and too disruptive. Ronaldsway was chosen almost by default as, from the beginning of 1935, the newly created Isle of Man Air Services Ltd carried mail to and from Ronaldsway and had already built a hangar and air traffic control building.

Flying was fashionable and useful for improving links with the island. Isle of Man air races were organised, either round the island or from various towns across the water. Ominously the rise of Nazi Germany was apparent even during sporting events. The London to Isle of Man air race in 1937, for example, was won by Major Hans Seidemann, a German pilot flying a Messerschmitt sporting a swastika.

War again

Despite Neville Chamberlain's pronouncement on 30 September 1938 of 'peace for our time', despite the *Daily Express* headline on 7 August 1939 stating 'no war this year', most people knew that war was coming. Negotiations had already taken place between Tynwald and Westminster about the creation of an RAF base on Mann in the event of another war. In 1938, work started on creating an airfield at Jurby, which was ready when war was declared in September the following year. It opened as No. 5 Air Observer School, but, by 1 December 1939, had changed to No. 5 Bombing and Gunnery School (B&GS). There were thirteen B&GS schools in total; the first four were all in Canada at Jarvis Ontario, Mossbank Saskatchewan, Macdonald Manitoba and Fingal Ontario respectively.

Top right: Spitfire (top) and Avro Anson etched into the glass in Jurby church
Below: wartime buildings at Andreas airport are being reclaimed and reused

ISLE OF MAN

36p

SPITFIRE

A second wartime airfield was needed and the Hall Caine aerodrome was considered, but rejected as being too close to the potential hazard of Skyhill. Instead, Andreas was chosen for the new airfield, this time as a base for fighters and air-sea rescue, as well as No. 11 Air Gunnery School. The layout of Andreas airfield is completely different to that at Jurby. Built in 1941, wartime experience had led to auxiliary buildings being scattered around the airfield rather than lined up as easy bombing targets as at Jurby. Land for the Andreas aerodrome was requisitioned from local farmers, and waste from the Laxey and Foxdale mines used as hardcore for the runways. Not only farmers were affected. The tower of Andreas church, St Andrew's, was a landmark throughout the northern plain, but, at 120 feet high, it was in the way of planes using the new airfield. It was reduced to half its height, not merely by demolishing the top, but by removing three quarters of the tower and then rebuilding the more decorated upper portion on the lower base.

Jurby continued as an RAF training station until 1963 and was officially closed on 30 April 1964. The Hall Caine airfield never re-opened after the war and, by 1951, as much as possible of the Andreas airfield went back to being farmed.

A different sort of visitor

Only two decades separated the first and second world wars, so wartime arrangements were fresh in many memories. It was little surprise to the Manx people that the island was again called on to host internees and prisoners of war. Again Knockaloe was used, but WW2 also saw the hotels, empty of tourists, requisitioned, fenced off with barbed wire and turned into internment camps. Mann is not alone in using hotels in this way – German internees were housed in hotels in Vittel, France, and representatives of the Vichy French government were interned for a while in Hotel Hershey in the US for example – but nowhere else have hotels been so comprehensively requisitioned for internment.

The first to open, in May 1940, was Mooragh camp, a fenced off section of the Mooragh promenade in Ramsey. Hoteliers were told to leave their properties, taking personal effects with them but leaving furniture and fittings. Later that year, Douglas front became a series of camps centred around its hotels and there were more camps at Onchan, Port Erin, Port St Mary and Peel. The Port Erin camp was devoted to women and some Port Erin landladies were allowed to stay to run their boarding houses for the female internees. In all other cases hoteliers were sometimes given only a few days' notice to arrange alternative accommodation for themselves and their families.

The largest number of internees were in Douglas and Onchan. Camps were kept separate to make guarding them easier and to minimise trouble between warring elements, e.g. Jewish refugees and Nazi sympathisers. The Castle Mona shops became the military stores, the Crescent Cinema (the imposing white-tiled façade on Central Promenade, now Spectrum Apartments) a depot for camp food, while the Falcon Cliff Hotel, now Falcon Cliff Court, became the camps' hospital. 'Mereside', a small hotel in Empire Terrace, was used as Camp HQ. By October 1940 approximately 85% of all aliens of enemy nationality living in Britain were interned in the Isle of Man.

Some internees were permitted to work on farms or take over certain civilian jobs while Manxmen were away fighting. Although the Manx generally welcomed those detained on the island, and were liked and respected in return, some circumstances did cause friction. For example, gas attacks had long been feared throughout Great Britain and civilian respirators were standard issue across the water. Not on Mann however. At first the only people on the island to have gasmasks were the internees who had been issued with them before they arrived. There was also general concern that internees should not receive more food than the civilians outside the wire. Partly to stem British questions on the matter, and partly to counter allegations made in a broadcast in English on German radio, Osbert Peake, the Under-Secretary of State for the Home Department in Westminster, on 25 February 1941 issued an official statement about the daily rations and diet of internees on the Isle of Man. According to his statement, internees were provided per week with, among other foodstuffs, 2oz of tea, just over 6lbs of bread, 14oz of jam and 4oz of meat on five days, but no butter, bacon or eggs. Kosher meat was provided when possible, and internees who declined non-kosher meat could be offered instead fish, lentils, cheese or rice when available. By contrast civilians received per week the same amount of tea, less jam (1lb every two months was usual), and often had to manage on roughly half of the meat given to internees, including the 4oz per week bacon ration. However, bread outside the camps was not rationed, and civilians were entitled to 2oz of butter and 1 egg per week.

Many of those enjoying an enforced stay on Mann were famous in their own sphere. Internees included hotelier Charles Forte, dada artist Kurt Schwitters (who made sculptures out of porridge), Alfonso Conti (actor Tom Conti's father) and even, it was rumoured, Lionel Logue, the Austrian speech therapist who had cured the king's stammer. The internee who had the biggest effect on Mann, however, was German archaeologist Gerhard Bersu.

Jewish ancestry meant that Bersu had been forced to leave his post at the *Deutsches Archäologisches Institut* (German Archaeological Institute) in Frankfurt-am-Main, and he was working in England when war was declared. Being German, he and his wife were interned. However, for Bersu, unlike many, being interned on the Isle of Man formed an unplanned but successful addition to his career. Bersu was a world expert in prehistoric archaeology, and the Isle of Man has a lot – most of it, at the time, unexcavated. Bersu, his wife and a motley group of volunteers spent most of the war trundling round the Isle of Man happily excavating. Much of the island's knowledge of its past, and the preservation of its prehistoric remains is thanks to the expert German professor and his wartime dedication.

Post-war problems – and opportunities

The desire of the Manx to run their own affairs had not gone away and, just as after the First World War more independence was granted to Tynwald, so more was expected after the Second. Samuel Norris, Member of the House of Keys for North Douglas, had kept the question alive when on 1 December 1942 he proposed forming a Manx Cabinet to share power with the Lieutenant Governor. Allied victories were growing, particularly in Africa where the Manx Regiment was fighting, and much had been said about fighting for freedom and democracy, but Norris was premature in expecting much to change when party politics had been largely shelved, and the wartime British government was a cross-party coalition.

Even before the war ended the British monarchy acknowledged the island's part in the defence of the realm by making it the destination of the first royal visit outside the UK since the war began. Victory in Europe (V later VE) day was 8 May 1945, Victory in Japan (VJ) day was 14 August the same year. Between the two, on 4 July 1945, King George VI and Queen Elizabeth arrived by

Wartime bunkers, Cranstal, Bride. Built of brick and reinforced concrete, and camouflaged by soil and grass, the bunkers formed part of an extensive radar complex

boat for a three-day visit. The visit wasn't completely official; Lieutenant Governor Granville's wife was the queen's elder sister. During the visit the king became the first monarch to preside on Tynwald Hill since the days of the Vikings.

In 1946, after general elections in both Mann and the United Kingdom, the time was right for change. The new UK Home Secretary allowed the creation of a Manx Executive Council to be made up of the chairmen of the five boards: Agriculture and Fisheries; Highways and Transport: Social Services; Local Government; Education, plus two further members of Tynwald voted to the post by their peers. On 16 October 1946 the new Executive Board came into being to act as a Manx 'Cabinet' and advise the Lieutenant Governor.

After the war the Manx people struggled to get the island back to welcoming holiday makers. Only a few of those interned on the island wanted to stay there, camps were dismantled and hotel owners reclaimed their hotels. After the overcrowding, trauma and damage of wartime, properties were at best extremely shabby and at worst badly damaged with neither the internees nor the military respecting the private hotels they had inhabited. The Manx government had promised to make good any damage but what the government thought of as adequate compensation was not what the hoteliers thought they would need. In addition the war had exhausted all stocks of raw materials so even simple things like paint were extremely scarce. Food rationing was also still in force. Nevertheless hoteliers smartened up their properties and, in 1946 welcomed a huge number of visitors eager to have fun and take their first real holiday for seven years.

Sliding into recession...

For over a hundred years the Manx had catered for the huge numbers of visitors who came to spend their holidays on the island. The TT had resumed in 1947 after the hiatus of wartime and continued to draw thousands to Mann but some attractions, such as the Marine Drive tramway (see chapter 7) had not re-opened after the war, and others, such as the Douglas Head Theatre attracted far less custom. Not only that but the 1950s saw holidays abroad begin to grow in popularity. The weather in southern Europe was predictably sunny, travel was often less expensive than to the Isle of Man, and the newly-built European hotels were often fitted out to a higher standard. Jugs/ basins and a bathroom at the end of the corridor in Victorian hotels in Douglas, could not compete with *en-suite* facilities in new hotels in Spain. Visitor numbers began to decline.

Not only that, the holiday season was just that – seasonal. Finding employment for the winter months had always been a problem on the Isle of Man and to some extent still is. As holiday makers began to go elsewhere, year-round unemployment became more of a problem. Emigration, the island's barometer of economic stability, once again began to increase. Around 7,000 people, around 13% of the population, most of them young, left Mann during the 1950s. The economic problem was made worse by the galloping inflation of the 1970s when prices rose steeply and earnings didn't keep up.

Several schemes which would be unthinkable now were actively proposed to try to improve the island's finances. Although the Isle of Man has no oil of its own, Tynwald was in favour of constructing an oil refinery on the Ayres to process oil shipped from the Middle East on behalf of an American company; a rare and fragile ecosystem would have been lost. The Gaiety Theatre, one of the best surviving Victorian theatres in the world, was planned for demolition and replacement with a shopping mall, flats and offices. Other schemes were allowed to go ahead, including the demolition of Derby Castle dance hall and entertainment complex; the demolition of Fort Anne, former home of William Hillary; the sale of The Nunnery, former home of the Goldie Taubman family since 1776, to racehorse owner and breeder Robert Sangster; the sale of Bishopscourt, home to the Bishops of Sodor and Man since the thirteenth century, to millionaire Gerard Fairhurst.

Despite the island's financial concerns, the Manx still wanted independence from their UK overlords. Small steps had been taken to secure greater independence but, until the 1970s, the outward signs of UK dominance – the stamps and coinage – still existed. The Manx government had been printing their own banknotes since 1961, but the island's coinage remained firmly that of the UK. That changed with the introduction of decimal coinage to Britain in 1971. For the first time for around 130 years the Isle of Man coins carried specifically Manx designs.

The first stamp with a Manx identity had been issued in 1958, but was issued by the UK post office, rather as it distinguished Scottish, Welsh and Northern Irish regional identities. In the spring of 1971 a postal strike in the UK interrupted Manx mail. Just as, in the seventeenth century John Murrey had led the way by privately producing 'Murrey's pence' (see chapter 6), two centuries later Gordon Quirk provided Quirk's stamps; a temporary *Post Manninagh*. It was no amateur attempt. Mr Quirk received an official Letter of Authority to 'operate a private collection and delivery service for letters' and did so from 20 January to 8 March, which was the length of the strike. He produced a special First Day Cover for the official introduction of decimal coinage on 15 February and, perhaps tongue-in-cheek, a Last Day Cover for the last day of his private postal service. For stamps Quirk used the paper covers from souvenir matchbox covers which he had been printing in advance of the tourist season. Cancellation franks were provided by a numbering machine previously used for invoices. Later that same year Tynwald began negotiating a separate and official Manx postal service. Not only was the government aiming to emphasise the island's independent identity, it also saw the production of Isle of Man stamps as a way to raise money with stamp collectors around the world. Appropriately, the Manx Post Office came into being on Tynwald day (5 July) 1973.

...and climbing out again

Improving the island's finances became increasingly imperative as the numbers of holidaymakers dwindled. Today only around 5% of Mann's income now stems from tourism, but it is still considered important to the Manx economy. The major annual tourist event is of course the TT, but during the last half of the twentieth century, efforts were made to provide many more attractions for visitors. Such diversification was obviously intended to increase visitor numbers by varying the experiences on offer and lengthening the season which the island's location and weather tends to make short. Summerland, for example, opened in 1971 on the old Derby Castle site, and was designed to provide artificially sunny conditions year round in the hope of attracting holidaymakers who might defect to Spain. Summerland's design and construction was frankly experimental and in 1973 it was destroyed in one of the worst peacetime fires in twentieth century Britain. Today visitors are much more likely to discount the weather and come to Mann for the scenery, walking, sport such as diving, cycling, fell running or golf, to ride on the heritage transport, visit the unique heritage sites or to view rare marine life such as the basking sharks. Even the motorbike events have diversified with the Southern Hundred and Manx Grand Prix tempting enthusiasts to visit the island at different times of the year.

Mann is also one of the few places in Britain to offer American-style casino facilities. First proposed in 1956, a casino was approved in 1961 and opened in 1963 in the Castle Mona hotel. It closed temporarily in 1965 as the American syndicate which operated it was accused of financial irregularity. Rebuilt, it moved to a new venue next door and was opened in 1966 by 'James Bond' or rather the actor who played him, Sean Connery. Today online gambling is big business, and e-gaming forms the single biggest source of income for the Isle of Man.

Another big earner for the island is the Manx film industry. Many visitors don't realise that Isle of Man Film is one of the busiest film producers in Britain. The Isle of Man has stood in for Ireland (*Waking Ned*), the Lake District (*Miss Potter*), Yorkshire (*Lassie*), 18th century England (*Belle*), futuristic England (*Stormbreaker*) and all over the place (*Spooks: the Greater Good*)! It's about time the island was filmed as itself.

Manx skills in information and communication technology have led to the island being one of the world leaders in the space industry. The Isle of Man is fifth after China, the US,

Russia and India in the race to return to the Moon. The highest capacity satellite in the world, ViaSat-1, was placed in space by an Isle of Man team and is now providing broadband access to rural areas of the United States. The Isle of Man aerospace team was also involved with the Phoenix Mars Lander. Astronomy is flourishing on the island too, as Mann has relatively few street lights to obscure the night sky. The lack of light pollution has led to seven places around the island being internationally designated Dark Sky Discovery Sites.

Although now overtaken by e-gaming, for many years the Isle of Man's income has been boosted by providing financial services. The island had long been known as a place of financial advantage and for centuries was often the refuge of UK debtors who knew that their creditors could not legally enforce recovery from debtors across the water. Financial manoeuvrability was after all one of the reasons the Dumbell family came to the island (see chapter 7). History may have repeated itself in 1982 and 1983 when the Isle of Man's Savings and Investment Bank, Investors Mercantile Ltd and Chancellor Finance all collapsed, but new legislation to supervise and control financiers, while still offering them better tax breaks than in the UK, made the island attractive to financiers. By the early 1980s a quarter of the Manx national income came from the financial sector; today the figure is closer to 40%. Recognised by the International Monetary Fund as an offshore financial centre of excellence, in 2015 the Isle of Man was named Best International Finance Centre by *Professional Adviser*, an information service for financial advisors.

Back to basics

Over the centuries, the three traditional supports for the Manx economy have been fishing, farming and mining. Mining largely ended on the island when the Great Laxey Mine closed in 1929, although the Snaefell mine was briefly reworked in the 1950s, without success. Fishing and farming continue to flourish however and form part of an increasingly successful food industry. Although the island no longer has the large fleets which fished the seas around Scandinavia and Iceland, Mann has become known for producing high quality shellfish, particularly Queen Scallops, known locally as Queenies, as well as the more traditional Manx kippers.

Visitors only need to look around to see that farming is hugely important to the island, and often ask whether the Isle of Man is or could be self-sufficient in food. There's no easy answer, as it depends on what people want to eat! Cows and sheep are the main animals farmed, with relatively few pigs being kept on the island and Mann exports slightly more than half the meat and slightly less than half the milk it produces. There are some large producers of eggs on Mann such as Gellings which specialises in free range eggs and bacon, but, with no foxes on the island, many people keep a few chickens and sell or swop eggs for other produce, as country people have done for thousands of years. Even then this only accounts for about a third of the number of eggs used. The Isle of Man also imports almost all the chicken eaten on the island plus a lot of the vegetables, as it doesn't produce enough for the island's needs and certainly not all the year round. On the other hand 80% of the bread eaten on the island is produced from island-grown cereal crops. The land and the animals are healthy, and Manx exports tend to be viewed as the luxury end of the market. Manx scallops are sold in Spain and France, for example, whelk exported to the far east, and Manx cheese to the US.

From food to drink. Brewing was traditionally a cottage industry and as well as, Okells, the large commercial brewer, the island also has a few micro breweries such as the Old Laxey Brewery attached to the Shore Hotel. The Manx Brewing Purity Law of 1874 still stands which states that 'no brewer shall use in the brewing, making, mixing with, recovering or

In the shelter of North Barrule a farmer feeds his sheep during the winter months

colouring, any beer or any liquid made to resemble beer, or have in his possession ... any article, ingredient, or preparation whatever for, or as a substitute for malt, sugar or hops'. The Campaign for Real Ale (CAMRA) approves!

Relationship with Britain and Europe

The Isle of Man is not independent of British rule, but nearly so. Like Jersey and Guernsey, Mann is a Crown Dependency, which means that it is neither part of the United Kingdom nor of Great Britain but is a British Island (a political entity into which the Channel Islands fall) and part of the British Isles, which is a geographical term referring to the islands off the north west coast of Europe. The Isle of Man is self governing – its brand new jail opened at Jurby in 2008 – but Manx legislation requires royal assent to become law. Since 1981 the Lieutenant Governor, as the Queen's representative, has been permitted to grant royal assent on her behalf. As royal assent has not been refused since 1707 it is deemed to be largely automatic.

Tynwald, the Manx parliament, is divided into two chambers, the House of Keys and the Legislative Council. The two chambers are roughly equivalent to the Houses of Commons and Lords in the Westminster parliament, although they do not have precisely the same executive function. Together the Keys and the Legislative Council form the Tynwald Court which is the highest court in the land as well as authorising and managing island expenditure. The Council of Ministers, formerly the Executive Council, is similar to the Cabinet in the Westminster government, although again does not have a precisely similar function. The Council of Ministers is the highest-level decision-making body within the Isle of Man government, and sets national and international policy.

The Isle of Man is not a member of the European Union (EU), although it is part of the European Economic Area. Under the UK's Treaty of Accession Mann was allowed to trade freely with the EU, as the British Crown Dependencies were granted associate membership of the Economic Community. The Isle of Man's independent status and the fact that it was not a member of the EU in its own right, meant that the Manx were denied a vote in the 2016 referendum to decide whether the UK should leave the EU. Now that the UK has voted for 'Brexit', the Manx have to consider how their relationship with Europe will change.

Foreseeing the Future

From being batted about between warring neighbours the Isle of Man has emerged as a small independent country fiercely proud of its language, heritage and traditions. Much less reliant than it used to be on the sea for communication, food and trade, its island status still quarantines Mann from developments in which it wishes to take no part. The foot and mouth crises which hit the UK in 2001, for example, did not spread to the island as the Manx took great care to protect their island from infection, even going to the lengths of cancelling that year's TT. Neither does the Isle of Man have a particular problem with illegal immigration although the island's population is certainly fluid. Foreign nationals are employed in areas where the Manx have no specialist workers of their own, and young people leave the island to study and work overseas. However many Manx return later in life, and those which don't usually maintain close contact with their roots. Such has been the Manx way for hundreds of years. No-one has a crystal ball, but one or two predictions may be attempted – and probably with the usual inaccurate results.

As the UK voted to leave the EU, any advantages to trading with Europe will cease on Mann. The EU was already making life difficult for offshore financial centres, and Mann had responded by tightening controls. With EU controls removed, the island might work to become a more attractive financial proposition again. At the same time non-European countries, in particular those in the Commonwealth, have shown interest in forming trade agreements. The Isle of Man has an established aerospace industry and could well form lucrative partnerships with India and China in the space race. Much of space exploration relies on robotics and Manx industry could develop in that area too; in 2016 the island government encouraged driverless cars to be tested on the island's roads.

The Isle of Man is also known for the excellence of its agriculture and the fact that much of the food it produces is organic. The country purchasing the largest amount of organic produce per capita in the world is Switzerland – which is not a member of the EU. Neither is Liechtenstein, fifth in the list of consumers of organic produce. Scandinavians also buy a lot of organic food, so Manx produce could find a niche market in areas where the island already has established trade routes.

Global warming continues to be of global concern. Depending on which research is accepted, the British Isles are either going to become much colder or much warmer. One of the predictions made is that global warming could disrupt the warm waters of the Gulf Stream which would result in the temperature dropping around five degrees in the latitude of the Irish Sea. The British islands would have much in common with Greenland today, so Mann's impressive range of hills might make it into a popular ski resort.

Colder temperatures 15,000 years ago caused the Isle of Man's expansion as glacial deposits formed the northern plain to Point of Ayre. 5,000 years later melting ice caused by a warmer climate caused the seas to rise and turned Mann into an island. Over the next fifty years or so global warming might cause the sea to rise still further and reclaim much of the northern plain, including the Lhen Trench, the Curraghs and the town of Ramsey. Further south, the lower parts of Douglas and Ronaldsway could also be swamped. The Tynwald building might end up on the sea shore. The wheel of time turns and the Manx will be ready for whatever is turned up. As they say: *myr shegin dy ve, bee eh*; what must be, will be.

CHAPTER 9

THE ALTERNATIVE HISTORY; SELECTED MYTHS & MYSTERIES

If you stand on the summit of Snaefell on a clear day you can see seven kingdoms, or so the story goes: Mann (of course), England, Wales, Scotland, Ireland, the ocean, which is Neptune's Kingdom and heaven, the Kingdom of God. From Snaefell you can see the great panorama of neighbouring islands circling around Mann in the centre, like the rim of a tea cup circling the bubbles in the middle. If the light is right – and it doesn't happen often – the islands of Britain seem close enough for you to reach out your hand and pluck Scafell Pike from the Lake District or cradle the Mountains of Mourne in the palm of your hand.

The creation of an island

Of course, standing on the Mountains of Mourne it just as naturally appears possible to pick up the Isle of Man, and an Irish giant once did just that. Fionn mac Cumhaill (Finn MacCooil) had fallen out with his neighbour giant in Scotland. During the ensuing fight the anonymous Scottish giant fled Ireland by way of the giant's causeway. Enraged at his escape Fionn scooped up a handful of earth to hurl at his retreating back but missed. A giant's handful is a lot of earth and, when it landed in the middle of the Irish Sea, it created the Isle of Man. The hole left in Ireland filled with water and became Lough Neagh, the third largest lake in Europe.

Fionn had a lot to do with shaping the island he created. He lived on it for a while, until a buggane decided to drive him away. A buggane is like a Manx ogre and enjoys evil. From sunrise to sunset the giant fought the buggane right on the southern-most tip of the island. Up until then the Calf of Man had been part of the Manx mainland but, as the fight went on, Fionn's feet wore away the ground and Calf Sound and Little Sound were carved out on either side of Kitterland. The buggane had taken his stand between Bradda Mooar and Meayll Hill, so his feet wore away the rock to create Port Erin Bay. Fionn was eventually defeated and fled back to Ireland. The giant could walk on the sea, but bugganes can't cross water or stand on hallowed land. Frustrated that Finn was getting away, the buggane pulled out one of his own teeth and flung it after him. The tooth bounced off Fionn and landed in the sea where it turned into the Chicken Rock. Partly because it stemmed from a buggane, and partly because Fionn cursed it, the rock has been a hazard to sailors ever since.

Chicken rock lighthouse from Spanish Head

Fionn mac Cumhaill might be credited with creating the Isle of Man, but it's another figure of legend who gave the island its name. According to mediaeval texts Mannin McLir was a celebrated merchant and sea pilot who lived on the island and was skilled at reading the weather. Over the years Mannin became confused with Manannan, the Celtic equivalent of Neptune, and McLir transmogrified into Mac y Leir or son of the sea. As Manannan Mac y Leir he's credited with being the island's first ruler and after whom Mann is named.

Legend says that Manannan protected his kingdom by enveloping it in mist so that enemies couldn't find it and invade. Even today, low cloud is often referred to as the cloak of Manannan (not, as one visitor claimed, King Orry's shroud!). The marram grass spread on the processional way each Tynwald Day (see appendix 4) is a traditional tribute to Mann's traditional protector. Loosely referred to as 'rushes', the traditional name for the marram grass is 'bent' and tradition also plays a part in how it's provided for Tynwald Day. The bent came from Ballaleece Farm, about half a mile west of St John's along the current A1, and its supply for use on Tynwald Day was a condition of the farm's tenancy.

Manannan is also the traditional creator of the three legs of Mann. According to one version of the legend the sea god turned himself into a three-legged fiery hoop which rolled down from North Barrule to rout Manx invaders. Another tale claims the triskelion to be the result of what we should now recognise as a visit by a flying saucer. Back in the time of the Druids a group of fishermen was driven ashore by a storm and set up camp on a Manx beach. As they were huddled around their fire, a huge fiery wheel supported on three armoured legs emerged from the stormclouds, hovered above them partially obscured by mist, and then floated up the cliff and inland. The seamen took the apparition to be a good omen and the three mailed legs became a lucky symbol thereafter.

If a god gave his name to a large island, a man gave his name to a tiny one. Baron Kitter supposedly lived in Mann around eight hundred years ago. He lived in a castle on the top of South Barrule and, while he was out hunting on the Calf one day, his castle caught fire. His cook shouted for help and alerted the Baron who set off immediately to cross the Sound. Reckless in his haste Baron Kitter sailed carelessly and his boat struck a rock about half-way across and sank. Unable to cross either to the Manx mainland or to the Calf, the baron clung to the tiny scrap of land until he died. It has been called Kitterland ever since.

Christianity arrives...

By tradition the first people to arrive on Mann landed at what is now Castletown, although their landing was hotly disputed by the little people or fairies who lived there. Gradually the human invaders won the day, possessing first the land in Rushen and gradually extending their rule over the whole island. Not that the fairies, or as the Manx say 'themselves', left the island of course, but they took care to hide from view.

Castletown has long been their stronghold and of course fairies built

Fairy entrance, Bank Street, Castletown

the castle's foundations. Unmapped by men, the castle is rumoured to have numerous fairy-built subterranean tunnels and chambers, making it larger below ground than it is above. Those attempting to explore the fairy passages return out of their senses or not at all. The lowest dungeons of the castle were of course inhabited by giants. Some say they are still.

St Maughold,
Braddan New
Church

St Patrick himself was supposed to have taken time out from converting Ireland to bring Christianity to Mann; St Patrick's Isle was named in his honour. Great saints perform great miracles and he crossed to Mann on horseback. He was also in something of a hurry as he was being chased by a sea monster at the time. Taking a great leap to avoid the monster the horse landed on Corrin's Hill. The sea beast crashed into the cliff below, turning into stone as it did so. It's still there, *Carrick yn Ardnieu*, the rock of the serpent. As both horse and rider were thirsty after their gallop across the Irish Sea, a spring of fresh water gushed out of the rock where the horse's feet had landed. The spring became known as the Holy Well of St Patrick, or occasionally as *Chibbyr Sheeant* (Blessed Well) or *Chibbr yn Argid* (Well of the Silver). The first Christians on the island were said to have been baptised in the well by the saint. The spring was also reputed to have healing properties, particularly for eyes, and modern analysis has found some basis for the claim. The water contains silver compounds, and silver is noted for being able to purify water.

Like many visitors to Mann, St Patrick had a look round while he was on the island and visited a keeill on Ballafreer Farm not far from Colby Glen. It's said that the saint trod on a thorn while on his way to the keeill and cursed the land on which the thorn had grown saying that it would never bear a crop. Apparently it never has.

St Patrick's visit is the stuff of legend, but St Maughold, one of Patrick's disciples really did come to the Isle of Man, although in a rather unusual way. Maughold started life as a thief and murderer living in Ulster, where he decided to expose St Patrick as a fraud. Maughold hid one of his men in a shroud and asked Patrick to raise the supposed dead man to life. In a reversal of form, St Patrick laid a hand on the man who promptly died. Frightened and apologetic Maughold and his bandits asked the saint's forgiveness and Patrick gave the man in the shroud back his life. Unsurprisingly Maughold was convinced and converted. He begged to atone for his previous wickedness and so was cast adrift in a small coracle, with his feet shackled together. Drifting with the tide he eventually washed ashore on the Isle of Man. St Maughold's Well or *Chibbyr Vaghal* marks where he landed and gave thanks for his deliverance. The key to his shackles was found in the belly of a fish and, strengthened by this miracle, St Maughold began his holy work on the island, finally becoming its first Bishop around AD500.

...as do the Vikings

The Vikings arrived in the latter part of the eighth century, and some of the most abiding Manx myths arose around Godred Crovan. In Manx, Godred becomes *Goree* and King Godred is therefore King Gorree, or King Orry. When he landed in Lhen in 1079, it was a brilliant star-lit night. People gathered to see who he was and where he came from. With fine theatricality he pointed upward to the Milky Way, saying that it led to his home. Ever since then the Milky

Way has been known as *Raad Mooar Ree Goree*, or the Great Way of King Orry. The largest Neolithic monument on Mann, the chambered cairn Gretch Veg, is said to be his grave.

King Orry fought the battle which eventually gave him the island at Sky Hill. The hill was well known as the setting for a large fairy city, but there is no rumour of themselves having influenced the outcome. Although…?

One hundred and fifty years after Godred Crovan his namesake Godred II was King of Mann and the Isles. His brother-in-law, Somerled, sought to oust Godred from the throne and landed at Ramsey in 1158. Locals stacked valuables in Maughold Church, placed their livestock in the churchyard, and trusted to the great saint to protect them from harm. Gilcolm, one of Somerled's generals, decided to raid the church and planned to attack at first light. Learning of it, the people of Maughold spent the night pleading for the saint's aid. St. Maughold answered their prayers and appeared to Gilcolm in a dream, dressed in white and holding a shepherd's staff. The saint then stabbed the general three times in the chest with his staff. His men fled the island in terror, and Gilcolm lived only long enough to tell what had happened.

Fairies, witches... and something worse

The Christian church considered itself to be constantly fighting an invisible battle between the belief in fairies on the one hand, and the fairies themselves on the other. A traveller in Malew had been lured by strange music to a place where the little people were feasting. Among them he saw former neighbours who had disappeared in mysterious circumstances. One warned him not to eat or drink anything as he would be unable to return home. The traveller was provided with a silver cup filled with sweet-smelling drink, but, despite his raging thirst, he resisted tasting it. Throwing the liquid onto the ground, the fairies rose in dismay and disappeared, leaving him with the cup. Frightened of its possible power he asked his vicar what he should do with it. The vicar, unsurprisingly, suggested that it could have no power if devoted to the service of the church so the traveller gave the cup to him. Malew Parish Church certainly once possessed a communion cup dating from around 1781 but it seems unlikely to be of fairy provenance. Pity.

Fairies seem to make good construction workers and a number of Manx builders appear to have had supernatural help. The landowner at Tholt-y-Will wanted to build a large house below Snaefell and employed men to quarry the requisite stones from the beach. The quarried material

Isle of Man E II R

43

fynoderee

Joh. Enschede

1997

Colleen Corlett

included one large white block which he intended to use as a hearth stone. As it was too large to move with the muscle power available, the team knocked off for the night. On the following day they gathered more men to heave the stones up from the beach. When the crowd assembled they found that a phynnodderee, a Manx creature, half man, half beast and with prodigious strength, had been before them and moved the two hundred tons of stone to the building site in a single night. Grateful to the phynnodderee the gentleman built his house.

The oldest house in a Manx village was obviously the first to be built and was often called the *thie ferrishyn* (fairies' house) as the occupants would have had to have a good a relationship with the little people in order to be allowed to build there. The little people retained a fondness for the old dwellings and occupants could often hear haunting music.

Greeba was an area well known for supernatural happenings. The Curragh Glass or marshy pool situated in the valley below Greeba Mountain was a favourite place for testing for witchcraft. If the unfortunate woman did not suffocate in the marsh she was guilty of being a witch. Witches were also killed by being put into a spiked barrel and rolled down the steep slopes of Slieau Whallian, near St John's. For many years there was a bare track down the hill where nothing would grow. Folk said that the witches' way had been cursed by the witches who had died on it.

Punishment for witchcraft on the Isle of Man was often much lighter than in the islands across, probably because so many Manx people believed in them and used their services. A famously skilled group of Manx witches, or herb doctors, was the Teare family of Ballawhane. The skill was passed down from at least the seventeenth century and even as late as the 1930s people were using charms and remedies originating from the Teares.

As well as a testing station for witchcraft, Greeba is also the site of a more famous supernatural happening. While St Trinian's church was being built, the local buggane decided

St Trinian's church, Greeba. Still roofless after 300 years

that he didn't like the idea of being woken up by church bells ringing at all hours so came and tore the roof off; he knew that people wouldn't use the church if it wasn't finished as it wouldn't have received the bishop's blessing. Every time the roof was completed the buggane came down the mountain and tore it off again. Timothy, a poor tailor trying to earn a little extra money, wagered that the next time the roof was finished he would spend the night in the church making a pair of breeches.

Arriving at dusk he began work. He cut and sewed as fast as he could and all the time kept a sharp eye open for the buggane. Towards midnight the head of the buggane rose out of the beaten earth of the church floor. Faster and faster sewed the tailor and higher and higher rose the buggane. Just as the monster pulled himself out of the ground the tailor put in the last stitch. Scooping up his sewing kit Timothy ran from the church as the buggane ripped off the roof and gave chase. Knowing that his pursuer could not enter consecrated ground Timothy fled to St Runius's Church, now known as Marown Old Church, and hid in the churchyard. So incensed was the buggane that it tore off its own head and threw it after the tailor. It missed but hit the ground and exploded presumably destroying the buggane. Nevertheless no-one wanted to tempt fate by replacing the roof on St Trinian's and it has remained unfinished since the seventeenth century.

Saltwater...

During the time of Oliver Cromwell fewer ships visited the Isle of Man and the lack of sea traffic gave merpeople the opportunity of visiting the Manx shore uninterrupted. The Manx call them simply *ben varrey* and *dooiney varrey*, women of the sea and men of the sea, and they were considered particularly common around the Chasms.

Sailors are notoriously superstitious and were concerned to propitiate whatever lived in the sea in order to get a good catch. Some boats would curry favour with the merpeople by throwing some of the catch overboard as a gift. Merpeople were particularly fond of crabs, but herring would do. Whistling was never permitted at sea as it upset the merpeople and they might retaliate by sending strong winds. The protective mist which hides the island from its enemies is a gift from Manannan, but the mist which rises up from the sea to confuse the seafarer and make the trader miss the Manx ports is the work of offended mermaids and mermen.

Bad weather was a constant worry, of course, and having a cat on board was considered to bring a vessel good luck. Manx cats were popular ships' cats, as a common naval belief was that a cat could start a storm using magic stored in its tail. No tail, no storm-starting powers!

Up until the end of the nineteenth century, fishermen would light a fire of dry heather inside their boat, touching every part of the boat with the burning fronds to exorcise evil spirits. Sometimes a herb doctor would give them herbs which had to be prepared and drunk on board by the whole crew, with the remaining brew thrown over the nets. On the last day of April a cross of rowan – *crosh cuirn* – would be hidden in the boat, the one from the previous year being removed at the same time. No boat would leave harbour for the fishing grounds on a Friday, and no Peel fishing boat would leave the harbour third in the fleet, so the third and fourth boats out often roped themselves together temporarily to count as one.

...and blood

Many countries have a belief in the magical properties of blood, particularly the blood of a leader. When Charles I of England was executed on 30 January 1649 the scaffold and floor were covered with black cloth. After the beheading the executioner sold pieces of cloth soaked in the king's blood to the crowd. A similar scene occurred at the execution of William Christian, aka Illiam Dhone, by firing squad on 2 January 1663 (see chapter 6). According to tradition, blankets were spread where Christian stood so that his blood did not fall onto the ground. No records appear to exist about what was done with the blankets but, presuming they were used to wrap the body, one or more might well have been kept by his supporters. Even if the English garrison was formally instructed to destroy them, there is such a thing as bribery…

Calendar customs

Every year on 5 July, old midsummer's day, Manx dignitaries meet on Tynwald Hill, St John's to proclaim new laws. The Tynwald ceremony stretches back more than a thousand years and marks the world's oldest parliament, but its timing owes much to Scandinavian legend. People living within the Arctic circle experience twenty-four hours of darkness during the winter, so midsummer with its twenty-four hours of daylight had special significance. According to Norse mythology Baldr was the son of Odin and Frigg. He was famed for his goodness, peace and joy, and associated with the beneficial effects of the sun. His life culminated at midsummer, during which fires were lit to prefigure Baldr's funeral pyre and hoops of fire were rolled down the hillside to symbolise the sun's decline – we're back to the origins of the three legs of Mann again (see above). As was usual, the Christian church, unable to stop such pagan celebrations, adopted and used them for its own ends. St John ousted Baldr and the midsummer celebrations officially honoured the saint. In some stories, sacred wells appeared from the

The real *Fairy Bridge, Kewaigue*

hoofprints of Baldr's horse and there is a Manx saying: *Lane croie cabbyl dy ushtey L'aal Eoin feeu mayl Vannin*, or 'a full horseshoe of water on John's feast day is worth the rent of Mann'.

Not only is St John's church integral to the Tynwald ceremonies (see appendix 4) but every Tynwald participant also wears a buttonhole of *Bollan-feaill-Eoin* (the wort of the vigil of John) or mugwort. Sometimes called bollan bane it is not the same as St John's Wort which does not grow naturally on Mann. Traditionally worn in the hat or on the head, mugwort protects against supernatural harm. By Scandinavian custom, wearers of bollan bane are also demonstrating loyalty to their monarch.

Modern Myths

The nineteenth and twentieth centuries have also had their share of supernatural interest, much of it created to provide attractions for tourists. Several parishes claim to have a Fairy Bridge, for example. The celebrated bridge over Santon Burn where everyone is exhorted to greet the fairies for fear of bad luck is thought to have been a nineteenth century tourist attraction. Locals will tell you that the original fairy bridge is actually a mediaeval bridge in Kewaigue, but wherever you are the little people still like to be greeted.

Myths continue to be created. Sulby Glen has a stone circle, which wasn't there a few years ago. Standing stones have sprung up in a garden in Crowcreen, and fairy homes at Summerhill. The gnarled spirit of the woodland has been made manifest in Groudle and Ballaglass Glens. Recent myths have less to do with recording the history of the island, and more to do with affecting it. Early tales explain the island's creation, later ones draw visitors who bring wealth to the island – a modern development on 'crossing the palm with silver', perhaps. Perhaps a legend cannot really be a legend until it has time on its side. Even so, by supporting the island's tourist industry, the little people continue to influence its history.

Fortune telling

A great witch, or some say a great wizard, who lived many years ago was known for the accuracy of her prophecy. *Caillagh-ny-Faashagh* (sometimes *Caillagh-ny-Ghueshag*) lived in Foxdale but is said to have foretold many events which subsequently came to pass. She prophesied the Battle of Santwat in 1098 and foretold the founding of the mines in Foxdale. She said that the mountains of Mann would be cut over with roads and iron horses would gallop over them to the inn at the top of Snaefell. In her last prophesies she said that Mann and Scotland will come so close that a Scotswoman and a Manxwoman would be able to fold washing across the gap. Sand and shingle is indeed building up on the Point of Ayre, although there's long way to go before it meets Scotland. *Caillagh-ny-Faashagh* also said that the rulers of Mann will be compelled to flee. Perhaps the separation from the European Union…?

Above: Ballaglass Glen
Right: New stone circle, Sulby Glen

KINGS AND THINGS

Almost any community or group of people will have a leader, whether formalised or not. Kings and, later, Pharaohs had ruled Ancient Egypt from as early as 3,000 BC, but it was not until the late Bronze Age, and the development of a perceived need to defend settled homesteads, that rulers of lands, rather than tribal leaders, became the norm in most parts of Northern Europe. The following is a list of rulers who believed that the Isle of Man fell under their domain, plus their other holdings and country of origin if applicable. It should be remembered, however, that Mann was often not considered as a separate identity by the countries which surrounded it, so the idea of formal rule probably didn't exist before the advent of the Vikings, and was often not taken into account after it. As the ruling dynasties of the Scandinavian countries were all interrelated, holdings could pass from, for example, England to Mann to Denmark and back again merely by succession. In addition, the uncertainty of some of the records mean that dates, particularly the earlier ones, may vary by a year or two. Note: the dates given are the dates of the reign, not the life-span of the ruler.

Dates	Ruler	Country/holdings
445-452	Niall	High King of Ireland
452-463	Lóegaire	High King of Ireland
463-482	Ailill Molt	High King of Ireland
482-507	Lugaid	High King of Ireland
507-534	Muirchertach I	High King of Ireland
534-544	Tuathal Máelgarb	High King of Ireland
544-565	Diarmait I	High King of Ireland
565-566	Forggus	High King of Ireland (co-regent)
	Domnall Ilchelgach	High King of Ireland (co-regent)
566-569	Ainmire	High King of Ireland
569-572	Báetán I	High King of Ireland (co-regent)
	Eochaid	High King of Ireland (co-regent)
572-586	Báetán II	High King of Ireland
586-598	Áed	High King of Ireland
598-604	Áed Sláine	High King of Ireland (co-regent)
	Colmán Rímid	High King of Ireland (co-regent)
604-612	Áed Uaridnach	High King of Ireland
612-615	Máel Cobo	High King of Ireland
615-628	Suibne Menn	High King of Ireland
616-633	Edwin	King of Northumbria (claimed Mann)
628-642	Domnall	High King of Ireland
642-654	Conall Cáel	High King of Ireland (co-regent)
642-658	Cellach	High King of Ireland (co-regent; ruled alone 654-658)
658-665	Diarmait II	High King of Ireland (co-regent)
	Blathmac	High King of Ireland (co-regent)
665-671	Sechnussach	High King of Ireland
671-675	Cennfáelad	High King of Ireland
675-695	Fínsnechta Fledach	High King of Ireland
695-704	Loingsech	High King of Ireland
704-710	Congal Cenmagair	High King of Ireland
710-722	Fergal	High King of Ireland
722-724	Fogartach	High King of Ireland
724-728	Cináed	High King of Ireland
728-734	Flaithbertach	High King of Ireland (deposed)
734-743	Áed Allán	High King of Ireland
743-763	Domnall Midi	High King of Ireland
763-770	Niall Frossach	High King of Ireland
770-797	Donnchad Midi	High King of Ireland
797-800	Áed Oirdnide	High King of Ireland (deposed)

Between 800 and 841 Vikings ruled Mann. They were originally from Norway, but by this time also based in

Ireland. The Norwegian monarchy was founded in 841 when Halfdan subjected his peers and created the first ruling family. The King of Norway often sent a deputy to rule Mann in his stead, with greater or lesser success. Nominally under Norwegian rule, the Isle of Man was actually often under the thumb of whoever had the power to take and hold it.

841-858	Halfdan the Black	King of Norway (abdicated)
858-928	Harald I, 'Fairhair'	King of Norway
928-933	Eirik I, 'Bloodaxe'	King of Norway (deposed)
933-959	Haakon I, 'the Good'	King of Norway
959-974	Harald II, 'Greycloak'	King of Norway
974-994	Earl Haakan Sigurdsson	King of Norway
994-999	Olaf I	King of Norway
999-1015	Earl Eirik	King of Norway (abdicated)
1015-1016	Earl Svein	King of Norway (deposed)
1016-1028	St Olaf II	King of Norway
1028-1035	Cnut, 'the Great'	King of Denmark, England and Norway
1035-1040	Harold I, 'Harefoot'	King of England (regent 1035-1037)
1040-1042	Harthacnut	King of England
1042-1066	St Edward, 'the Confessor'	King of England
?-1070	Godred, 'son of Sitric'	King of Mann
1070-1079	Fingal	King of Mann
1079-1088	Godred, 'Crovan'	King of Mann, Dublin, Leinster and parts of Scotland
1088-1095	Lagman	King of Mann and the Isles
1095-1098	Muirchertach II	High King of Ireland (sent Donald son of Teige to be caretaker King of the Isles. He proved a tyrant and was driven away.)
1098-1103	Magnus III, 'Barelegs'	King of Norway, Mann and the Isles
1103-1153	Olaf I, 'the Dwarf'	King of Mann and the Isles (beheaded)
1153-1154	Reginald plus two brothers	Kings in Mann (co-regents)
1154-1158	Godred II	King of Mann and the Isles (defeated)
1158-1164	Somerled	King of Argyll, Mann and the Isles
1164	Reginald	King of Mann and the Isles (for four days – defeated)
1164-1187	Godred II	King of Mann and the Isles (resumed the throne)
1187-1226	Reginald I	King of Mann and the Isles (defeated)
1226-1237	Olaf II	King of Mann and the Isles
1237-1249	Harald	King of Mann and the Isles (drowned)
1249	Reginald II	ing of Mann and the Isles (for twenty-four days – defeated)
1249-1250	Harald II	King of Mann and the Isles
1250-1252	John	King of Mann and the Isles (claimant)
1252-1265	Magnus IV	King of Mann and the Isles (1263-1265 King of Mann only)
1266-1286	Alexander III	King of Scotland
1286-1290	Margaret	Queen of Scotland (died aged 7)
1290-1307	Edward I	King of England
1307-1313	Edward II	King of England
1313-1316	Robert I 'the Bruce'	King of Scotland
1317-?	Edward II	King of England

Between 1317 and 1329 the Scots and the English both claimed Mann and its rule passed backwards and forwards between them.

?-1329	Robert I 'the Bruce'	King of Scotland
1329-1334	Edward III	King of England

In 1334 the right to rule in Mann was first granted to a member of the English nobility by the English crown. Although holding the title by the grace of the English king of the time, the King of Mann became in fact, if not in law, absolute ruler of the island. Where appropriate, members of the nobility are therefore listed as rulers of Mann, rather than the English kings to whom they at least nominally owed allegiance.

1334-1344	William Montecute	King of Mann,1st Earl of Salisbury
1344-1393	William Montecute	Lord of the Isles of Mann and Wight, 2nd Earl of Salisbury (sold Mann)
1393-1399	William le Scrope	King of Mann, 1st Earl of Wiltshire
1399-1405	Henry Percy	King of Mann, 1st Earl of Northumberland
1405-1414	John Stanley	King of Mann, Knight
1414-1437	John Stanley	King of Mann, Knight
1437-1459	Thomas Stanley	King of Mann, 1st Baron Stanley
1459-1504	Thomas Stanley	King of Mann, 1st Earl of Derby
1504-1521	Thomas Stanley	Lord of Mann, 2nd Earl of Derby
1521-1572	Edward Stanley	Lord of Mann, 3rd Earl of Derby
1572-1593	Henry Stanley	Lord of Mann, 4th Earl of Derby
1593-1594	Ferdinando Stanley	Lord of Mann, 5th Earl of Derby
1594-1603	Elizabeth I	Queen of England, Lord of Mann
1603-1607	James VI and I	King of Scotland and England, Lord of Mann
1607-1608	Henry Howard	Lord of Mann, 1st Earl of Northampton,
1608-1609	Robert Cecil	Lord of Mann, 1st Earl of Salisbury
		(Howard and Cecil caretaker Lords appointed by King James VI and I)
1610-1642	William Stanley	Lord of Mann, 6th Earl of Derby
[1612-1627	Elizabeth Stanley	Wife of the 6th Earl, she largely ruled Mann in her husband's stead.
1627-1642	James Stanley	Son of Elizabeth and the 6th Earl. While still Lord Strange (i.e. before inheriting the earldom) he took over the administration of the island on his mother's death]
1642-1651	James Stanley	Lord of Mann, 7th Earl of Derby
1649-1660	Thomas Fairfax	Lord of Mann (during the Commonwealth and Protectorate; appointed by parliament before the earl's death), 3rd Baron Fairfax
1660-1672	Charles Stanley	Lord of Mann, 8th Earl of Derby
1672-1702	William Stanley	Lord of Mann, 9th Earl of Derby
1702-1736	James Stanley	Lord of Mann, 10th Earl of Derby
1736-1764	James Murray	Lord of Mann, 2nd Duke of Atholl
1764-1765	John Murray	Lord of Mann, 3rd Duke of Atholl (held in right of his wife Charlotte; sold Mann)
1765-1820	George III	King of England, Lord of Mann
1820-1830	George IV	King of England, Lord of Mann
1830-1837	William IV	King of England, Lord of Mann
1837-1901	Victoria	Queen of England, Lord of Mann (note: Victoria preferred to be called Lady of Mann)
1901-1910	Edward VII	King of England, Lord of Mann
1910-1936	George V	King of England, Lord of Mann
1936	Edward VIII	King of England, Lord of Mann (abdicated)
1936-1952	George VI	King of England, Lord of Mann
1952-	Elizabeth II	Queen of England, Lord of Mann

The Bishopric of Sodor and Man was ratified by the papal bull of Pope Anastastius IV in 1154 and was created out of territory traditionally ruled by bishops from York, England and Nidaros (Trondheim), Norway. The merger was not accepted by the archbishops of the old territories who insisted on retaining the right to consecrate bishops of their own choosing. The political tension between Scandinavia, Scotland, England and Ireland also influenced who appointed the bishops and whether they were accepted by everyone else. As a result Sodor and Man occasionally had two or more bishops. Many of the dates are therefore speculative and a few may overlap.

Dates	Bishop	Notes
c. 1050	Roolwer	Said to be buried in Maughold.
c. 1080	William Hamond	Manxman.
?1138	Wimund	Possibly Bishop of the Isles and not Mann
	Gamaliel	Buried at Peterborough, England
1152-1170	Reginald	Norwegian.
c.1158-c.1164	Christinus	From Argyll, Scotland. Died at Ulster, Ireland.
c.1164-1203	Michael	Manxman. Died at Fountains Abbey.
1203-1217	Nicholas	From Argyll, Scotland. Died at Ulster, Ireland.
1217-?	Reginald	Buried in Rushen Abbey.
d.1226	John	Died in a fire at Jervaulx, England.
1226-1247	Simon	From Argyll, Scotland. Died at the church of St Michael the Archangel. Buried in St German's church, St Patrick's Isle.
1247-1249	Laurence	Formerly Archdeacon in Mann. Drowned off Shetland with King Harald.
1249-1252	*Vacant*	
1252-1274	Richard	Died at Langley, Cumbria. Buried Furness Abbey. First Baron Bishop
1274-1303	Mark	From Galloway, Scotland. Buried in St German's church, St Patrick's Isle.
1303-1305	*Vacant*	
1305-1321	Alan	From Galloway, Scotland. Buried Rothesay, Isle of Bute, Scotland.
1321-1324	Gilbert MacLelan	From Galloway, Scotland. Buried Rothesay, Isle of Bute, Scotland.
1324-1327	Bernard	Scottish. Buried Kilwinning, Scotland.
1327-1348	Thomas de Rossy	Scottish. Buried Scone, Scotland.
1348-1374	William Russell	Manxman. Abbot of Rushen Abbey. Elected by the clergy of his diocese. Died at Ramshead, England. Buried Furness Abbey.
1374-?1381	John Donkan	Manxman. Previously served as Papal Nuncio in Ireland and as Seneschal of Ulster. Translated to Derry and then, in 1394, to Down.
1381-1387	Robert Waldby	Translated to Aire in France, and then, in 1391, to Dublin
1387-1392	*Possibly vacant*	
?1392-1409	John Sprotton	
1410-1429	Richard Payl	Previously Bishop of Dromore. Possibly reigned longer in Mann
1429-1448	*Unknown*	
1448-1453	John Green	Also Vicar of Dunchurch, Warks and Suffragan Bishop of Lichfield
1453-1455	*Vacant*	
1455-1458	Thomas Burton	Franciscan
1458-1480	Thomas of Kirkham	Abbot of Vale Royal Cheshire
1480-1486	Richard Oldham	Formerly Abbot of St Werburgh, Chester
1487- c.1521	Huan Hesketh	
1523-1542	John Howden	
1542-1545	Thomas Stanley	First installation. Probably the illegitimate second cousin of the 3rd Earl. Deposed, ostensibly because he objected to the diocese being transferred from the Province of Canterbury to that of York
1545-1548	Robert Ferrar	Translated to St Davids. Martyred 1555
1548-1556	Henry Mann	Dean of Chester
1556-1568	Thomas Stanley	Restored. Noted pluralist.
1569-1573	John Salisbury	The last abbot of Titchfield Abbey. Held deanery of Norwich concurrently with title of Bishop
1573-1576	James Stanley	

1576-1599	John Meyrick	Previously vicar of Hornchurch
1599-1604	George Lloyd	Translated to Chester
1604-1633	John Phillips	Archdeacon of Mann from 1587. Also Archdeacon of Cleveland 1601-1619. Translated Book of Common Prayer and Bible into Manx
1634-1635	William Forster	Possible Prebendary of Chester
1635-1643	Richard Parr	
1643-1661	*Vacant*	Commonwealth; puritans do not recognise bishops
1661-1662/3	Samuel Rutter	Archdeacon of Mann from 1640; may have been acting as bishop after the death of Richard Parr
1663-1671	Isaac Barrow	Also Governor. Translated to St Asaph in North Wales
1671-1682	Henry Bridgeman	Also Dean of Chester
1682-1684	John Lake	Formerly Archdeacon of Cleveland. Translated to Bristol and Chichester
1685-1692	Baptist Levinz	Became Prebendary of Winchester
1693-1697	*Vacant*	
1698-1755	Thomas Wilson	Had been personal chaplain to 9th Earl of Derby and tutor to his son. Declined preferment to the much wealthier Exeter in 1724.
1755-1772	Mark Hildesley	Formerly Rector of Hitchin. Oversaw translation of Bible into Manx
1773-1780	Richard Richmond	Formerly Chaplain to the 3rd Duke of Atholl. Nominated by Charlotte Murray, the Duchess
1780-1783	George Mason	Nominated by Charlotte Murray now Dowager Duchess
1784-1813	Claudius Crigan	Formerly Rector of St Anne's, Liverpool. Nominated by Charlotte Murray.
1814-1827	George Murray	Nephew to the 4th Duke of Atholl. Translated to Rochester
1828-1838	William Ward	Concurrently Rector of Great Horkesley, Essex. Defended see against merger with Carlisle
1838-1840	James Bowstead	Fellow of Corpus Christi College, Cambridge. Translated to Lichfield
1840-1841	Henry Pepys	Prebendary of Wells. Translated to Worcester
1841-1846	Thomas Vowler Short	Tutor at Christ Church, Oxford. Translated to St Asaph which he had administered for some years as its bishop was ill
1847	Walter Shirley	Rector of the family livings of Shirley and Brailsford and Archdeacon of Derby. Died of pneumonia after a wet journey to Mann. Reigned only two months and nineteen days
1847-1854	Robert Eden	3rd Lord Auckland. Formerly Chaplain to Queen Victoria. Translated to Bath & Wells
1854-1877	Horatio Powys	Formerly Rector and Rural Dean of Warrington
1877-1887	Rowley Hill	Formerly Rector and Rural Dean of Sheffield. Proposed merger with Liverpool
1887-1892	John Bardsley	Numerous previous church appointments. Translated to Carlisle
1892-1907	Norman Straton	Formerly Archdeacon of Wakefield. Translated to Newcastle
1907-1911	Thomas Drury	Manxman. Had held various church posts on Mann and been Mathematics master at King William's College. Principal of Ridley Hall, Cambridge. Translated to Ripon
1911-1925	James Denton Thompson	Formerly Vicar of Birmingham
1925-1928	Charles Thornton-Duesbury	Manxman. Formerly Rector of Holy Trinity, Marylebone
1928-1943	William Jones	Formerly Archdeacon of Bradford
1943-1954	John Strickland Taylor	Formerly Principal of Wycliffe Hall, Oxford
1954-1966	Benjamin Pollard	Formerly Bishop of Lancaster
1966-1974	(George) Eric Gordon	Formerly Rector of Chelmsford and Provost of Chelmsford Cathedral
1974-1983	Vernon Nicholls	Formerly Archdeacon of Birmingham. Sold Bishopscourt
1983-1989	Arthur Attwell	Formerly Rector of St Michael's, Workington
1989-2003	Noel Jones	Formerly Archdeacon for the Royal Navy and Chaplain for the Fleet
2003-2007	Graham Knowles	Formerly Dean of Carlisle. Became Dean of St Paul's Cathedral
2008-2016	Robert Paterson	Formerly Canon of the Province of Wales, and Chaplain and Researcher to the Archbishop of York
2017	*Vacant*	at the time of writing

APPENDIX 3   GOVERNORS, LIEUTENANT AND OTHERWISE

Today the most senior figure on the Isle of Man is the largely ceremonial position of Lieutenant Governor who represents the English crown. Various different titles, including Captain, Commissioner, Bailiff and Governor, have been used for the post which is below the ruler but above everyone else. The job was occasionally held quite informally, and often in conjunction with some other office in one of Mann's neighbouring islands. This list is intended to give some idea of those who had responsibility for day-to-day governance of the island, rather than those who held the more exalted and often less involved title of Lord of Mann.

Dates	Name	Notes
1290	Richard de Burgh	Earl of Ulster, Lord of Connach, known as the 'Red Earl'
1290-1293	Walter de Huntercombe	
1293-1294	John Balliol	King of Scots, vassal of Edward I of England
1294-1307	Anthony de Bek	Bishop of Durham
1307-1308	Simon de Montacute	father of William Montecute, future ruler of Mann (see appendix 1)
1308-1310	Henry de Bello Monte	Also known as Henry de Beaumont, second cousin of Edward II of England
1310	Gilbert Makaskel	possibly working for Anthony de Bek
1311	Piers Gaveston	Earl of Cornwall, favourite of Edward II of England
1310	Gilbert Makaskel	Again!
1312-1313	Henry de Bello Monte	Again!
1313	Gilbert Makaskel	Yet again!
1313-1317	Thomas Randolf	Earl of Moray
1317-1329	John de Athy	Also captain of the fleet in the Irish Sea and Constable of Carrickfergus Castle
1329-1334	Edmund Mortayn	Escheator of Ireland. Possibly also known as MacToyn, Martolene or Martholine. Possibly continued as governor under William Montecute (see below)
1334-1344	William Montecute	Also King of Mann (see appendix 1)
1344-1393	William Montecute	Also King of Mann (see appendix 1)
1393-1399	Stephen le Scrope	Brother of ruler William le Scrope
1399-1405	Henry Percy	Also King of Mann (see appendix 1)
1405	Michael Blundell	
1405-1417	John Letherland	
1418-1422	John of Fazakerley	
1422-1428	John Walton	
1428	Henry of Byrom	
1428-1496		*No information*
1496-1497	Peter Dutton	
1497-1505	Henry Radcliffe	Abbot of Rushen
1505-1511	Ralph Rushton	
1511-1517	Sir John Ireland	
1517-1521	Ralph Rushton Again!	
1521-1522	Thomas Denisport	Also known as Danport
1522-1526	Sir John Ireland	Again!
1526-1529	Richard Holt	
1529-1530	John Fleming	
1530-1532	Thomas Sherburne	Also High Sheriff of Lancashire
1532-1533	Henry Bradley	
1533-1535	Henry Stanley	Related to the ruling family
1535-1537	George Stanley	Related to the ruling family
1537	Sir Thomas Stanley	Related to the ruling family
1537-1539	George Stanley	Again!
1540-1544	Thomas Tyldsley	
1544-1552	William Stanley	Related to the ruling family
1552-1556	Henry Stanley	

1556-1558	Thomas Stanley	Bishop of Sodor and Man. Illegitimate. Cousin of Lord of Mann
		Appointed by Queen Mary I of England
1558-1566	Richard Ashton	
1566-1570	Henry Stanley	Again!
1570-1576	Edward Tarbock	Married to Anne, daughter of Henry Stanley
1576-1580	John Hanmer	Also known as Harmer
1580	Richard Sherburne	Catholic. Owned Stoneyhurst and Mitton in Lancashire
1580-1592	John Meyrick	Bishop of Sodor and Man. May have been advisory post only
1592-1593	Cuthbert Gerrard	
1593-1594	William Stanley	Later 6th Earl of Derby
1594	Thomas of Burcough	Burcough Priory was the traditional burying ground of the Earls of Derby
1594-1595	Randulph Stanley	
1595-1608	Thomas Gerard	1st Baron Gerard, English MP, Landowner in Staffordshire and Lancashire
1609-1610	John Ireland &	Joint governors by patent from Scottish/English King James VI/I
	John Birchall	
1610-1623	John Ireland	
1623-1624	Sir Ferdinando Leigh	From Middleton. Gentleman of the Privy Chamber to Charles I
1624-1625	Edward Fletcher	Possibly from Braddan, Isle of Man
1625-1627	Edward Holmewood	
1628-1634	Edward Christian	From the influential Manx family
1634-1638	Sir Charles Gerard	Of Hallsall, uncle to the Earl of Macclesfield
1639	Radcliffe Gerard	Younger brother of Sir Charles
1640-1651	John Greenhalgh	Of Brandlesome Hall, Bury, Lancs
1651	Robert Duckenfield	Lieutenant Colonel with Parliamentarian forces
1651	James Chaloner,	Joint commissioners (not governors) appointed by Lord Fairfax
	Robert Dynely &	
	Joshua Witton (Rev)	
1652-1656	Matthew Cadwell	
1656-1658	William Christian	Also known as Illiam Dhone
1658-1660	James Chaloner	Former commissioner
1660	Richard Stevenson	Major, of Balladoole, Isle of Man
1660-1664	Roger Nowell	Possibly of Read, Lancashire
1664-1673	Isaac Barrow	Also Bishop of Sodor and Man
1673-1676	Henry Nowell	Also of the Lancashire Read family
1677-1678	Henry Stanley	Cousin of William Stanley, Lord of Mann
1678-1690	Robert Heywood	Grandson of Governor John Greenhalgh
1691-1693	Roger Kenyon	Of Kenyon Peel Hall, Lytham St Anne's
1693-1696	William Sacheverell	Close relation of the Sitwell family
1696-1701	Nicholas Sankey	Colonel
1701-1703	James Cranston	
1703-1713	Robert Mawdesley	
1713-1715	Charles Zedenno	Uncle of James Stanley, Lord of Mann Stanley and
		Member of Parliament in Westminster
1715-1723	Alexander Horne	Deputy governor from 1713
1723-1725	John Lloyd	
1725-1736	Thomas Horton	From Chadderton, Lancashire, England
1736-1743	James Murray	Not the James Murray who was Lord of Mann
1744-1751	Patrick Lindsay	Provost of Edinburgh
1751-1761	Basil Cochrane	Brother of 8th Earl of Dundonald

While Wood, Smith and Murray (see below) retained the post of Governor (G), several Lieutenant Governors (LG) were appointed under them. Deputy governors had been appointed from time to time, but this was the first consistent use of a supportive office.

1761-1777	John Wood (G)	From Carse near Dumfries
1773-1775	Henry Hope (LG)	
1775-1790	Richard Dawson (LG)	Major in the Royal Engineers
1777-1793	Edward Smith (G)	Colonel of the 4th Regiment of Horse
1790-1804	Alexander Shaw (LG)	Colonel and Chief of Clan Shaw
1804-1805	Henry Murray (LG)	Brother of Governor
1793-1828	John Murray (G)	4th Duke of Atholl, son of the last non-royal Lord of Man
1805-1832	Cornelius Smelt (LG)	First royally-appointed Lieutenant Governor

After 1828 no governors were appointed and the title Lieutenant Governor was always used.

1832-1845	John Ready	Former Lieutenant Governor of Prince Edward Island, Canada
1845-1860	Charles Hope	Husband of Lady Isabella!
1860	Mark Hildesley Quayle	Judge. Acting Lieutenant Governor
1860-1863	Francis Stainsby- Conant-Pigott	Sometimes known as Francis Pigott Stainsby Conant
1863	Mark Hildesley Quayle	Again! Acting Lieutenant Governor
1863-1882	Henry Loch	Sir Henry from 1880
1882-1893	Spencer Walpole	Author of *A History of England*
1893-1895	Joseph West Ridgeway	Became Governor of Ceylon (now Sri Lanka)
1896-1902	John Major Henniker-Major	5th Baron Henniker
1902	John James Gell	Clerk of the Rolls. Acting Lieutenant Governor
1902-1919	George Somerset	3rd Baron Raglan
1919-1926	William Fry	First time tenure was restricted (to 7 years)
1926-1933	Claude Hill	
1933-1937	Montagu Butler	Father of Rab Butler
1937-1945	William Leveson-Gower	4th Earl Granville. Naval commander. Uncle by marriage to Queen Elizabeth
1945-1952	Geoffrey Bromet	Air Vice Marshall. Son-in-law of Sir Arthur Conan Doyle
1952-1959	Ambrose Dundas	Involved in the growth of Bracknell New Town pre 1952 and post 1959
1959-1966	Ronald Garvey	Previously Administrator of St Vincent and Governor successively of British Honduras (now Belize) and Fiji
1966-1973	Peter Stallard	Son of Manxwoman Eleanor Gawne. Had been Governor of British Honduras (now Belize)
1973	Hugh Norman-Walker	Appointed but had to decline as his wife would not accompany him.
1973-1974	Peter Stallard	Again!
1974-1980	John Paul	Had been Governor of British Honduras (now Belize). Oversaw the independence of Gambia and the Bahamas, and encouraged that of Mann
1980-1985	Nigel Cecil	Rear Admiral
1985-1990	Laurence New	Major General. Educated King William's College
1990-1995	Laurence Jones	Air Marshall
1995-2000	Timothy Daunt	Father of James Daunt of Daunt bookshops
2000	Thomas Cain	First Deemster. Acting Lieutenant Governor
2000-2005	Ian Macfadyen	Air Marshall. From Mann he became Constable and Governor of Windsor Castle
2005	John 'Mike' Kerruish	First Deemster. Acting Lieutenant Governor
2005-2011	Paul Haddacks	Vice Admiral
2011	David Doyle	First Deemster. Acting Lieutenant Governor
2011-2016	Adam Wood	Career diplomat mainly serving in Africa
2016	David Doyle	Again! First Deemster. Acting Lieutenant Governor
2016-	Richard Gozney	Career diplomat. Speaks Indonesian

Although not strictly relevant to a book about the history of the Isle of Man, many readers may be interested to learn a little more about a ceremony which has not changed in essence for hundreds of years. The following, although far from comprehensive, provides a brief summary.

The Tynwald ceremony is held at St John's each year on 5 July, or on 6 July if the fifth is a Sunday. It starts with a service held in the Royal Chapel of St John's and conducted in a mix of English and Manx. Dignitaries then proceed to Tynwald Hill along the processional way which is strewn with marram grass, the local name for which is 'bent'. All those taking part in the Tynwald Day Ceremony also wear a sprig of mugwort (see chapter 9).

Two processions leave the church largely in reverse order of seniority. Tynwald Hill has four tiers and the first procession is made up of those seated on the lowest two. The second procession, often called the Tynwald Court Procession, consists of those seated on the top two tiers of Tynwald Hill. The Manx National Standard precedes the President of Tynwald and the Sword of State precedes the Lord of Mann or his/her representative which is usually the Lieutenant Governor.

Before they reach the war memorial, about half way down the processional way on the north side, the two processions halt and face inwards. The Lord of Man passes between the two lines and the processions reform behind him, effectively turning themselves inside out so that the Lord may be the first to step onto Tynwald Hill.

Seating on Tynwald Hill

Seated on the top tier of Tynwald Hill is the Lord of Man and their consort, or the Lord's representative the Lieutenant Governor and his assistant if necessary. Also seated on the top tier is the President of Tynwald, the Lord Bishop of Sodor & Man, Members and Clerk of the Legislative Council, the Surgeon to the Household and the Sword Bearer.

On the second tier down is seated the Speaker, Members and Secretary of the House of Keys and their chaplain.

The third tier is occupied by the High Bailiff, the representative of the Commission of the Peace, the Chief Registrar, the Mayor of Douglas, the Chairmen of Commissioners from Castletown, Peel, Ramsey, Laxey, Onchan, Port Erin and Port St Mary, the Archdeacon, the Vicar General, clergy of various denominations and the Chief Constable.

Seated on the fourth and lowest tier are the four Coroners, Yn Lhaihder (The Reader), and the Captains of the Parish. The fourth tier also carries the two lecterns used by the two deemsters.

Ceremony on Tynwald Hill

One of the coroners and Yn Lhaihder 'fences' the court, the coroner in English and Yn Lhaihder in Manx. Fencing is a proclamation to all those present that no disturbance will be tolerated and that everyone should answer to their names when called. Traditionally no weapons, apart from the Sword of State, were permitted within the symbolic fence.

The four coroners are first sworn in for the next year and receive their staves of office.

The two deemsters then proclaim the laws enacted during the previous year. The First Deemster stands at the lectern on the south side of the hill to promulgate the new laws in English, while the Second Deemster stands at the lectern on the north side to promulgate them in Manx.

The Lord of Man or their representative then invites any members of the public who have a petition for redress of grievance to come forward and hand them to the Clerk of Tynwald who receives them at the foot of the Hill. Such petitions are considered by the Standing Orders Committee of Tynwald at a later date.

At this point the business on the Hill is deemed to have been completed. The processions leave the Hill in the same order and with the same procedure as that used when leaving the church. By this means the Lord, preceded by the Sword of State, is the first to re-enter the church.

Captioning Ceremony

The Court of Tynwald is formed of the President of Tynwald, Legislative Council, Speaker and Members of the House of Keys. Once it has reassembled in the Royal Chapel, the Acts promulgated on Tynwald Hill are captioned. Certificates for each Act are signed first by the Lord of Mann or the Lieutenant Governor, then by the President and finally by the Speaker. The Court is then adjourned and the Lord of Mann or their representative, the President and Legislative Council retire. The Keys remain to transact any remaining business.

APPENDIX 5

O land of our birth,
O gem of God's earth,
O Island so strong and so fair;
Built firm as Barrule,
Thy Throne of Home Rule
Makes us free as thy sweet mountain air.

When Orry, the Dane,
In Mannin did reign,
'Twas said he had come from above;
For wisdom from Heav'n
To him had been giv'n
To rule us with justice and love.

Our fathers have told
How Saints came of old,
Proclaiming the Gospel of Peace;
That sinful desires,
Like false Baal fires,
Must die ere our troubles can cease.

Ye sons of the soil,
In hardship and toil,
That plough both the land and the sea,
Take heart while you can,
And think of the Man
Who toiled by the Lake Galilee.

When fierce tempests smote
That frail little boat,
They ceased at His gentle command;
Despite all our fear,
The Saviour is near
To safeguard our dear Fatherland.

Let storm-winds rejoice,
And lift up their voice,
No danger our homes can befall;
Our green hills and rocks
Encircle our flocks,
And keep out the sea like a wall.

Our Island, thus blest, No foe can molest;
Our grain and our fish shall increase;
From battle and sword Protecteth the Lord,
And crowneth our nation with peace.

Then let us rejoice
With heart, soul and voice,
And in The Lord's promise confide;
That each single hour
We trust in His power,
No evil our souls can betide.

O' Halloo nyn ghooie,
O' Ch'liegeen ny s'bwaaie
Ry gheddyn er ooir aalin Yee,
Ta dt' Ardstoyl Reill Thie
Myr Barrool er nyc hoie
Dy reayl shin ayns seyrsnys as shee.

Tra Gorree yn Dane
Haink er traie ec y Lhane
Son Ree Mannin v'eh er ny reih
'S va creenaght veih Heose
Er ny chur huggey neose
Dy reill harrin lesh cairys as graih.

Ren nyn ayryn g'imraa
Va Nooghyn shenn traa
Yn Sushtal dy Hee fockley magh
Shegin yeearree peccoil
Myr far aileyn Vaal,
Ve er ny chur mow son dy bragh.

Vec ooasle yn Theihll
Ayns creoighys tooilleil
Ta traaue ooir as faarkey, Gow cree
Ny jarrood yn fer mie
Ta coadey 'n lught-thie
Ren tooilleil liorish Logh Galilee.

D'eiyr yn sterrm noon as noal
Yn baatey beg moal
Fo-harey hug Eh geay as keayn
Trooid ooilley nyn ghaue
Ta'n Saualtagh ec laue
Dy choadey nyn Vannin veg veen.

Lhig dorrinyn bra
Troggal seose nyn goraa
As brishey magh ayns ard arrane
Ta nyn groink aalin glass
Yn vooir cummal ass
As coadey lught-thie as shioltane.

Nyn Ellan fo-hee, Cha boir noidyn ee
Dy bishee nyn eeastyn as grain
Nee'n Chiarn shin y reayll
Voish strieughyn yn theihll
As crooinnagh lesh shee 'n ashoon ain.

Lhig dooin boggoil bee,
Lesh annym as cree,
As croghey er gialdyn yn Chiarn;
Dy vodmayd dagh oor,
Treish teil er e phooar,
Dagh olk ass nyn anmeenyn 'hayrn.

ACKNOWLEDGEMENTS

I am indebted to several organisations and individuals who gave up their time to provide help, information and/ or photographic material. They include, individuals: Pippa Bradley, Neil Burridge, William Short, Melanie Stern, Jon Wornham and organisations: Hurstwic Viking Group; Wessex Archaeology.

Always of course I am grateful for the support and photographic expertise of my husband, George Hobbs.

Thank you all for your help and assistance; any mistakes are entirely mine.

SELECTED BIBLIOGRAPHY

The information for this book has been derived from a number of sources. In addition to the selected bibliography in the first edition, the author acknowledges with gratitude the debt she owes to the following:

Bersu, Gerhard and Wilson, David M., *Three Viking Graves in the Isle of Man*, The Society for Medieval Archaeology, Monograph Series: No 1, 1966

Chaloner, James, *A Short Treatise of the Isle of Man, 1656*, Lily Publications, 2013

Crellin, Rachael Joanne, *Changing times: the emergence of a Bronze Age on the Isle of Man*, unpublished thesis, Newcastle University, 2014

Crow, Captain Hugh, *The Memoirs of Captain Hugh Crow*, reprint from 1830, Bodleian Library, 2007

Cummings, Vicki & Fowler, Chris (eds), *The Neolithic of the Irish Sea; materiality and traditions of practice*, Oxbow Books, 2004

Draskau, Jannifer Kewley, *Illiam Dhone; patriot or traitor?*, Profile Books, 2012

Francis, Paul, *Isle of Man 20th Century Military Archaeology, Part 1: Island Defence*, and *Part 4: Ronaldsway Airport*, Manx Heritage Foundation, 2006

Gawne, C.W., *Controversy 1651-1895, from Smuggling to the Common Purse*, Manx Heritage Foundation, 2009

Hulme, Peter J. *Government Houses in the Isle of Man*, The Manx Experience, undated but c.1990

Kelly, Robert C. and Kniveton, Gordon N., *Sir William Hillary and the Isle of Man Lifeboat Stations*, The Manx Experience, undated c. 1995

Lamplugh, George William, *Economic Geology of the Isle of Man, with special reference to the metalliferous mines*, HMSO, 1903

Moore, A.W., *The Folk-Lore of the Isle of Man*, Brown & Son, 1891

Phillips, Bishop John, *The Book of Common Prayer in Manx Gaelic, 1610*, facsimile edition, General books LLC, 2012

Talbot, Rev. Theophilus (translator), *The Manorial Role of the Isle of Man 1511-1515*, Humphry Milford, 1924

Thompson, Steve & Hall, Naomi, *Speke Keeill, Mount Murray Hotel, Isle of Man; archaeological evaluation and assessment of results*, Wessex Archaeology, July 2007

Wilkins, Frances, *Manx Slave Traders*, Wyre Forest Press, 1999

Periodicals and papers

The Journal of the Manx Museum, Vol VI, Number 80, 1964, The Franciscan Friary at Bymacan, J.K. Barratt

Norsk Tidsskrift for Sprogvidenskap Bind VIII, Oslo 1937, summary in English of paper in Norwegian about Treens and Keeills, Prof Carl J.S. Markstander

INDEX

Page numbers refer only to the most significant references within the text. Pages numbers in *italics* indicate illustrations; italicised pages may also contain relevant text.